Rethinking Play and Pedagogy in Early Childhood Education

Concepts, contexts and cultures

Edited by Sue Rogers

Routledge
Taylor & Francis Group

LONDON AND NEW YORK

KH

This first edition published 2011
by Routledge
2 Park Square, Milton Park, Abingdon, Oxon OX14 4RN

Simultaneously published in the USA and Canada
by Routledge

270 Madison Avenue, New York, NY 10016
Routledge is an imprint of the Taylor & Francis Group,
an informa business

Typeset in Garamond and Gill Sans by Swales & Willis Ltd, Exeter, Devon
Printed and bound in Great Britain by TJ International Ltd, Padstow, Cornwall

British Library Cataloguing in Publication Data
A catalogue record for this book is available
from the British Library

Library of Congress Cataloging-in-Publication Data
Rethinking play and pedagogy in early childhood education: concepts,
contexts and cultures / edited by Sue Rogers.
  p. cm.
  1. Play. 2. Early childhood education. 3. Critical pedagogy.
  I. Rogers, Sue, 1961–
  LB1139.35.P55R47 2010
  372.21 – dc22
  2010019468

ISBN13: 978–0–415–48075–8 (hbk)
ISBN13: 978–0–415–48076–5 (pbk)
ISBN13: 978–0–203–83947–8 (ebk)

2/28/12

Contents

Notes on Contributors   vii

Introduction   1

1. Play and pedagogy: a conflict of interests?   5
   SUE ROGERS

2. It's about power: researching play, pedagogy and participation
   in the early years of school   19
   JO AILWOOD

3. The challenge of play for early childhood educators   32
   SUE DOCKETT

4. 'We are hunters and gatherers of values': dramatic play, early
   childhood pedagogy, and the formation of ethical identities   48
   BRIAN EDMISTON

5. Revisiting Vygotskian perspectives on play and pedagogy   60
   ELENA BODROVA AND DEBORAH J. LEONG

6. Exploring culture, play, and early childhood education practice
   in African contexts   73
   KOFI MARFO AND LINDA BIERSTEKER

7. Play and pedagogy framed within India's historical, socio-cultural
   and pedagogical context   86
   AMITA GUPTA

8. Learning through play in Hong Kong: policy or practice?   100
   DORIS CHENG PUI-WAH

 9. Meeting at the crossroads: postmodern pedagogy greets children's
     aesthetic play-culture   112
     FAITH GABRIELLE GUSS

10. Deconstructing the metaphysics of play theories: towards a
     pedagogy of play aesthetics   126
     HAE-RYUNG YEU

11. Digital play in the classroom: a twenty-first century pedagogy? 139
     TIM WALLER

12. Taking play seriously   152
     LIZ BROOKER

     Index   165

Contributors

Jo Ailwood is Senior Lecturer at the University of Newcastle, Australia. She has taught in early years settings in London and in Queensland. Dr Ailwood teaches, researches and publishes in theories of childhood, play, pedagogy and policy. Her current research focus is upon children's participation, rights and citizenship.

Linda Biersteker is Head of Research at the Early Learning Resource Unit, an ECD NGO specializing in policy, advocacy and programme development located in Cape Town, South Africa.

Elena Bodrova is a Senior Research Fellow, NIEER, MCREL. She has published widely in the field of Vygotskian perspectives on play. She has coauthored (with Deborah Leong) *Tools of the Mind: the Vygotskian Approach to Early Childhood Education.*

Liz Brooker is a Senior Lecturer at the Institute of Education, London. Her research is concerned with young children's learning in their home and community environments; their transitions into preschool and school settings; and their development of a complex cultural identity and sense of belonging.

Sue Dockett is Professor, Early Childhood Education, Charles Sturt University, Australia. Sue began her career as an early childhood teacher and, since 1988, has been involved in early childhood teacher education. Sue has researched and published widely in the areas of children's play and educational transitions.

Brian Edmiston is Associate Professor of Teaching and Learning at The Ohio State University, USA. The winner of research and teaching awards and the author of three books, including *Forming Ethical Identities in Early Childhood Education*, he specializes in pedagogical uses of dramatic play and inquiry across the curriculum.

Amita Gupta is a Fulbright Scholar and Associate Professor at The City University of New York. She is an experienced early childhood teacher and teacher educator in cross-cultural contexts and has published extensively in the areas of international and comparative education, postcolonial theory, and socio-cultural constructivism of teaching.

Faith Gabrielle Guss has taught drama and theatre for children in early childhood studies since 1978, currently at Oslo University College, Norway. She has created theatre for young children and published extensively about the aesthetics of playing and the parallels between playing and theatre arts.

Deborah J. Leong is a Senior Research Fellow, NIEER, Metropolitan State College at Denver, Department of Psychology and a professor of psychology at Metropolitan State College of Denver. Her interests include the application of the Vygotskian approach to early childhood education and authentic assessment. She has coauthored (with Elena Bodrova) *Tools of the Mind: the Vygotskian Approach to Early Childhood Education*.

Kofi Marfo is Professor of Educational Psychology at the University of South Florida, USA, and has published widely on early intervention/early childhood development, parent-child interaction, childhood disability, cognition and education, and internationally adopted children's development. His current interests include developmental science and social policy and supporting child development research in Africa.

Doris Cheng Pui-wah serves in the Department of Early Childhood Education in the Hong Kong Institute of Education. She has worked in Higher Education since 1985 and has been interested in researching and publishing the enactment of play and learning.

Sue Rogers is based at the Institute of Education, University of London. A qualified primary school teacher and experienced researcher. She has worked in Higher Education since 1995 and has published widely in the field of early childhood pedagogy and play.

Hae-Ryung Yeu majored in curriculum studies at the University of Alberta, Canada, and is a professor in the Department of Early Childhood Education, Youngnam University, Korea. Her research interests and publications include phenomenological-hermeneutic understanding of play, childhood education, and interpretive qualitative research methodology.

Tim Waller is Reader in early years education in the School of Education, University of Wolverhampton, England. Previously he taught in nursery, infant and primary schools in London and has also worked in the USA. His research interests include outdoor learning, children's perspectives, pedagogy, ICT and social justice.

Introduction

Sue Rogers

The aim of this book is to stimulate debate about the relationship between play and pedagogy in early childhood education. In essence, it will explore how play is transformed by institutional and pedagogical discourses from a range of cultural and conceptual perspectives, which delineate and ultimately govern how play is presented and, it follows, how it is experienced by children. With these points in mind, the absence of discussion of play in relation to 'subjects' and curriculum requirements is deliberate, in order to consider alternative conceptions of play that may be both difficult to manage and difficult to measure in early childhood pedagogy.

Global concerns about the nature and purposes of education for young children inevitably raise questions about the extent to which and how play is valued as a vehicle for early learning. In many ways the coupling of play with pedagogy is problematic, not least because traditionally in Western discourses of early childhood, the concept of play has been positioned in opposition to its apparently more worthwhile counterpart, work. This division is marked not simply by the ways in which play is often relegated to specific times and places, but also in the ways in which play, wherever it is enacted in early childhood settings, is shaped by the pedagogical and contextual features which surround it (Rogers, 2010). A 'pedagogy of play' might be characterised by complexity and diversity of practice, the locus of interactions between the needs and desires of the children and those of adults, between ideological and pragmatic imperatives, between spontaneous and intrinsically motivated actions of the child and the demands of a standardised and politicised curriculum. Moreover, pedagogy tends to be defined principally from the adults' perspective with less attention to how children respond to and make sense of pedagogical practices within the contexts of their play, remembering that play is described widely in the Western early childhood literature as a child-initiated activity, free from externally imposed rules. Against this background, the chapters in this book problematise the intersection of play and pedagogy and draw on a range of perspectives including post-developmental, critical and cultural analyses of that intersection. With this in mind, the chapters address some emerging issues surrounding play and pedagogy in the twenty-first century. These include:

- Application of critical and socio-cultural analyses to play in early childhood;
- Renewed interest in the ethical, aesthetic and affective dimensions of play in early childhood education;

- Competing discourses of 'performativity', market forces, social reconstruction and child-centredness;
- Children's voice and participation within educational settings;
- Globalisation, migration and cultural pluralism;
- The role of digital technology in early childhood education;
- Diversity, identity and social justice within early childhood settings.

The discussions presented in this book are not intended to be conclusive. Nor is the intent to offer a panacea for overcoming many of the (well documented) tensions that exist in offering play pedagogy that is simultaneously meaningful to young children and valued by adults and society in general. It is hoped that the book will encourage further cross-national/cultural debate and will contribute to future global debates about the (sometimes) vexed relationship between play and pedagogy in early childhood education.

How the book is organised

Each author adopts a particular cultural, conceptual or contextual perspective on play and pedagogy. In this way, each chapter can be read as a distinctive and separate discussion of the topic. Equally, however, the chapters have much in common particularly with regard to the issues they raise around adult roles and attitudes to play, difficulties in reconciling dominant pedagogical discourses and children's spontaneous play. Chapter 1 problematises the relationship between play and traditional notions of pedagogy as a 'conflict of interests' and notes that increasingly, pedagogic practices are determined by economic terms with an emphasis on standards, accountability and testing (Edwards and Usher, 2008). The chapter questions dominant approaches to play pedagogy which tend to start from the perspective of the adult's role in providing an environment and strategies that support the processes of teaching and learning, rather than looking at play from the 'inside'. It proposes that taking a relational and co-constructed approach may be one way to rethink pedagogy in relation to play. In Chapter 2, Jo Ailwood examines the interconnected themes of power, play, participation and pedagogy, illustrated with examples from a research project conducted in Australia. Drawing on the work of Foucault, she challenges dominant Western discourses of play in early childhood education, exploring two main concepts: the conditions of possibility, and relationships of power. These concepts are explored in relation to children's play, participation and competence in early childhood pedagogy. In Chapter 3 we turn our attention to the perspective of teachers. Sue Dockett explores perceptions of play and play-based pedagogies among a group of teachers in Australia in order to shed light on some of the assumptions held about play and how their involvement in a research project provided a starting point for challenging, changing and reconceptualising their approach to play and pedagogy. In Chapter 4, Brian Edmiston examines adults' active participation in dramatic play with children, at home and in classrooms, arguing that it can be highly significant in the formation of powerful morally persuasive identities. His chapter begins with a very personal account of his experience of growing up in a divided society in Northern Ireland and of his experience of playing with his son Michael. From this highly personal and autobiographical perspective, Edmiston develops a compelling case for viewing dramatic play between adults and children as a powerful site for the development of ethical identities. The theme of adult roles continues in Chapter 5 where Elena Bodrova and Deborah J. Leong revist Vygotskian perspectives on play and pedagogy. They argue that with increasing pressure for formal pedagogies in early childhood classrooms, opportunities for the most elaborate forms of play, the ones that take longer for children to develop are most at risk. From the perspective of Cultural-Historical Psychology they utilise Vygotskian insights and post-Vygotskian contributions to research on play to argue for a pedagogy of play that allows for adults to help children to acquire the necessary skills to play in ways that are beneficial to the development of self-regulation and imagination.

Perspectives from contexts that lie 'outside' the Western traditions of early childhood play are still relatively rare in the literature. Chapters 6, 7 and 8 move away from Western early childhood settings to three post-colonial contexts, Africa, India and Hong Kong respectively. In Chapter 6, Kofi Marfo and Linda Biersteker offer a cultural-historical, contextualist perspective to the discourse on play pedagogy and early childhood education. They examine the relationship between culture and play drawing attention to 'the perennial *problem of relevance* – the degree to which exclusively Euro-American models of ECE practice are appropriate for Africa', arguing for the inclusion of cultural differences and local realities in the development of pedagogy and curriculum design. Though they acknowledge that there are many 'Africas' the authors present a case study of early childhood education policy and practice trends in South Africa to exemplify some of the key issues and tensions that exist in developing play pedagogy. Chapter 7 continues to examine the relationship between play pedagogy and post-colonialism. Amita Gupta offers a detailed examination of the ideas which appear to have shaped the relationship between play and pedagogy within the Indian context. Drawing on post-colonial theory, she gives empirical examples from a study of early childhood teachers' perceptions of play in India to consider the extent to which it is desirable or indeed possible to import a child-centred, play-based pedagogy to the Indian context, without causing other rifts, inequities, and impediments to social justice. Similarly in Chapter 8, Doris Cheng Pui-wah problematises the relationship between play and policy in the Hong Kong context. She asks: Has the official policy recommendation to introduce a play-based pedagogy in the Hong Kong early childhood curriculum led to a paradigm shift in how teachers teach and young children learn? In Chapter 9, we return to the question: 'what kind of pedagogy is a pedagogy of play?' posed in Chapter 1. From the perspective of drama and dramatic play, Faith Gabrielle Guss argues for a pedagogy of play that is 'inspired by insight into the ways in which children express themselves, interpret experience, and construct knowledge in their autonomous play-culture'. Guss gives extended examples of children's dramatic play in a Norwegian preschool to support an aesthetic reconceptualisation of play from a postmodern perspective. Hae-Ryung Yeu in Chapter 10, continues the discussion of the aesthetic in play by deconstructing classic play theories in order to consider how and in what ways we might discuss the aesthetic quality of children's play in a contemporary context. Through examples of play in Korean early childhood contexts, the complex, multi-faceted, and dynamic nature of children's role play is illustrated. In Chapter 11, Tim Waller offers a critical account of the function and role of digital technology in early years pedagogy, with particular reference to children's play experiences both inside and outside the setting. He argues in favour of developing a transformative play pedagogy in early childhood that can embrace fully the opportunities offered to children and adults in new technologies, both indoors and outdoors. Finally, in Chapter 12 Liz Brooker revisits the current fragile consensus on play, before discussing issues of 'culture and diversity, of power and pleasure, of home and school pedagogies, and of the work/play dichotomy'. She gives examples of young children's self-initiated and serious play in early childhood settings, and asks us to consider the challenges which these play behaviours offer to conventional understandings of the play/pedagogy nexus. It seems apt to end with this chapter, which reminds us of the need to take children's play seriously in early childhood and to recognise the very extensive powers they bring to their play in spite of the numerous and complex pedagogical processes that comprise contemporary early childhood settings.

References

Edwards, R and Usher, R. (2008) *Globalisation and Pedagogy*, 2nd edition, Abingdon: Routledge.

Rogers, S. (2010) 'Powerful pedagogies and playful resistance: children's experience of role play in early childhood education,' in E. Brooker and S. Edwards, (Eds) *Engaging Play*, Maidenhead: Open University Press.

Chapter 1

Play and pedagogy
A conflict of interests?

Sue Rogers

Introduction

> It is important for pedagogy not to be the prisoner of too much certainty, but instead to be aware of both the relativity of its powers and the difficulties of translating its ideals into practice.
>
> (Malaguzzi in Edwards *et al.,* 1998: 58)

What kind of pedagogy is a *'pedagogy of play'*? How and in what ways do pedagogical practices shape the play experiences of young children in early childhood classrooms? Answers to these questions are surprisingly difficult to find in spite of a vast literature on the subject of play in early childhood classrooms. Insights from theoretical and empirical studies illustrate powerfully that young children demonstrate an inherent capacity to play and that it appears to be central to their early learning. Few would dispute this. Yet how such insights are to be translated into pedagogical practices across diverse social and cultural contexts has presented the international early childhood field with some of its most enduring challenges. As I have argued elsewhere (Rogers, 2010), the coupling of play and pedagogy in early childhood education is problematic for several reasons: first because traditionally, the concept of play has been positioned in marked opposition to its apparently more worthwhile counterpart, work (play *versus* work). The division between play and work characteristic of many early childhood classrooms may prevent the integration of play into pedagogical practice. Second, theorising 'play *as* work' as Gibbons (2007: 303) argues, may in fact obscure the ways in which play may become 'a technique of social control and a means of transmitting assumptions and beliefs regarding the nature and purpose of childhood: the child must work at being a child' (see also Ailwood, 2003; Cannella and Viruru, 2004). Third, the *pedogogisation* of play (Rogers, 2010) seen in countries across the globe has meant that play has increasingly become an instrument for learning future competencies; emphasising social realism rather than the transformative, mimetic and life-enhancing qualities of play (see also Guss, this volume). These mixed and sometimes paradoxical conceptions of play provide an important context for this chapter and indeed this book. Put simply, a consensus about the value and benefits of play exists within dominant Western early childhood educational discourse. Yet there appear to be inherent and widespread difficulties, both conceptual and practical, in realising the potential benefits of play, what I have termed here a *conflict of interests* between the competing imperatives of play in early childhood pedagogy. Alongside these difficulties, there has been widespread migration of educational policy and pedagogy (Edwards and Usher, 2008) so that Western models have been imported into developing economies such as the Indian subcontinent (see Gupta, this volume). By the same token within the West, alternative pedagogic practices have been widely disseminated and influential (see for example the Reggio Emilia approach).

One possible alternative to recontextualising play into traditional models of pedagogy is to rethink our understanding of pedagogy in relation to the characteristics and benefits of play. Taken separately, the words 'play' and 'pedagogy' hold diverse and distinct meanings in educational discourse, each invested with differential power potentially to shape the experiences of young children in early childhood settings. If we take the concept of 'play' in early childhood, we are likely to imagine an activity that is spontaneous, child led and intrinsically motivated. In contrast, common understandings of 'pedagogy' usually take as their starting point the adult's role in providing an environment and strategies that support the processes of teaching and learning. Increasingly pedagogic practices are determined by economic terms with an emphasis on standards, accountability and testing (Edwards and Usher, 2008). We can perhaps see already a tension between our understanding of play on the one hand and pedagogy on the other. The question underscoring this chapter is, then, how can we reconcile two apparently divergent imperatives in the early childhood classroom?

Building on earlier work on play and pedagogy in English reception classes (Rogers and Evans, 2008), this chapter will explore how pedagogy is co-constructed between children and adults and between children, when spaces are opened up for meaning to be negotiated in the context of play, drawing on the concept of relational pedagogy now well-established in the literature (for a recent example see Papatheodorou and Moyles, 2009), and enacted in the innovative pedagogical practices of Reggio Emilia in Northern Italy, Te Whariki in New Zealand. Broadly speaking, a relational pedagogy offers the possibility of overcoming the traditional division between play and work in the early childhood classroom because it is responsive to the 'needs passions and interests of the learners' (Gold, 2005 cited in Papatheodorou, 2009), and, moreover, for challenging traditional concepts of power in the classroom (Fraser *et al.*, 2007).

An alternative approach, suggested in this chapter, is to view play from the 'inside' (Rogers and Evans, 2008). In part, this would mean adults seeking and reflecting upon the perspectives of children on the meaning and value of play. This would enable the content, nature and dynamic of play to inform pedagogy in a reciprocal and relational way. To illustrate, I draw on empirical examples gathered as part of a larger study of children's perspectives of play conducted in English reception classes (Rogers and Evans, 2008). My reason for focusing on this particular context is two-fold: first, the reception class, a term with particular currency in countries of the UK (but also in Australia), has been identified in numerous studies as offering children conflicting and competing pedagogic discourses; play *versus* work; child-centred *versus* formal instruction. Second, the reception class is a highly specific educational context, catering as it does for the very young and unschooled child, while at the same time operating within the social and institutional context of the school. Located in the borderlands between nursery or pre-school education and statutory schooling, children's play activity occupies a rather precarious, unstable and sometimes ambiguous position in relation to the pedagogical processes of teaching and learning common to primary school classrooms. The study demonstrated that for young children play is mainly about connecting with others, forming relationships with friends and exploring multiple identities through pretend roles. However, meeting these aspirations in practice was problematic and suggested a series of tensions between child-adult objectives. Conceptualising these here as a 'conflict of interests', I will explore how these tensions might be resolved by foregrounding relationships within play, thus seeing play pedagogy as emergent, co-constructed and relational. In this way children's play might inform classroom pedagogy rather than, as is the case in many early childhood classrooms and in some accounts of pedagogy in the literature, pedagogy informing children's play. It seems to me that this is an important distinction in meaning. Children invest huge energy and commitment in their play to achieve their goals and desired outcomes, both collective and individual. Often these desires are rooted in friendships that emerge in the course of play, friendships that may be fleeting or lasting but that interact with the play frame in a symbiotic relationship. By 'friendship' I am referring to the making and breaking of relationships that are characteristic of early childhood play and inferring also the possibility for exclusion as well as inclusion in play relationships.

Many of the issues raised in this chapter resonate with international provision, in particular the USA and Australia, but also in postcolonial contexts such as the Indian subcontinent, where Western discourses about young children and play continue to exert considerable influence in the development of early childhood curriculum and pedagogy (see for example the chapters by Gupta and Cheng in this volume). However, I will undertake to sketch briefly for the international reader some of the key landmarks in recent policy developments in the early childhood education sector in the UK and more particularly in England.

Play, policy and pedagogy: the English 'reception class'

Educational discourses of play, particularly those contained within official policy documents sometimes offer contradictory messages about what is meant by play and the purposes to which it might be put. In England, educational policy has focused intensively on play, not only in early childhood settings, but in the wider community. This commitment is informed by the view that engagement in play activities can make a valuable and lasting contribution to the well-being of children, young people and communities, exemplified in the statement 'a community where children are playing is a healthy and sustainable community . . .' (DCSF/DCMS 2008: 4). However, in spite of this commitment, a discourse of instrumentalism permeates policy documentation on play. The definition of play adopted within current policy is 'What children and young people do when they follow their own ideas and interests in their own way for their own reasons balancing fun with a sense of respect for themselves and others' (DCSF/DCMS, 2008), in other words, a spontaneous and child-led activity. But as Powell (2008) argues in an analysis of policy statements on play, the dominant discourse is one which links play instrumentally to the particular priorities of relevant government departments in the UK including health and fitness, cognitive, social, emotional development and learning. Powell concludes from her analysis that

> although the government has repeatedly voiced its support from play in recent years, what is actually meant by 'play' and why it should be supported is unclear from policy documentation, whereas structured activities are more clearly defined . . . For play to be truly beneficial it must actually be play and not some other activity – this may mean relinquishing some control over what, where, why and how children are playing.
>
> (Powell, 2008: 41)

It is fair to say that there has been major and long-overdue capital investment in the early years sector in the UK in the past decade and a genuine will on the part of policy makers to acknowledge the importance of early childhood education and care in relation to economic success, individual achievement and well being across the life span. A raft of recent policy documents and initiatives emanate from a national commitment to improving the education and care for young children and their families and the impact such investment can make on the life-chances of young children. One such initiative is the English *Early Years Foundation Stage* (EYFS) (DCSF, 2007), a curricular framework for children from birth to statutory school age, currently set 'in the term after a child's fifth birthday'. In practice, however, most children in England start school before the statutory age of five, joining reception classes in primary schools as four-year-olds. The *EYFS* framework in England has established a long-awaited and distinct educational phase for young children from birth to five and clarifies for all practitioners working with young children key areas of learning and appropriate progression towards Key Stage One of the National Curriculum in England. It provides a bridge between the diverse pre-statutory school settings characteristic of provision in England, and statutory schooling at Key Stage One, stressing flexibility and informality in the reception year, and focusing on child development, practical play and outdoor activity. However, studies have highlighted the continued division between pre-school provision and reception classes in spite of the fact that the EYFS was designed precisely to overcome such divisions. Key challenges can include diverse admission policies have led to uneven quality of provision for four-year-olds in reception classes; a reduction in adult attention is due to reduced adult to child ratios in reception classes; a lack of appropriately trained staff in reception classes may lead to over-formal activities; there may be a reduction in the availability of choice of activity, outdoor play, appropriate resources and equipment and time and space for active play; changes in teaching style and classroom ethos (Rogers and Rose, 2007; Riggall and Sharp, 2008).

Although the EYFS is an avowedly play-based curricular framework, the dominant discourse running through the documentation promotes play that is well-planned, purposeful and potentially instructive, aspirations that may run counter to the discourses of free play expressed by many early childhood practitioners (Bennett *et al.*,1997; Rogers and Evans, 2008). What we are left with is the dual aim to meet adult-determined goals for play (which in turn link with the wider socio-political agendas of closing the disadvantage gap), and at the same time engage children in meaningful and intrinsically motivating play activities. This is pedagogically challenging if we want to avoid the play/work dichotomy that persists in early childhood or risk 'pedagogising' play to the extent that we lose sight of its inherent, life-enhancing qualities, what play *might* be rather than prescriptions for what it is. As many of the authors argue in this book, the experience of play may offer other and different learning opportunities to those that are 'well planned' and 'potentially instructive', that lie outside of what is measurable in curricular terms but which may be immeasurable in terms of the benefits to children. For example, children's moral development and formation of ethical identities (see Edmiston, 2008 and this volume), are increasingly viewed as lacking in early childhood discourse and policy documents. Similarly, aesthetic expression (see Guss and Yeu, this volume) is equally neglected in the early childhood literature. Yet it is argued in other educational spheres that play, viewed as part of the range of expressive and artistic endeavours offer a range of human experiences that help us develop aesthetic and ethical judgements and are crucial in making us who we are in diverse and multiple subjectivities/identities (Mission and Morgan, 2007). Within a relational pedagogic framework, it might be possible to overcome the 'false dichotomy between outcomes-based and process-oriented pedagogical practice' (Papatheodorou, 2009: 14) that underscores play pedagogy in practice.

Play and pedagogical practices

The point was made in the introduction to this chapter that there is a substantial and well-documented empirical and theoretical research literature to support the view that play is a highly significant activity in human experience and development. Further, the research literature also demonstrates that a distinctly human type of play develops most noticeably in children aged 2–5. This is the development of imagination and with it a 'theory of mind' which is most obvious in the early pretend play of toddlers but which quickly transforms into the complex social pretence that characterises the play of children aged 3–5 and which defines and underpins much human activity across the life span. The ability to play in this way is profound and unique to humans, and lays the foundations for crucial life skills such as empathy, problem solving, creativity and innovation. Alongside psycho-biological developmentalist perspectives on play, a growing body of literature has contested dominant ways of the knowing the child and of understanding childhood play (see for example Ailwood, 2003; Gibbons, 2007; Grieshaber, 2008; Lofdahl, 2006), though as Walsh (2005) has argued it is not an 'either/or' situation. Rather we can draw on multiple sources to understand the ways in which children learn, grow and develop within diverse social and cultural contexts. The application of post-structuralist frameworks to early childhood structures and practices views the ideological commitment to subjects such as play, prevalent in early childhood discourse as 'regimes of truth' in the Foucauldian sense that generate an authoritative consensus about what needs to be done in that field and how it should be done (Ailwood, 2003; Cohen, 2008). In the contemporary literature it is often argued that a specific Western ideology persists in early childhood education theory, research and practice stemming largely from re-configurations of the work of successive pioneer educators. This ideology has been variously formulated over time by critics within the field as 'received wisdom', (Tizard, 1977) a 'common law inheritance', (McAuley and Jackson, 1992), and, more recently, as engendering a kind of 'rhetoric' which bears little relationship to practice (Wood and Attfield, 2005, Bennett *et al.*, 1997). The concept of 'learning through play' has a long and established history/tradition in educational contexts. How far such ideas were realised in practice is difficult to ascertain in any precise way and it is likely that most young children across the globe continued to be educated in more traditional ways. These principles for practice, however, are more difficult to translate into pedagogical contexts since they offer little in the way of practical insight into how play is managed, organised and integrated into the early childhood curriculum, what meaning it has for teachers in terms of children's learning and development and how children experience play in early childhood pedagogy.

Research has shown fairly consistently over the years that in many early childhood classrooms and in particular reception classes of primary schools, competing pedagogies (Aubrey, 2004) exist between free play and formal teacher-led activity. More recently integrated approaches to play pedagogy have been suggested by Sylva *et al.* (2004) and Wood (2009) allowing for a continuum from free play and structured play. However, evidence suggests that realising this in practice is challenging, particularly as children approach statutory school age and the pressure for teachers to prepare children for formal schooling increases, remembering that classrooms are complex social worlds and not simply places where pedagogical practices, curriculum guidelines, educational theory and beliefs are put neatly into practice. One possible way forward is to look not only at how play fits into our existing understanding of pedagogy but also how play itself may inform and shape new understandings of pedagogy so that play pedagogy 'connects with culture, social structures and human agency, and thus acquires educational meaning' (Alexander, 2008: 46).

From the perspective of a relational pedagogy, play has the potential to provide opportunities for children's social experience, but the way in which play is structured pedagogically in early childhood settings may severely limit the opportunities available to children to explore relationships within their play or alternatively fail to offer the support that some children need in establishing the social contact they desire. For example, research by Trawick Smith (1998) distinguishes between play at home or in the neighbourhood and school-based play. He contends that while the former is sufficiently open-ended and child-directed to allow for social learning, school-based play is more limited in this respect (1998) because of the common organisational strategies observed in early childhood classrooms, which may constrain rather than enable children's opportunities to develop socially. The first of these relates to grouping practices and classroom organisation. The practice which he calls 'assign and rotate' means that children are routinely sent to particular play areas and play groups by the teacher. The second strategy relates to classroom rules about exclusion in play. Some teachers establish the rule that all children must include all other children. This is reminiscent of Paley's rule that 'you can't say you can't play' (1992), a strategy introduced in order to address the exclusion of certain children from play groups. The counter-argument is that an inclusive strategy while important, may in fact serve to deny children the freedom to terminate interactions and play situations, to move in and out of play and to resolve conflicts and disagreements. Finally, Trawick Smith describes 'match-making strategies', which involve teachers in social engineering, such as 'assigning a withdrawn child and an outgoing child to play together' (1998: 242–43). Clearly there are times when it is appropriate for educators to intervene in children's play choices and to support those children who remain for the most part at the fringes of play and who may lack the skills and confidence to gain access into certain peer groups. And it is important to note that Paley's rule is based on her detailed knowledge of a particular class, their group dynamics and children's individual social needs and emerging relationships emphasising the point that pedagogical decisions need to be based on local contexts and educators' knowledge about specific groups of children rather than only on broad understandings of what constitutes effective pedagogy. A balance needs to be struck, therefore, between broad pedagogical priorities and the provision of play activities that enable children to exercise their developing social competencies, establish authentic relationships and make real choices about where, what and with whom they will play. Without such opportunities it seems that the social and affective dimensions of play will be severely curtailed.

In many early childhood settings, play takes place alongside other work-like activities often within 'choosing time', offered to children as an alternative to, or reward for, work. This choice, however, is often controlled by the teacher and other adults who select groups of children and direct them to specific areas of the play provision, a pedagogical strategy which simultaneously offers the prospect of choice and exercises social control (Rogers, 2010). Tobin (1995) likens this approach to an 'auction', sketching a picture of the teacher (auctioneer) 'selling' the activities to the children (the bidders) as they sit in front of her at choosing time.

> Each time a child puts in a bid for dramatic play area, another one of the teacher's fingers goes down . . . as higher and lower status children make their bids, the value of the dramatic area rises and falls like a commodity.
>
> (1995: 232)

Children's positioning in the social order of the classroom also determines the outcome of the 'auction', in other words where children play and with whom. For example, Steven aged 4 watched Tony closely while he chose another child in the class. Tony took a while to choose but eventually chose Martin to help him. Steven said:

Steven: I knew he would choose Martin.
Joe: How did you know that Steven?

Steven: I knew he would choose him 'cos he's Tony's friend.

Rogers and Evans (2008) identified two distinctive pedagogies operating simultaneously in the English reception class. These can be described as a free play pedagogy in which children appeared to exercise choice and control over where, with whom and what they played. By contrast, a work-oriented pedagogy operated in parallel to the free play activities in which activities were adult led with clear learning objectives and outcomes derived from official curriculum documents. This observation is not new of course, replicating the findings of many studies of reception class practice. However, close observation of pedagogical practices manifest in classroom routines and the interactions between children and adults, and importantly the ways in which children navigated these within their play, showed that the children's free play was governed by the official and rational pedagogic discourse of teaching and learning objectives.

For example, Kevin plays in the role play area set up as a 'travel agency'. He announces to his teacher 'I'm a policeman', but the teacher responds to Kevin, 'no you're in the travel agents. There are no policemen in the travel shop.' Here we see a conflict of interests between Kevin's desire to be a policeman and the teacher's desire to meet the objectives for children to play at being a travel agent or customer. The activity was presented to the children as free play or 'choosing time', yet the dominant discursive practice in this classroom is one of control, in which Kevin is learning what the teacher wants. This approach limits the possible subject positions available to both the teacher and child. Kevin cannot position himself as the policeman in the game. The teacher cannot fulfil her desire for children to engage in free play. Nor will she learn about Kevin's desire to be a policeman and what this might signify for him (Rogers, 2010). A relational pedagogic approach might have enabled the teacher to play with Kevin and to explore together a repertoire of identities and ethical positions, opening up what Bibby (2009) terms 'the unknown and inchoate' aspects of education. Moreover, when adults adopt roles in play the traditional power relations shift (Edmiston, 2008) and in so doing create new pedagogic relationships. Seeing play pedagogy as relational might also allow space for children to explore the aesthetic and affective dimension of play (what is it like to be a policeman?) *and* a rational/ utilitarian approach (what does a travel agent and or policeman do?). In an 'aesthetic way of knowing, the rational is not contrasted with the emotional, rather the affective and intellectual are held together in a dialectical relationship' .

Kevin's teacher's valued highly children's free play for its capacity to foster children's independence, sense of ownership and the 'success built in' factor. Yet her practice prioritised a more structured approach to play, one in which she set the parameters – material, temporal and social – even when children had some freedom to approach the task in their own way. Free play took place only when children had finished teacher-directed tasks, in the form of 'choosing time'. Her practice presented a 'conflict of interests', between the demands placed upon her to meet particular objectives in preparation for entry into statutory schooling and her belief that children should have opportunities for free play with peers. She explained that you're conscious that they are [the children] going into year one and things are going to be a bit different in Year one . . . I think towards the end of the year maybe we're a little bit more conscious that there is less time for play, maybe is free choice play, although we do still try and get it into the activity that we're doing.

Note also the example of Cobi who is in the 'hospital' as the doctor when he is called away to read to an adult. He is reluctant to go, but knows he must so moves the boundary of the role play area so that he can retain his position in the play while he reads to a teacher: a foot in each camp. Or Milly who, bored with the class Pet Shop, carefully and surreptitiously moves the domestic play equipment, off limits in her classroom, into the role play area, transforming the space into a kitchen so that she can serve dinner to her friends while they play at being 'a family'. Through revisiting even the most mundane roles such as 'mother', 'baby' and 'teenager', children explore and experience multiple subject positions in relation to others in the context of the play. In the case of Milly, the pet shop play which was stilted and quickly disintegrating, found new life in the 'home corner', was more sustained and generated a richer and more lasting narrative. So, left to their own devices children can and do find ways to develop play that is meaningful and which enables them to explore and consolidate relationships, real and imagined, in the classroom.

In spite of recent attempts to conceptualise a pedagogy of play that can overcome the difficulties identified earlier (for example, Wood, 2009), play pedagogy is described principally from the adults' perspective with little, if any, reference to how and in what ways children might (and indeed do) exercise agency through their active participation in the making of pedagogy in early childhood classrooms (Rogers and Evans, 2008). In practice, 'pedagogy' is implicitly tied up with the exercise of power between teachers and pupils and, as Bibby notes, 'even contemporary definitions of pedagogy fail to account for the ways relationships and subjectivity constitute knowledge, focusing on rational and conscious acts' (2009). Little attention is paid to how pedagogy in relation to children's play is structured by adult-determined regulatory practices (Powell *et al.*, 2006; Cannella and Viruru, 2004), which may suppress the physical, social and affective qualities of play, in order to meet the demands of a prescribed, externally evaluated, play pedagogy.

In contrast to the aforementioned pedagogic approaches suggested which prioritised the official curriculum above play, I give an example from a classroom in which the pedagogy could be described as relational, based on a 'pedagogy of listening' (Dahlberg and Moss, 2005: 98). The extract recalls my first meeting with Jessica, then aged 4 and new to school. For the benefit of the reader, I reproduce my field notes in full:

Ssshh . . . the lion's asleep'. Jessica, aged four took my hand as I entered her classroom for the first time, and led me on tiptoes towards the corner of the classroom where there was a 'cave' made out of cardboard, paper and paint. Inside the cave was a large toy lion, 'sleeping'. We sat together quietly in the cave for several minutes, until Jessica turned to me and said with some urgency 'he's waking up now . . . let's go'. This momentary suspension of reality required, that for a short time, both Jessica and I stepped out of the classroom and into a shared imaginary world.

(Rogers and Evans, 2008: 21)

The extract raises a key question: *what kind of pedagogy enables Jessica to initiate this playful encounter?* In Jessica's classroom the dominant pedagogical approach emphasised what *learners* do rather than what *teachers* do (Moore, 2004: 170). Following the approach adopted in Reggio Emilia preschools, the children in Jessica's classroom worked/played on projects throughout the year from ideas that they had voiced and discussed in negotiation with the teacher and each other. Planning projects was an integral part of the culture of listening fostered by the teacher and other adults. Relationships were explored and established through the co-constructive process. Disagreement was encouraged and ethical dilemmas were examined by children with their teacher. The teacher frequently adopted roles in the children's play as a way of exploring different identities and subject positions, thus shifting the power relationships between players, between children and adults, believing that it is through the co-construction of pedagogic relationships that children learn to make decisions for themselves, and are able to explore different identities and relationships with others in a safe and encouraging environment. A relational approach to play pedagogy is a co-constructed pedagogy which allows for uncertainty and possibility, remembering that for young children, a principal reason for participating in play is to be with people you like and are interested in, and to make relationships (Rogers and Evans, 2008). From this perspective, play is viewed as one way towards developing pedagogies that are 'genuinely geared towards an uncertain, intriguing, yet-to-be constructed future . . . that prioritise the child rather than the curriculum, and that are more concerned with the creation of democratic, culturally inclusive classrooms, than with cultural and behavioural conformity' (Moore, 2004: 171). My point here is that by making play fit into already existing, traditional pedagogic frameworks we may miss the 'uncertain' and the more 'intriguing' aspects of play for both children and adults in early childhood classrooms.

Play and pedagogy: a conflict of interests?

Play pedagogy in many early childhood classrooms can be characterised by a range of dilemmas and tensions and can be conceptualised as a *conflict of interests*. This may seem unduly negative, but it is not the intention here to suggest that it is play *as such* which engenders such conflict. Rather conflict stems from multiple sources, in part at least from the ways in which play has been appropriated by the structures of schooling in its century-long history as an educational tool. Kevin's teacher felt disempowered by structural and macro political contexts, and the pressures it placed upon her to meet specific learning objectives even when she believed that child-led play was a more appropriate and beneficial pedagogical approach, a pedagogical 'conflict of interests'. As we have seen play also represented a conflict of interests for Kevin whose desire to be a policeman was 'not heard' by his teacher. Although Kevin did not resist the teacher's request to play at being a travel agent, we know that children exercise agency in adapting and reinterpreting adult conceptions of play contexts, in resisting adult requests and negotiating with adults to achieve a 'balanced compliance' (Rogers and Evans, 2008), in other words a way of resolving conflict so that the needs of both children and teachers are met. Like those T.V. shows that show the 'out-takes', the things that go badly wrong (they are often the best bits!), it is of value to look at children's responses to pedagogic practices implemented by adults and to examples of subversive play, play that does not fit the class theme, but which may be of relevance and meaning to the child as with Kevin's role as the policeman. We know that too much direction on the part of adults can diminish children's play experiences. So too, I would suggest, can over-prescription and inflexibility in early childhood classrooms that offer free play alongside more formal activities. On the one hand, we talk of structured play, or put another way, play in which adults intervene at the level of planning, resourcing and initial implementation (what Steiner educators call the 'the pre-cooked play fare' approach, quoted in Drummond, 1999: 52). On the other hand research shows that teachers do not as a rule intervene in play once they have set it up. Yet as we have seen Kevin's teacher clearly had intentions for, and expectations of how and in what ways he should play.

An alternative vision of what play *might* be is given by Drummond's characteristically eloquent account of her observations in a Steiner kindergarten. Children did not engage in the 'cognitive learn as you play' regime which characterises much early childhood practice, but rather in highly 'imaginative, transformative and exploratory acts' (*ibid*, 53), play which according to Steiner educators will help children to avoid 'cultural, personal and social deprivation' (*ibid*, 53). Utilising play in relation to a broader interpretation of children's intellectual and social development rather than attempting to make it fit narrowly prescribed educational agendas, may be the most satisfactory means by which to resolve the conflict of interests that surrounds play, particularly in reception classes. I suggest that to overcome the conflict of interests that appears to exist between children's play and adults' pedagogical imperatives that an alternative view of play pedagogy might be as a negotiated and relational 'space', both physical and conceptual, for children and teachers to explore identities and desires, and consider questions of voice and power in the classroom. But how would this work in practice? Play would not be viewed simply as a vehicle for delivering the curriculum, under the guise of 'play-based learning'. The starting point would be to see the value of play from the children's perspective, as a powerful context for understanding emerging and shifting subjectivities within classroom relationships. Play pedagogy as a negotiated practice, co-constructed between children and adults, might also help to overcome the play/work dualism that persists in early childhood classrooms (Cannella and Viruru, 2004), which perpetuates the resistance evident in children's responses to the pedagogical structures surrounding their play. This will require adults to recognise and value the different ways in which children play, including play which is 'not nice' from an adult perspective but which may be of interest and value to the children (Lester and Russell, 2008: 42). The seemingly chaotic and anarchic qualities of play may be disconcerting and cause adults to feel a loss of control, yet it is precisely these features that for many define the very nature of play. Again Lester and Russell, make this point, that the essence of play – 'flexibility, unpredictability, spontaneity and imagination' (2008: 42) – is precisely what makes it of such benefit to children's development and well-being: there is a fine balance to be struck between adult involvement and the 'adulteration' of play.

Conclusion

The concept of a play pedagogy that is relational and co-constructed, which allows time for children to engage with others and their environment in meaningful ways, though persuasive, is challenging in practice. Evidence indicates that practice remains remarkably resistant to change and that the relationship between theory and research on the one hand and practice on the other is a problematic one. For ideas to take hold they have to have meaning to the specific context and local conditions. Moreover, in the current policy context of England there are still very real difficulties in reception classes where teachers feel under pressure to complete assessment profiles in which the targets do not necessarily match the play-based pedagogy of the EYFS framework. Part of the imperative to play is tied up with social recognition and acceptance within a social group. Relationships underpin much of what it means to be human. Play is also an occasion for children to demonstrate to their peers their autonomy from teachers, to display boundaries of inclusion and exclusion from shifting peer groups, and to experience power and control; friendships developed in and sustained by play are tied up with power and desire. We have seen how children exercise agency in shaping the play pedagogy of their settings even when it means they resist and risk conflict with adults. By adopting a relational and co-constructive approach to play pedagogy we may resolve some of the conflicts of interest that arise between play and pedagogic practice. In doing so we might rethink what we mean by pedagogy in relation to play in early childhood.

References

Ailwood, J. (2003) 'Governing early childhood education through play', *Contemporary Issues in Early Childhood,* 4(3), pp. 286–99.

Alexander, R. J. (2008) *Essays on Pedagogy,* London: Routledge.

Aubrey, C. (2004) 'Implementing the Foundation Stage in reception classes', *British Educational Research Journal.* 30(5), pp. 633–56.

Bennett, N., Wood, L. and Rogers, S. (1997) *Teaching Through Play,* Bucks: Open University Press.

Bibby, T. (2009) 'How do pedagogic practices impact on learner identities in mathematics? A psychoanalytically framed response', In L. Black, H. Mendick and Y. Solomon (Eds), *Mathematical Relationships in Education: Identities and Participation,* London: Routledge, pp. 123–35.

Cannella, G. and Viruru, R. (2004) *Childhood and Postcolonisation,* New York/London: Routledge.

Cohen, L. (2008) 'Foucault and the Early Childhood Classroom' *Educational Studies,* 44, pp. 7–21.

Dahlberg, G. and Moss, P. (2005) *Ethics and Politics in Early Childhood Education,* London: Routledge.

Department for Children, Schools and Families (DCSF) (2007) *Early Years Foundation Stage,* Nottingham: DCSF.

—— (2008) *Fair Play: A consultation on the play strategy.* London: DCSF.

Drummond, M. (1999) 'Another way of seeing: perceptions of play in a Steiner kindergarten', in L. Abbott and H. Moylett (Eds), *Early Education Transformed,* London: Falmer Press.

Edmiston, B. (2008) *Forming Ethical Identities in Early Childhood Play,* London: Routledge.

Edwards, R. and Usher, R. (2008) *Globalisation and Pedagogy,* 2nd edition, London: Routledge.

Edwards, C., Gandini, L. and Forman, G. (1998) *The Hundred Languages of Children: Reggio Emilia Approach – Advanced Reflections,* London: JAI Press Ltd.

Fraser, D., Price, G., Aitken, V., with Gilbert, G., Klemick, A., Rose, L. and Tyson, S. (2007) 'Relational pedagogy and the arts. Set: Research Information for Teachers (1)', *Waikato Journal of Education,* 11 (1), pp. 2–6.

Gibbons, A. (2007) 'The politics and processes of education: an early childhood metanarrative crisis', *Educational Philosophy and Theory,* 39(3), pp. 301–11.

Grieshaber, S. (2008). 'Interrupting stereotypes: teaching and the education of young children', *Early Childhood Education and Development,* 19(3), pp. 505–18.

Lester, M. and Russell, W. (2008) *Play for a change – Play, Policy and Practice: A review of contemporary perspectives,* London: Play England.

Lofdahl, A. (2006) 'Grounds for values and attitudes: children's play and peer-cultures in pre-school', *Journal of Early Childhood Research,* 4 (1), pp.77–88.

McAuley, H. and Jackson, P. (1992) *Educating Young Children: A structured approach,* London: David Fulton.

Mission, R. and Morgan, W. (2007) 'How critical is the aesthetic? The role of literature in English' in V. Ellis, G. Fox and B. Sweet (Eds) *Rethinking English in Schools, London: Continuum,* pp. 73–87.

Moore, A. (2004) *'The Good Teacher': Dominant Discourses in Teaching and Teacher Education.* London: RoutledgeFalmer.

Paley, V. G. (1992) *You can't say you can't play,* Cambridge: Harvard University Press.

Papatheodorou, T. (2009) 'Exploring relational pedagogy', in T. Papatheodorou and J. Moyles, (Eds) *Learning Together in the Early Years: Exploring Relational Pedagogy,* London: Routledge. pp. 3–17.

Papatheodorou, T. and Moyles, J. (Eds) (2009) *Learning Together in the Early Years: Exploring Relational Pedagogy,* London: Routledge.

Powell, S. (2008) 'The Value of Play: Constructions of Play in England's National Policies' *Children and Society,* 23(1), pp. 29–42.

Powell, K., Danby, S. and Farrell, A. (2006) 'Investigating an account of children passing: how boys and girls operate differently in relation to an everyday, classroom regulatory practice', *Journal of Early Childhood Research,* 4(3), pp. 259–75.

Riggall, A. and Sharp, C. (2008) 'The structure of primary education: England and other countries', *Primary Review Interim Report Research Survey 9/1,* Cambridge: University of Cambridge.

Rogers, S. (2010) 'Powerful pedagogies and playful resistance' in E. Brooker and S. Edwards (Eds) *Engaging Play,* Maidenhead: Open University Press, pp. 152–65.

Rogers, S. and Evans, J. (2008) *Inside Role Play in Early Childhood Education: Researching children's perspectives,* London: Routledge.

Rogers, S. and Rose, J. (2007) 'Ready for Reception? The advantages and disadvantages of single-point entry to school', *Early Years*, 27(1), March, pp. 47–63.

Sylva, K., Melhuish, E. C., Sammons, P., Siraj-Blatchford, I. and Taggart, B. (2004) 'The Effective Provision of Pre-school Education (EPPE) Project', *Technical Paper 12 – The Final Report: Effective Pre-school Education*. London: DfES/Institute of Education, University of London.

Tizard, B. (1977) 'Play: the child's way of learning?' in B. Tizard and D. Harvey (Eds) *The Biology of Play*, London: SIMP.

Tobin, J. (1995) 'Post-structural research in early childhood settings', in J. A. Hatch (Ed.) *Qualitative Research in Early Childhood Settings,* Greenwood Publishing Group,Westport CT.

Trawick Smith, J. (1998) 'School-based play and social interactions' in D.F. Fromberg and D. Bergen (Eds) *Play from Birth to Twelve and Beyond,* New York: Garland Publishing.

Walsh, D. (2005) 'Developmental theory and early childhood education: Necessary but not sufficient' in N. Yelland (Ed.) *Critical Issues in Early Childhood Education* Bucks: Open University Press.

Wood, E. (2009) 'Developing a Pedagogy of Play' in A. Anning, M. Fleer, and J. Cullen (Eds) *Early Childhood Education: Society and Culture*, London: Sage.

Wood, E. and Attfield, J. (2005) *Play, Learning and the Early Childhood Curriculum*, London: Paul Chapman.

Chapter 2

It's about power

Researching play, pedagogy and participation in the early years of school

Jo Ailwood

Play is a point at which many ideas in early childhood education converge. It can be a point of cohesion and friendship, of marginalization and exclusion, a place of pretence or of quiet solitude. How the range of different players in early childhood educational settings understand play is based in powerful sets of discourses and relationships. My interest is in investigating these discourses and relationships, particularly with regard to how relationships of power between adults and children or between children and children may be produced and managed.

In this chapter I will pursue a part of this agenda, examining the interconnected themes of power, play, participation and pedagogy in one small research project. As I consider these ideas I am aiming to do two things. First, I aim to continue my ongoing questioning of the discourses of play in early childhood education. Second, I aim to begin unpacking how young children play outside in the early years of school. As I am interested in discourses, relationships of power and conditions of possibility, my analytical focus is upon the context in which the research took place, what was possible to see, to say, to do in that location at that time – as child, teacher or researcher. To begin my discussion I first turn to two analytical ideas provided through the work of Foucault: conditions of possibility and relationships of power. I then turn to discuss play, participation, children's competence and pedagogy in early childhood settings, making use of a research project investigating children's views about playing outside at school.

Conditions of possibility and relationships of power

How we, as adults, think about young children is both enabled and constrained by the discursive possibilities we make use of to develop and justify our practice. These discourses form the conditions of possibility for thinking about, and acting within, our world. As Alldred and Burman (2005: 178) point out, our 'social world can only be accessed and interpreted via language'. The language and discourses of, for example, developmental psychology or the Reggio Emilia approach are well rehearsed in the early years literature (see for example, Bredekamp and Copple,1997; Dahlberg *et al.*, 2007). These discourses contribute to and also form the various conditions of possibility – the practices that are/are not possible in early years settings. In school sites, the early years of school operate within long established conditions of possibility, including regulation via bells, timetables and the disciplinary boundaries of subjects. Schools are institutional sites where relations of power and discourses of regulation have been produced and reproduced over decades, indeed centuries, functioning to govern the everyday lives of the children and adults who inhabit these sites. This broader context provides the conditions of possibility for what happens in the early years of school, in terms of research, play and pedagogy.

Gallagher (2008: 395) suggests that 'thinking about what power is and how it can be analysed is crucial for understanding children's participation'. While he was writing about participatory research methods with children, the point about power should also be extended to understanding children's play. From a Foucauldian perspective, power operates through relationships and actions – both our action upon ourselves and our actions upon and relationships with others (Foucault, 1982; 1977). In the early years a crucial point where these power relationships and actions flow is through children's play. A simple, everyday example of this is the setting up of a room with play activities and resources where adults are in a position to decide (perhaps in con-sultation with children, perhaps not) what resources are made available and will then often enforce limits on the numbers of children accessing the materials at any one time. These power relationships and actions function within and are dependent upon a field of regulated possibilities; that is there are a range of conditions of possibility that children and adults can and cannot draw upon to 'do' school. These possibilities function within relations of power, and the available discourses can be mobilized by some but not others. A further example is provided by Danby and Baker (1998), who describe how the 'big boys' in the block corner have access to a range of violent and exclusionary discourses that send the 'small boys' away from the block play and crying to the teacher, leaving the 'big boys' holding their ground in the block corner. For these boys, 'bigness' matters and it is a powerful condition of possibility that only some of the boys can draw upon. This unevenness is linked to relationships and contexts – who has the authority to speak, in what situations and upon what terms? This can also be contextualized through such things as geography, space or time: all of which set up conditions of possibility that enable and constrain relations of power.

These ideas of power, discourses and conditions of possibility are based in Foucault's work where power is relational and productive but also dependent upon freedoms. Foucault argues on several occasions that where there is power there is also the potential for resistance (e.g. 1977, 1978, 1982). An individual's freedom to resist the exertion of power, regulated within conditions of possibility, is central to this web-like understanding of power. In this understanding there are a multitude of relations of power in human societies, and these power relations operate in mobile ways that can be transformed and modified. In such power relationships, power and freedom are not mutually exclusive, but rather mutually constitutive.

Power can be understood in terms of a series of flows, networks and circularities that are spread throughout social relations. Power is integral to the management of populations and individuals. However, this understanding of power is not a deter-ministic one in which some hold more power than others and exercise it at will, and without resistance, to gain their desired ends. While the state and institutions certainly exercise particular relations of power, these are by no means the only relations of power in societies (Foucault, 2000/1978). One of the key analytical tools provided by Foucault is that power is more complex and intricate than can be conceptualized via a top down or commodified formulation. In major social institutions such as schools, power relationships may seem 'frozen' within the historical location of that institution (O'Farrell, 2008). For example, the principal or headteacher of a school maintains access to particular relations of power through his or her role – as adult, as leader of the school and as teacher – while teachers and children have access to different relationships of power. However, to stretch the metaphor, what is frozen can defrost, in other words these relations of power are not necessarily static or fixed.

Poststructural theories and the work of Foucault in particular, have formed the theoretical basis for a body of research that provides a challenge to 'traditional' early years theories and practices (e.g. Ailwood, 2003, 2008, 2010; Ryan, 2005; Sumsion, 2005; Mac Naughton, 2005). Such work can produce powerful and valuable ways of thinking in order to challenge received knowledge – the commonsense – by providing us with a way of thinking and language for asking political questions in new ways. The process of asking these questions and drawing on Foucault to develop analyses could be considered an optimistic process. For as the statement below indicates, Foucault was positive about the idea that power is about relationships:

> I say that power is a relation. A relation in which one guides the behavior of others. And there's no reason why this manner of guiding the behavior of others should not ultimately have results which are positive, valuable, interesting, and so on.
>
> (Foucault, 1988)

His ideas and the analytical tools that are his legacy reflect a hopefulness that knowing the historicity and changeability of situations can serve as a reminder that things do not necessarily need to stay as they are, and at the same time help us acknowledge that relations of power are not always and necessarily negative. From a Foucauldian perspective it is always necessary to consider the historicity of a setting, discourses, or the ways in which relations of power have arisen and are maintained in that site, for what purposes and with what effects (in the case of play see for example Ailwood, 2003).

Further in depth analysis of the relations of power, the capillaries and networks that work to produce conditions of possibility is an important aspect of the ongoing work of poststructural research in early childhood education. In our work with young children in education settings, the power relationships between adults and children are often taken as commonsense, and therefore easily ignored, marginalized or forgotten in the intense pace of our daily lives working with young children. How often do we question (especially in school-based early years settings) what choices or decisions children are enabled to make regarding very basic human necessities, for example what they'd like to eat or when to go to the bathroom. Do we provide spaces for children to be private – to play without being subject to an adult gaze? How rigid is the timetable and/or system of playtimes, are these managed by the ringing of a bell? In many Australian schools, young children have to learn how to eat their lunch while balancing their lunch box on their lap because lunch is eaten outside in a covered area with benches for sitting, but no tables. These are examples of common adult decisions, and adult built environments, that have material effects upon the daily life experiences of children. Many of these examples are so much a part of our lives with children that we take them for granted. However, when we forget that children operate in a world where all adults have greater access to political, social and economic relations of power, we fail to recognize that children, and particularly very young children, continue to live in a world where the conditions of possibility for their daily lives are produced and managed by adults.

Playing at school: a research project[1]

In Australia, most state and territory governments provide a non-compulsory year of school for children turning five. This year of provision goes by a number of different titles: for example the preparatory, reception or kindergarten year. Kindergarten in New South Wales is a year of voluntary, formal schooling for children turning five by July 31 in the year they attend and is part of the formal primary school setting, located in a classroom within the school site. School is not compulsory until the year the children turn six. I chose this school because of its size (having only 92 children (K-6) enrolled), and its rural location. The school playground included a large playing field, a concrete area, sandpit and climbing fort. At the time, I was working in a rural university and a focus on rural experience was valued within the local academic community. The town close by this school was in decline, as were many country towns in Australia, particularly during the period of extended drought at that time. This particular kindergarten class had 16 children enrolled, although, at the time of my visits, there was never full attendance.

In this project my aim was to investigate how children use play to organize and manage their relationships in the school playground. In my first meeting with the principal to discuss my project and seek entry to the school, I explained that I wanted the children to take photos of each other playing outside of the classroom and I would then have the photos developed and interview the children using the photos as stimulus for discussion. The principal gave me access to the school and the class, but suggested somewhat dismissively that 'I would just get photos of the concrete'. On talking to the classroom teacher, I found that she was also skeptical that the children would be able to take 'worthwhile' photos. Despite this initial sense of skepticism and disbelief from the principal and the teacher I gained access to the school and the class.

Formal written consent was sought from parents and the classroom teacher. Informal consent was sought from the children during initial discussions. During these discussions we sat together and talked about play, the research and taking photos. The children were reminded of consent issues again at the time of the interviews. The initial discussions aimed to ensure that the children who did not want to be photographed knew they could refuse. Given the institutional setting of a school and the powerful relationships between adults and children, gaining children's informed consent for research in a school setting may be considered a debatable process, for once parents and teachers have consented, young children may find it difficult to refuse (Morrow, 2005 and for further discussion of ethical considerations in interviews with children see also Danby and Farrell, 2005). One of the subsequent interviews included a moment when at least one of the children resisted and refused the photography aspect of the research:

Laura: Emma, you runned away from this one, didn't you Emma? She didn't want to be in there.
Emma: I runned away.

When I asked the children what they knew about cameras and how to use them the responses clearly showed knowledge of photography and cameras. As a group, the children demonstrated detailed, step-by-step instructions about how to use the cameras and take photographs. One child stood up and volunteered to explain, using the camera as he went:

> You close one eye [closed his eye]. You hold the camera up here [held the camera to his open eye] and you look through the hole and you click your finger here [pretended to click the picture button].

> (field notes)

Once we had established that the children were able to take photos of anything they liked to do during outside playtime at school, and that they all knew how to use cameras, I left the children with one disposable camera between small friendship groups of two or three. I returned a week later to gather cameras, had the film developed then returned another week later. There were around 200 photos – and only a small number were blurred or 'of the concrete'. I took friendship groups of children apart to show them their photos and ask them why they took them and about their play and games at school. I interviewed three groups of two children and one group of three children. These were audio recorded and transcribed. In total I interviewed nine children, five girls and four boys. All the names in this chapter are, of course, pseudonyms.

On this visit with the developed photos, I also brought with me a display folder with plastic slides, coloured card and other decorative materials for the children to create a class book about playing at school. This activity was intended to be a way to leave a token of thanks behind in the form of a literacy activity; I was playing the education/classroom game, drawing on powerful pedagogical discourses to establish myself and my own legitimacy in the classroom environment. In the end, it was this 'polished product' that impressed the teacher the most (personal communication with teacher). Indeed she was so proud of what the children had produced that we all had our photo taken with the book and she sent the photo and a story to the local newspaper reporting on the research and book-making. The teacher's decision to send a photo and article to the local newspaper also reflects different relationships of power in research process. As researcher I could not, ethically, have published the research in this way as it identified all participants to anyone who read the paper. The teacher, however, in a proud moment could make use of her position as classroom teacher to produce an ethically acceptable local news story.

Who's telling this story anyway?

Initially, I considered my interviews a profound failure. I slipped into 'teacher mode'. I attempted to keep order, manage the children, the discussion and the sharing out of the photos the children had taken. This was my first experience of interviewing children, and I simply was not prepared – despite my reading about conducting interviews with children – for the children's deep lack of interest in anything I was interested in. I wanted the children to tell me what they played outside at school, how and why. I was attempting to conduct my research with the idea of children's competence and participation as central, and I did not want to have to manage the interview conversation in the way I would manage a classroom conversation as teacher. If I was aiming for participatory research based in the idea that children were competent and capable – why didn't this feel right?

The interviews took place in a room next door to the classroom, with the door open at the school; my status as a teacher, or more specifically a teacher educator, was potentially on display. I felt the need to be 'teacherish' and 'in control' – at least to anyone wandering by. As an outsider in the physical environment of a school I was trying to establish myself within the more dominant, and powerful, discourse of what a 'good' teacher might look like. I was working within, or governing myself within, the conditions of possibility provided through existing power relationships and my own historical knowledge and experience of the complex relationships between universities, teaching and schools. My personal and adult agendas were foregrounded here, as I struggled to reconcile my resistance of a dominant discourse of children (as not able to undertake an adult activity such as photography) and the consequences of that resistance (other adults' dismissiveness) in the school site.

These feelings of uneasiness when researching with children in 'participatory' ways are not unique and have been reported elsewhere in the literature, for example, by Haudrup Christensen (2004) and Gallacher and Gallagher (2008). Furthermore, as I reflected on these interviews I decided that while they may have felt like a failure for me, they were not necessarily a failure for the children. The children successfully evaded my questions and maintained their focus on their own agenda at that time. To do this the children drew on powerful tactics – of ignoring and evading – and to some degree they could draw on these tactics because I was not their classroom teacher. As a visiting adult of obscure status, the children made use of the ambiguous power relationship with a non-teacher adult to pursue their own agendas.

The children were interested in the photos of themselves and their friends, sharing the photos between them and working out which ones to use in the book-making and which ones to take home. The discussion in the interviews reflected these nego-tiations between the children as they chose their photos and shared the copies out between themselves:

Jo: Can you choose a favourite one each that you'd like to tell me a little bit about?

Emma: I want this one.

Laura: Where's the big girl? I want that one.

Emma: I'm going to have two.

Jo: You're going to choose two are you? Okay.

Laura: Yeah, I'm going to pick two too.

Jo: Okay, you can pick two. Which one would you like?

Laura: I have to pick one first.

Luke: I'm choosing one, I get some good ones.

Blake: Not that one, no way.

Luke: I've got 1,2,3,4.

Blake: 4,5,6.

Luke: 7, I picked 7.

Blake: I picked 6.

Luke: I'll swap one.

The negotiation for ownership of the photos was enthusiastically and vociferously undertaken by the children, reflecting Clark and Moss (2001) who also suggest that children enjoyed the process of photography, reporting the excitement children expressed when presented with their photos. Once the excitement of seeing the pho-tos and of negotiating ownership over the prints abated, I was able to begin asking the children questions. I asked the children about why they picked particular photos, what games they like to play at school and what they like to do with their friends in the playground. They talked about friends, school games and pretending. Three of the four groups of children raised 'traditional' school games such as duck duck goose, crocodile crocodile, ring around the rosy or teddy bear teddy bear turn around.

Jo: So what are your favourite games when you come to school? What do you like playing best?

Blake: I like playing best, playing with my friends and that.

Jo: Just playing with friends and that? Do you have a particular game you like to play with your friends?

Blake: Lucky where is he, pocket full of daisies, crocodile crocodile, duck duck goose.

Jo: Oh, duck duck goose? You like those games?

Blake: Yeah

Jo: What about you Luke?

Luke: Oh, I usually play, I usually play soccer, and play with my friends.

Jo: what would you say is your favourite game to play outside at school?

Sonia: I'd say crocodile, crocodile.
Jo: What kind of games do you like playing together at school?
Emma: Ring around the rosy.
Laura: I know, I'm duck, duck, goose

The games the children listed, some of which I had played myself as a child or played with children in my class when I was teaching, have a long history. Children's folklore has been documented at least since Opie and Opie (1955) and variations on the games mentioned by the children in the interviews have been noted by children's folklorists for many years (e.g. Factor, 2004). The nostalgia of these games reflects a powerful discourse of 'traditional' childhood, a discourse the children drew upon to respond to my questioning about games and play at school.

Alldred and Burman (2005: 193) point out that 'we need to ask through what cultural understandings of children are the words of any child "heard", and how our account of them will be heard'. In other words, as adults we are listening to and hearing children through our own cultural understandings of who we think children are. Perhaps in these interviews the children were making careful use of what they perceived to be the acceptable discourses available to them in a discussion about play with an adult located in the setting of the school. My responses in the interviews indicate surprise that the children raised these organized and traditional games as their favourite thing to play at school rather than play of imagination and pretence. Discussion of traditional and organized games was not a response I expected and I was not necessarily hearing what I wanted to hear or indeed asking the right sort of questions (is 'playing a game' the same as 'playing'?).

As the interviews progressed pretence was also raised and discussed at length by many of the children. One pair of girls liked to play in the 'cubby house', in this case the cubby house was a wooden outside climbing fort with an enclosed space. In this cubby house, the girls could trick others by hiding:

Jo: Yeah, so why do you like playing in the cubby house Sonia?
Sonia: Because you can hide in the cubby
Jo: Hide from who?
Rebecca: Your friends
Sonia: The teachers or friends. You can trick everybody
Jo: You can pretend you're not really there at all
Sonia: Yeah
             Sonia also pretended to be a horse:
Sonia: Yep – I'm a horse
Jo: You're being a horse there?
Sonia: Exercising

A pair of boys discussed their pretend play at home with machine guns, play that took place in a ditch near both home and the school. This play was interrupted by one of their mothers. The pretend aspect became clear when I asked how and why they played the 'machine gun' game:

Luke: One time he played a game at home with me with machine guns, you know.
Blake: We didn't know the game before we played it.
Luke: No.
Jo: So how did you play it, when you didn't know it before you played it?
Blake: We just pretended.
Jo: You just pretended? You made it up as you went along?
Blake: And then my mum comes out . . .
Jo: So you tricked her?
Blake: No, she saw what the game was.
Luke: We didn't redo the game but.

A second group of boys discussed their favourite game at school as 'going down the toilet':

Jo: What's your favourite game to play at school?
Neil: Go down the toilet, that's the toilet [points to the fireman's pole in the climbing fort].
Ian: Oh yeah
Jo: What is it?
Ian: We call it the toilet
Jo: Oh, you call it the toilet
Ian: Going down the toilet
Jo: It looks like the fireman's pole
Neil: You go straight down and you go, ooohhh . . .

I attempted to extend the discussion with a joking statement of 'the real' and said 'it looks like the fireman's pole'. The children, however, ignored me and continued to describe in ribald terms how they 'play the bum game' and go 'down the toilet' and land at the bottom. In the playful moment, I was ignored by the boys as they continued to develop the storyline of their pretence. For children of this age, pretence is a dominant and powerful discourse that they can draw upon to maintain their play, providing the potential for excluding and resisting adult agendas (Rogers and Evans, 2008). Hiding from others was also a form of pretence and, potentially, refusal.

Pretending and hiding can be powerful discourses of play that are acceptable to many adults as a playful, child-like or childish activity. It should be remembered also, that this play took place outside the classroom, in the school playground during breaktime. Learning of course does not stop at the classroom door and the pedagogy of play outside at school continues, as does the teachers' regulatory gaze. In Australia, 'playground duty' is part of a teachers' role and teachers are timetabled to supervise all eating and play breaks. Policing the social life between children in the playground is an integral function of children's play, and adults remain part of these policing relationships outside of the classroom. Despite this, there is very little education-based literature about play in school playgrounds for this age group (Rogers and Evans 2008; but see for example Blatchford, 1994).

Living with the tensions: relationships of power, participation and pedagogy

By making use of the 'disposable camera' method my aim was for the children to have an active and participatory role within the research process. Burman (2008: 17) suggests that, 'representation is always a practice of power'. Enabling the children to take the photos did alter some of the power relationships between children and adults, for example, the principal and teacher recognized and were pleasantly surprised by, and proud of, the children's ability to take successful photos. However, in and of itself the use of cameras as a data generation method for young children is not necessarily altering power relationships in any significant way. Providing children with disposable cameras was an attempt on my part to enable children to have control over what photos they took; that is, over what representations of themselves at play in school playgrounds they decided to record. However, my representations of the photos, interviews and my analytic choices all reflect my greater access to institutional power in terms of writing and publication. As the adult and the researcher, I get to speak. The children may not have represented the play as I did or have chosen the aspects of their play as of importance for analysis. The analysis provided in this chapter then is a representation of a representation – as the children represent themselves through photography and the interview discussions and I then re-represent these. After reflecting upon this research experience I would concur with Burman (2008: 16) who points out that 'there are major political and methodological challenges ahead in elaborating, implementing and evaluating practices of self-representation'.

Using photography as a data generation method, with young children, is one key way through which researchers are encouraged to enable children to participate in the research process. It is a seemingly unproblematic means for enabling children's self-representation, usually based in an often unproblematized philosophy of children's participation. It is presented as one way to 'empower' or 'give voice to' children and for them to be part of, and sometimes lead, the research process. 'Giving children a voice' or 'empowering children' is now a fairly common call, however, it nonetheless points towards the sturdiness of relationships of power between adults and children. For adults to 'give voice' they first have to be conceptualized as holding the power and the voice – a conceptualization that implies children have none or little of either. As Gallagher (2008) has also argued, if we accept that there are complex power relationships at play when we think of children's participation, then we must problematise the assumption that enable us to suggest that adults are able to 'give a voice' to children. 'Giving voice' also focuses upon the adult/child relationship, which tends to marginalize the complexity and ambiguity of the web of power relations that make up a classroom, school or other sort of early childhood setting, including the significance of relationships of power between children. A powerful relationship between the children that I did not explore but that I think warrants exploration, is that of who gets to be in the photo and who gets to take it, and what sort play and negotiation forms this decision-making process for children.

The doubt some adults hold about children's ability to engage effectively in social relationships or undertake perceived 'adult' practices, such as taking photos and being and discussing their play in interviews, is reflected in the comments of the principal and the teacher at this school who, at that time, did not have much confidence in the children's ability to successfully take part in the research. From this research experience, I would suggest that while the idea that young children are competent and their play reflects complex negotiations and social relationships has gained ground in some quarters, its uptake in school settings remains uneven. This is not surprising given that the ideas of children's participation and competence requires a significant shift in adults' thinking and conceptualizing about children, play and pedagogy. Bae (2009) reports a similar experience in the Norwegian context, suggesting that respect for children as competent beings, while embedded in policy, remains uneven in practice and dependent upon adult understandings and views of children and childhood.

Conclusion

Early years settings are sites of human interaction, where relationships of power are played out within particular conditions of possibility. When these settings are located within schools, there is a complex combination of 'school-like' and 'early childhood-like' possibilities swirling around the children and teacher. Within these conditions of possibility, relationships of power can be unpicked as children and adults seek to govern each other's behaviours. Play is a powerful discourse that has relatively recently become subject to a critical eye within the field. The conditions of possibility for children and adults that are enabled or constrained through play vary widely. For the children in this study, play outside at school was a place of maintaining children's culture and folklore, of pretence, friendship and humour.

In the early years an increased understanding of, and critical engagement with, the complexities of children's play will enable new relationships and pedagogies to develop between young children and early years practitioners. The ideas of children's competence, children's participation and understanding the complexities of play also enable shifts in children's relationships with adults. The necessity of children's relationships with adults remains, and within social structures and institutions adults will always have greater access to positions of power than children. In the context of schools, adults have far greater access to socially and institutionally sanctioned positions of power. However, the power relationships between adults and children in schools depend also on children's freedoms and resistance. Play is a key site where these are negotiated. Hiding, pretending, maintaining playground folklore and side-stepping adult questions were all ways children in this study engaged with relationships of power and freedom through play. In continuing to question and problematize play, we can reveal relationships of power between children and adults, and between children and children. Through this process we begin to make new spaces for thinking about play, pedagogy and participation in the early years of school.

Note

1 The research discussed in this paper was undertaken with the assistance of a Faculty of Education Seed Grant, Charles Sturt University, 2003.

References

Ailwood, J. (2003) 'Governing early childhood through play', *Contemporary Issues in Early Childhood*, 4, 3: 286–99.

—— (2008) 'Earning or learning in the Smart State: Changing tactics for governing early childhood education', *Childhood*, 15, 4: 535–51.

—— (2010) 'Playing with some tensions: Poststructuralism, Foucault and early childhood education' in L. Brooker and S. Edwards (Eds) *Engaging Play*, Milton Keynes: Open University Press.

Alldred, P. and Burman, E. (2005) 'Analysing children's accounts using discourse analysis', in S. Greens and D. Hogan (Eds) *Researching Children's Experience, Approaches and Methods*, London: Sage.

Bae, B. (2009) 'Children's right to participate – challenges in everyday interactions', *European Early Childhood Education Research Journal*, 17, 3: 391–406.

Burman, E. (2008) *Developments: Child, Image, Nation*, London: Routledge.

Blatchford, P. (1994) 'Research on children's school playground behaviour in the United Kingdom: a review', in P. Blatchford and S. Sharp (Eds) *Breaktime and the School, Understanding and Changing Playground Behaviour*, London: Routledge.

Bredekamp, S. and Copple, C. (Eds) (1997) *Developmentally Appropriate Practice in Early Childhood Programs Serving Children From Birth Through Age 8*. (2nd Edition) Washington: National Association for the Education of Young Children.

Clark, A. and Moss, P. (2001) *Listening to Young Children: The Mosaic Approach*, London: National Children's Bureau.

Dahlberg, G., Moss, P. and Pence, A. (2007) *Beyond Quality in Early Childhood Education and Care: Languages of Evaluation* (2nd Edition), London: Falmer Press.

Danby, S. and Baker, C. (1998) 'How to be masculine in the block area', *Childhood*, 5, 2: 151–75.

Danby, S. and Farrell, A. (2005) 'Opening the research conversation' in A. Farrell (Ed.) *Ethical Research with Children*, Maidenhead: Open University Press.

Factor, J. (2004) 'Tree stumps, manhole covers and rubbish tins: the invisible play-lines of a primary school playground', *Childhood*, 11, 2: 142–54.

Foucault, M. (1977) *Discipline and Punish: The Birth of the Prison* (A. Sheridan, Trans.) Harmondsworth: Penguin.

—— (1978) *The History of Sexuality: 1, The Will to Knowledge*. London: Penguin.

—— (1982) 'The subject and power', in H. Dreyfuss and P. Rabinow (Eds) *Michel Foucault, Beyond Structuralism and Hermeneutics* (2nd edition), Chicago: Chicago University Press.

—— (1988) 'Power, Moral Values, and the Intellectual. An Interview with Michel Foucault by Michael Bess', *History of the Present* 4: 1 http://www.vanderbilt.edu/historydept/michaelbess/Foucault%20Interview (Accessed 5 November 2009).

—— (2000/1978) 'Governmentality' in J. D. Faubion (Ed.) *Power, the Essential Works of Foucault 1954–1984*, 3, London: The Penguin Press.

Gallacher, L. and Gallagher, M. (2008). Methodological immaturity in childhood research? Thinking through 'participatory methods', *Childhood*, 15, 4: 499–516.

Gallagher, M. (2008) 'Foucault, power and participation', *International Journal of Children's Rights*, 16: 395–406.

Haudrup Christensen, P. (2004) 'Children's participation in ethnographic research: Issues of power and representation', *Children & Society*, 18, 2: 165–76.

Mac Naughton, G. (2005) *Doing Foucault in Early Childhood Studies: Applying Poststructrual Ideas*, London: Routledge.

Morrow, V. (2005) 'Ethical issues in collaborative research with children' in A. Farrell (Ed.) *Ethical Research with Children*, Maidenhead: Open University Press.

O'Farrell, C. (2008) 'Foucault on Power and Resistance', Weblog. *Refracted Input*. 3 December 2008.   http://inputs.wordpress.com/2008/12/03/foucault-quote-for-december-2008/ (Accessed 5 November 2009).

Opie, J. and Opie, I. (1955) *The Oxford Nursery Rhyme Book*, London: Open University Press.

Rogers, S. and Evans, J. (2008) *Inside Role-play in Early Childhood Education: Researching Young Children's Perspectives*, London: Routledge.

Ryan, S. (2005) 'Freedom to choose, examining children's experiences in choice time' in N. Yelland (Ed.) *Critical Issues in Early Childhood Education*, Maidenhead: Open University Press.

Sumsion, J. (2005) 'Preschool children's portrayals of their male teacher: a poststructural analysis' in N. Yelland (Ed.) *Critical Issues in Early Childhood Education*, Maidenhead: Open University Press.

Chapter 3

The challenge of play for early childhood educators

Sue Dockett

Introduction

Play has a long history as an integral element of early childhood curriculum and pedagogy. There is consensus that play is both a vehicle for learning and a forum in which children can demonstrate their learning and development (Broadhead, 2006; *et al.*, 2002; Pramling-Samuelsson and Johansson, 2006; Wood, 2008). Traditional beliefs reiterate the value and positive nature of play, particularly the opportunities within play for children to exercise freedom, independence, choice and autonomy (Bennett *et al.*, 1997). While the benefits of play for children have been widely promoted, much less attention has been directed towards pedagogies of play and the role of educators within these. Indeed, traditional conceptualisations of play promote the role of educators as observers or facilitators of play, reflecting a focus on play as a child-directed, rather than teacher-directed, activity (Bennett *et al.*, 1997).

Recently, researchers have challenged assumptions about the universal efficacy of play and conceptualisations of freedom within play (Brooker, 2002; MacNaughton, 2004; Wood, 2007). Accompanying these challenges has been a growing focus on the role of play as a vehicle for teaching, as well as learning. Play-based pedagogies are not new in early childhood education: the significance of play for children has been noted by theorists including Froebel, Montessori, McMillan, Isaacs and many others (Dockett and Fleer, 1999). What is relatively new in seeking to understand the role of play in early childhood education is a focus on teaching, as well as learning, through play. Integral to this understanding is consideration of teachers' theories of play and the ways in which these impact on teachers' practice, for example in the implementation of curriculum, organisation of the learning environment and in the planned learning outcomes and as well as the pedagogical strategies employed (Bennett *et al.*, 1997). Wood (2008) reminds us that conceptualising play-based pedagogy presents challenges for early childhood educators. Of these, two are particularly pertinent to the study reported in this chapter. First, there is often a lack of clarity about pedagogies of play, defined as "provision for playful and play-based activities . . . design [of] play/learning environments, and all the pedagogical techniques and strategies [used] . . . to support or enhance learning through play" (Wood, 2004: 19). Second, there is also uncertainty about the place of play within contexts such as the first year of school, where 'play has always sat uneasily between the informal approaches that are typical in pre-school settings, and the more formal demands that are made in compulsory schooling' (Wood 2007: 311).

This chapter explores perceptions of play and play-based pedagogies among one group of teachers in Australia. As part of a larger, ongoing study, teachers in prior-to-school and first year of school settings shared their perspectives of play within their specific contexts. Opportunities to reflect on these perspectives provided impetus for a number of these teachers to engage in an ongoing process of practitioner inquiry, challenging their own and others' views of play, reconsidering their role in play and examining the barriers they encountered as they sought to implement play-based pedagogies. The aim in sharing these perspectives is to shed light on some of the assumptions these teachers shared about play and to provoke continued discussion about play-based pedagogies. For the teachers involved, the data reported in the chapter provide a record of their starting points in challenging, changing and reconceptualising their approach to play and pedagogy.

Background

During 2007, the South Australian Department of Education and Children's Services (DECS)[1] commenced a three-year project aimed at reforming pedagogy in the first year of school. Underlying this project was the view that the first year of school in South Australia (known as Reception) had changed a great deal since its introduction in 1981, when it was intended to provide a transitional learning context for children as they moved from prior-to-school experiences to compulsory schooling.

Children in South Australia may start school at the beginning of the school term after their fifth birthday, even though the compulsory school starting age is six years. Unlike most other states and territories in Australia, there are several intakes of children to school each year. However, there is only one intake into Year 1 each year, which means that the time children spend in Reception will vary – for example a child starting school in the last term of the year would usually spend a year and a term in Reception before progressing to Year 1.

Anecdotal evidence had suggested that the perceived purpose of Reception had shifted from a period of transition towards a programme with specified academic outcomes, and that this was reflected in both pedagogy and curriculum. Similar concerns have been reported in a range of other countries, with first year of school classes adopting more formal 'primary school' pedagogy rather than pedagogies of play most often associated with prior-to-school settings (Adams *et al.*, 2004; McLane, 2003; Morgan and Kennewell, 2006; Ranz-Smith, 2007; Rogers and Evans, 2007; Sharp, 2002; Walsh *et al.*, 2006). In this vein, Rogers and Evans (2008: 16) characterise play in school as having been 'hijacked for the purposes of delivering a subject-based curriculum where the demand is to produce tangible outcomes'. Reasons for the shift towards an academically oriented first year of school have been related to pressure for children to attain specific standards of performance (Rogers and Evans, 2008) and an associated emphasis on literacy and numeracy, often perceived to be at the expense of play (Fisher, 2000).

The South Australian project – *Early Years: Curriculum Continuity for Learning* – was designed to map perspectives and experiences of pedagogy in early childhood contexts (prior-to-school and Reception) and to use this to inform pedagogical change within Reception. The driving force for pedagogical change was to be teachers themselves, as they reflected on their own practice and engaged in cycles of practitioner inquiry to enact change in both their conceptualisation of pedagogy and their pedagogical practice. The overall aim was to seek a better match between pedagogy and the characteristics and dispositions of young children and their learning as they make the transition to school from prior-to-school experiences. Although the term *pedagogy* has not had a long history of use in Australian early childhood contexts, the project adopted both the use of the term and the definition proposed by Siraj-Blatchford, *et al.* (2002: 28) as 'that set of instructional techniques and strategies which enable learning to take place and provide opportunities for the acquisition of knowledge, skills, attitudes and dispositions within a particular social and material context'. Adopting this terminology served to connect early childhood teaching and learning with the broader field of education and pedagogy and signalled to teachers that the project was about provoking change around conceptualisations of learning and teaching. As part of the initial mapping phase of the project, a literature review (Dockett *et al.*, 2007), examining effective pedagogy in the early years was used to inform a series of focus group interviews with educators in prior-to-school and school contexts, parents of children in these settings, and their children. Within the interviews, there was a particular focus on play and the role of play in early childhood curriculum and pedagogy. The discussion in this chapter reports the teachers' perspective of play and their use of play-based pedagogy across both prior-to-school (PTS) and first year of school (FYOS) settings.

Play and pedagogy in the early years

In their review of effective pedagogy in the early years, the Early Years Special Interest Group of the British Educational Research Association (BERA-SIG) (2003: 13) described play as 'an almost hallowed concept for teachers of young children'. Despite this revered position, the place of play in early childhood education – particularly the early years of school – has been challenged in recent years. Underlying these challenges has been recognition of:

- changing understandings of play that question the developmental discourse that has characterised Western notions of play, particularly Developmentally Appropriate Practice (Ailwood, 2003; MacNaughton, 2004; Ryan, 2005) to emphasise the importance of the social and cultural contexts in which play occurs;
- diversity in the ways in which children learn. Play is not the only strategy used to promote children's learning in the early years, and it may well not be the preferred strategy for all children (Brooker, 2002; Wood, 2007);
- increasing demands to start academic education earlier, particularly for children from minority or marginalized groups who, in general, may not be perceived to be succeeding in school (McLane, 2003);

- the role of individual teachers, their beliefs and practices, and how these impact on the practice of play within early childhood education (Bennett *et al.*, 1997; Ranz-Smith, 2007; Rogers and Evans, 2008);
- the changing nature and experience of play as children engage with popular culture and a range of technologies (See Waller this volume, Marsh, 2005); and
- considerable variations in the quality of children's play, particularly in relation to child-adult interactions and cognitive challenge (Moyles, *et al.*, 2002; Sylva, *et al.*, 2004).

These challenges suggest that for play to retain its central place within early childhood pedagogy, there is a need to articulate clearly the rationale and purposes of play, as well as any limitations in the implementation of current play-based pedagogies. One approach to this task has been to explore teachers' theories of play and the alignment of these with practice. For example, Bennett *et al.* (1997: 126) note a strong commitment to play, largely derived from a Piagetian, constructivist orientation which emphasises the child actively constructing knowledge from interactions with the environment, resources and peers. In practice, this often meant that teachers adopted a reactive role in play, waiting for children to initiate experiences. While acknowledging a range of mediating factors that impacted on the implementation of play-based programmes, Bennett *et al.* (1997) also supported calls for a new pedagogy of play that incorporated socio-cultural models of learning and teaching with greater focus on the importance of social and cultural contexts in learning and teaching. Socio-cultural models of teaching and learning support a more pro-active and complex role for teachers in play and attach greater significance to teacher-directed interactions than constructivist models (Wood, 2007). In keeping with socio-cultural models, Siraj-Blatchford and Sylva (2004) have argued that educators need to provide appropriate scaffolding and support as children are challenged to co-construct new knowledge, skills and understandings. The changed role for educators underpins a call for a new pedagogy of play, where play is characterised as a planned and purposeful activity, built around a well resourced environment and rich interactions with adults (BERA-SIG, 2003).

Exploring teacher's perspectives of play

The *Early Years: Curriculum Continuity for Learning* project provided a context for the exploration of teachers' perspectives about play, the provisions they made in their contexts for play, challenges they faced in implementing play-based pedagogy and the nature of the play experiences in which their children engaged. Through the project, researchers visited six sites in South Australia and spoke with 15 teachers in prior-to-school settings (kindergarten or kindy, preschool, playgroup), 10 teachers of the first years of school and five school principals. The sites were diverse in terms of geography (urban, rural and remote), the social and cultural composition of the population, the educational needs of the children, and the experiences of the teachers.

Early childhood curriculum in South Australia is informed by the South Australian Curriculum Standards and Accountability framework (SACSA) (DECS, 2001), which outlines curriculum expectations for children aged from birth to Year 12. One of the four bands in the framework relates to early childhood, covering the period from birth to Year 2 (about age 8). Within this, three phases (0–3 years, 3–5 years, and Reception to Year 2) are outlined and the importance of children learning through play is noted. Learning outcomes are aligned with each phase. Those listed for the 3–5 years phase are framed as broad developmental learning statements. From the early years of school (Reception to Year 2), there is greater specificity in outcomes associated with designated curriculum areas. Despite this difference, there is a common curriculum framework across prior-to-school and school settings. Within this common framework, how do teachers define and use play?

Teacher definitions of play

Teachers across both PTS and FYOS settings stated beliefs in the value and importance of play in the early childhood years:

> The process of teaching children at 4 years of age has to be through a play-based curriculum . . . the processes of supporting and scaffolding children's learning through play is our fundamental pedagogy.
>
> [PTS teacher]

> [play] teaches kids so many things, just the being able to work in with others, the social skills part of it . . . They learn from each other and also they're learning at their own rate.
>
> [FYOS teacher]

These statements indicate that play is a 'pedagogical priority' (Bennett *et al.*, 1997) across both prior-to-school and school settings. While these two statements cannot be considered representative of all teachers involved in the project, they do reflect some diverse perspectives on play: from the PTS teacher there is a sense that play-based pedagogy involves teacher support and scaffolding; from the FYOS teacher there is a sense that play is an activity for children, controlled by the children, which may not require the involvement of an adult. It may well be that some of the mediating factors identified by Bennett *et al.* (1997), such as the pragmatics of organising a FYOS classroom with low staff to student ratios, also impinge on perspectives of play.

Despite a shared recognition of the importance of play, several teachers expressed the view that the FYOS was different from PTS settings, suggesting that there was a move away from play to a more formal, work based context.

> [in Reception we] start . . . to formalise things . . . getting some of those tools, of those basic skills.
>
> (FYOS teacher)

> [Reception] needs to be a little bit different because they are at school and it is a new step. They . . . learn a little bit more, like more on the educational side of things. I think by the time they get to school they need to have a bit more than just . . . playtime. It needs to be a little bit harder.
>
> (PTS teacher)

Teachers' definitions of play reflected elements identified in other studies (Ashiabi, 2007; Bennett *et al.*, 1997; Monighan-Nourot, 1997; Morgan and Kennewell, 2006), including:

- Choice
  [at kindy] we have lots of activities but we have free choice. But we don't really have free choice, everything they're doing is being programmed, planned, sorted out, individually for each child and they're working through a curriculum . . . We have to prepare the child for being ready for school. [PTS teacher]

- Activity
  . . . the most meaningful learning that happens . . . is actually through play and through the doing things . . . [FYOS teacher]

- Intrinsic motivation for the players
  play is our fundamental pedagogy . . . What we use is the innate desire to learn . . . The intrinsic motivation is what all good teaching is about. [PTS teacher]

The issue of choice was identified by Bennett *et al.* (1997) as a dilemma for teachers. On the one hand, teachers reported that much of the value of play related to children's freedom to make choices and hence, their control and ownership of play. On the other hand, there was realisation that any such freedom existed within the constraints of what was provided by teachers and the ways in which teachers managed the learning environment. The comment included here highlights the same dilemma: the importance of choice is noted, but so too is the qualification that the choice is, itself, limited – by the curriculum, demands to prepare children for school and the boundaries set by the teacher.

The other elements noted regularly by teachers – activity and intrinsic motivation – also feature in many lists of the characteristics of play (for example, Rubin, Fein, and Vandenberg, 1983). Ailwood (2003: 289) relates this focus to romantic/nostalgic understandings of play as a 'natural, intrinsic and free' process. Once again, the control and ownership of play is vested in the children; it is their activity and their intrinsic motivation that drives play. This view of play suggests a reactive role for adults – responding to children's interests and actions.

Play and learning

All participating teachers made connections between children's play and learning. When asked what children learned through play, teachers noted:

> Getting into a routine, starting to get into the mode of team work and friendships.
> [PTS teacher]

> [through play] they're getting the literacy and numeracy, social stuff, relational stuff, thinking, all of that is being built up in that . . . oral language . . . These children don't seem to come with those skills.
>
> [FYOS teacher]

[the children are] kind of learning through play and social skills . . . I quite like the idea of where children learn without them really knowing.

[PTS teacher]

For most of the participating teachers, there was an assumption that children who were playing were also learning, largely through discovery. While it was mentioned occasionally, the notion that children might engage in play to practice or master particular skills or activities (Fromberg, 2002) was much less prevalent.

Most teachers linked play with children's socialisation and their learning of specific skills related to literacy and numeracy. Teacher comments suggested that they regarded play as a context in which children could interact with their peers, in ways that were relevant for them, and engage in tasks or activities at a level that matched their levels of development and understanding. As reported by Bennett *et al.* (1997), these teachers regarded play as a context characterised by child control and choice, hence creating a situation where children 'couldn't fail'. Despite this, there was also a belief that some children did not have the prerequisite skills for success in play, and that these needed to be taught – much as Smilansky and Shefatya (1990) suggest in their notion of play training.

Overall, teacher comments reflected developmental discourses of play (Ailwood, 2003), referring to both stages of play and the connection between play and different developmental domains. Teachers across both PTS and FYOS expected children to possess a repertoire of skills to support their engagement in play, and also expected children to be able to engage in play independently.

Teacher provision for play varied considerably across contexts and sites. How teachers described this also depended on their definitions of play. For example, one teacher equated play with 'free play' and noted that the only time that children could choose their play and their companions in her Reception class was on Friday afternoons. Another teacher who described play as a daily occurrence equated play with children being able to choose an activity from the range she had set up, before moving on to the next activity. These differences reflect the different pedagogical orientations described by Wood (2008), which range from children having free choice of play materials, activities and partners, to teacher selected materials, activities and partners.

Teacher roles in play

Teachers' descriptions of their roles within play also varied considerably. Teacher roles in play are often described as a continuum, from indirect planning for play to direct involvement in play (Dockett and Fleer, 1999). For some teachers, there was a clear preference for non-interventionist roles.

[when they're playing] I'm normally doing reading . . . At times, I interact if I have time. Like they'll come and bring their cup of coffee or pretend . . . and so I interact in that way but it's their reward at the end of the thing . . .

[FYOS school teacher]

For others, play involved intervention in a range of ways.

> . . . our jobs would have to be to supply the resources so that if they were going to play at being, you know, a train driver or whatever, somehow, somewhere from your magic cupboard that's in the big room that you've got, you would be able to produce a couple of big boxes that with lots of imagination and perhaps you just throwing in the odd ideas. 'Well look here's a bit of a cylinder, what might you use this for?' . . . And then if they go so far with it, you need to be able either to say 'Ok that's the end of the trains' or to step in and say 'Perhaps we'll start planning, we'll go on a train'. So it would be just being subtle and being there beside them. Propping up the kids too, who have got no idea what happens on a train. Not letting them be run over by the kid whose father is a train driver. All those sorts of things, but providing the resources and being there.
>
> [FYOS teacher]

> To begin with it's right in there with them, showing them. It's highly structured play and then gradually pulling away . . . a lot of kids don't have play skills because the parents don't have play skills in the first place . . . it needs to be facilitated and supported and modelled and directed.
>
> [FYOS teacher]

These comments reflect two different approaches to play. The first comment draws from constructivist approaches to play, characterised by a focus on children's ownership of play and adult reluctance to intervene. Several teachers indicated that they used children's play time as an opportunity to engage in other tasks, such as reading with a small group or administrative tasks. In some instances, play was presented as a reward for completing 'work'. For these teachers, descriptions of their roles included words such as 'watching', 'observing' or 'facilitating' play. The pragmatics of managing a classroom may also influence this approach. Contrasting with the constructivist approach, the latter comments draw much more on socio-cultural theories, emphasising active adult involvement in play and high levels of scaffolding. There is still a sense from these teachers that providing resources and facilitating play is important, but also that their active engagement in play can provoke increasingly complex play and address some equity issues, such as assisting children to enter particular play contexts.

Regardless of their theoretical approach, there were some underlying issues related to the role of teachers in play. Overall, there was a general sense that play was owned and controlled by the children. Even when teachers made suggestions to extend or complicate the play, teachers believed that children had the right to choose whether or not to pursue these suggestions. In other words, child choice over-ruled teachers' pedagogical expertise (MacNaughton, 2004). There was also an expectation that children would have the skills to guide, plan and engage in play, often without adult help. Much of the teacher's role in scaffolding play related to assisting children deemed to be without these skills to engage in play. These results are not dissimilar from those reported by Bennett *et al.* (1997), in that they support teachers' general reluctance to engage in play and the expectation that children will demonstrate independence and autonomy in their play. Where children do not demonstrate these attributes, the role of the teacher is often described in terms of helping children to attain these.

Barriers to play

Alongside their views about the importance of play and children's learning through play, many teachers emphasised a range of barriers to implementing play-based pedagogy. Some of these barriers were contextually bound, and others were described as general societal or systemic barriers. Some teachers described different strategies to remove the barriers; others considered them insurmountable. It is important to note also that what were barriers for some teachers actually helped other teachers promote play. Common barriers included:

- School administration. While guided by the SACSA framework, teachers noted that the leaders within the school had an impact on their freedom to teach in particular ways. Some school leaders were particularly supportive of play-based pedagogy. Others were not: [some principals] don't understand . . . early childhood. [FYOS teacher]
- Systems issues. This barrier included expectations from the state-wide education system for teachers to engage with new programmes, skills and ways of doing things, as well as pressure to incorporate additional material into the curriculum. In addition, reporting and accountability requirements were seen to impinge on teachers' preferences for teaching and the time they had to implement pedagogies of play.

  . . . we are pressured with the technology . . . it's just the feeling of pressure, we are operating with computers in the classrooms, linked to the internet . . . and now we've been set up with smart boards in every classroom . . . and so you're trying to learn to use all this with the children . . . [we're] learning to cope . . . learning new things . . . how can I also set up for play and this and that and keep up with what I would like? [FYOS teacher]
- Curriculum expectations. Some teachers interpreted the SACSA curriculum framework in very prescriptive ways. In some cases, this led to teachers believing that play interfered with their attempts to teach to and for specific outcomes. Other teachers regarded play as a means of achieving these same outcomes. The pressure of curriculum expectation was felt by some teachers in PTS, as well as school settings.

  There is a bit of pressure that comes down on the kindergartens as well about curriculum and assessment . . . the curriculum pressure that leaves you with almost no space to move, is that its almost like childhood itself is being squeezed down to this shorter and shorter period of time. [Children] have to be always learning, learning, learning, being assessed. [FYOS teacher]

  . . . there's such a push down on literacy, in its very reading and writing sense . . . [PTS teacher]

- Parental expectations. There was a general view among teachers that parents did not value play as a means for promoting learning. This was more so from teachers of the first years of school, where parents were reported to focus on the work expected of their children at school.

    . . . there's pressure from parents which I think is driven by fear that if their children don't succeed then they won't do well in the world. [FYOS teacher]

    . . . the media has made parents believe they are failing parents if they haven't ticked all these boxes and got these kids moving along . . . we get it here 'When are you teaching my child to read?' [PTS teacher]

- Classroom management. In some sites, groups of children were described as disruptive, or not possessing skills deemed necessary for play. In these situations, teachers reported an unwillingness to make provisions for play.

    . . . coming from home where there's no structure or no routines and then being thrown into the classroom, they have never had anything like that . . . in my classroom . . . getting them to be used to routines, being comfortable with other kids, having to sit down and learn the rules like put your hand up and can I go to the toilet . . . [otherwise] off they go, they're wandering outside or . . . [FYOS teacher]

- Classroom organisation. In at least one school, teachers' commitment to play was countered by the level of organisation involved.

    . . . a year or so ago we did a big focus on play . . . We made up what we called play boxes. Beautiful boxes full of stuff and linked it to language and that. [But] it's the time factor, people say the boxes don't get taken into classrooms because there's a huge organisation . . . you have to organise it all and make a system work and people are running to find time to organise and again, the pressures, the time factor. It's not that the headset isn't there but . . . there's something blocking it. [FYOS teacher]

- Colleagues. Colleagues can offer support for implementing play-based programmes, or act as a barrier. In a number of schools, the views of colleagues teaching other grades often had an impact on Reception teachers, both in offering support (or not) for what happened in Reception and in their expectations for what children should have achieved by the time they had completed Reception. Part of the explanation for differences among colleagues in understanding the value of play was related to initial teacher education programmes.

    I just believe that a lot of teachers feel it's not learning. That if you don't have a piece of paper and a pencil in your hand kids aren't learning . . . [FYOS teacher]

    And you feel like you don't want to let the next wave of teachers down. You send children up from Reception to Year 1 and they haven't learnt all of their sounds and you sort of feel like . . . we've failed them. [FYOS teacher]

Several of these barriers reflect those noted by Kagan (1990) as attitudinal, structural, and functional barriers. Kagan (1990) argued that in addition to having a positive attitude towards play and a willingness to engage with play, the structure of learning environments (including time, space, resources, curricula) and functional elements (contextual factors) all impacted on teacher provisions for play. Bennett *et al.*

(1997) have also noted some similar barriers, particularly those related to the impact of national (or state) curriculum and the need for teachers to demonstrate children's learning outcomes.

Discussion

One of the aims of the *Early Years: Curriculum Continuity for Learning* project has been to explore teachers' perceptions of play in the context of reforming approaches to teaching and learning in the first year of school. Discussions with teachers in PTS settings and the FYOS highlighted different perceptions of play, different expectations about the role of teachers within play and a range of barriers to implementing play-based pedagogy, particularly in Reception. While all teachers were positive about play and were convinced that *children learn through play*, few were able to substantiate the power or significance of play beyond reference to general developmental areas, such as the benefit of play for children's learning of social skills or thinking skills.

Perhaps this is not surprising, as play has held a revered place in early childhood pedagogy, largely unquestioned until recent critiques (Ailwood, 2003; Fleer, 1998; Wood, 2007). As well, traditional approaches to play have focused on the importance of child choice, ownership and autonomy in play, suggesting minimal roles for teachers.

With current national and international focus on early childhood education and imperatives to improve both the quality and outcomes of early years education, there is an increasing need for early childhood educators to reconceptualise play and their role in play, to move away from romantic and nostalgic notions of play and to consider the complexities, challenges and potentially problematic nature of play. Armed with clear understandings of what constitutes positive play, the potential of play and its effectiveness in promoting children's learning and educational engagement, early childhood educators will then be well placed to engage in pedagogical debates in the broader field of education. One way in which this reconceptualisation is already occurring can be found in teachers' greater focus on the documentation of play, using strategies such as Learning Stories to record and analyse, from a range of perspectives, the learning within play (Carr, 2001; Perry, Dockett, and Harley, 2007).

Teachers who participated in this project described a range of roles for themselves in play-based pedagogy. These include roles as managers, facilitators and players. Some roles involved active engagement between adults and children with the aim of promoting rich and complex play. However, overall, these roles were not mentioned as often as less interactive, managerial roles. These results are in keeping with research indicating that many of children's play experiences do not offer high levels of cognitive challenge or high quality adult-child interactions (Bennett *et al.*, 1997; Plowman and Stephen, 2007; Siraj-Blatchford *et al.*, 2002). Some teachers described their hesitance to become involved in play, noting that they regarded play as the children's reward for finishing work, or the fear that what ensued would not be play if it involved the teacher (Rogers and Evans, 2008). Once again, these perspectives invoke romantic views of play as natural and free, and always positive and progressive (Ailwood, 2003). They omit views of play as times when children may require assistance to enter or remain included in play, engage effectively with others, understand play scripts or challenge stereotypes and discrimination in play. Also missing is recognition of the importance of sustained shared thinking (Siraj-Blatchford and Sylva, 2004) where adults and children co-construct understandings and explore cognitive challenges.

Educators teaching Reception classes were just as likely as PTS educators to refer to the value of play within curriculum, but they were also more likely than their PTS counterparts to state a range of reasons for not including play. These encompassed organisational and systems issues, as well as the expectations of colleagues and parents. The broader perception that curriculum and pedagogy in PTS and FYOS settings were influenced by more formal, academic school curriculum was confirmed by these teachers.

Internationally, as well as nationally, there is much focus on early childhood education both as a means of promoting equitable life outcomes and ensuring an appropriately skilled future workforce (Dahlberg and Moss, 2005; Office of Early Childhood Education and Child Care, 2008). One consequence is that what happens in early childhood education is under considerable scrutiny. School systems – and the teachers within them – are eager to demonstrate that the education they provide is of high quality and that all children are indeed learning. Consequences have already included questioning of the role and place of play, and the need for teachers to articulate their use and justification of play. This will require teachers to be clear about how teaching and learning can be accomplished through play. In conversations with teachers through this project, it was noticeable that the pedagogy of play was often conceptualised by teachers as 'what children get out of play' or 'what teachers did to set up the environment for play', rather than 'what teaching strategies teachers utilise during play'. Reflecting Moyles *et al.* (2002), teachers in this project were much more comfortable describing their practice (what they did) than they were describing what guided their own interactions. In other words, they were comfortable describing practice rather than pedagogy. If play is to be retained and celebrated as an effective approach to teaching and learning, it will be important for teachers to embrace the language of pedagogy and to develop confidence in exploring and reflecting upon their pedagogies of play.

In listing barriers to implementing play, there were also some comments from teachers relating to children themselves, with particular groups of children deemed unable to engage in play curriculum, either because they did not have the requisite skills, or because their behaviour was deemed inappropriate. In contrast, some teachers described play as providing opportunities to teach specific skills. The focus on skills and teaching children to play reflects a strong developmental focus, suggesting that teachers refer to a sequence of skills and types of play that children are expected to master. Where children do not have these skills, play training can be used to teach these (Smilansky and Shefatya, 1990). This perspective represents some challenges, including the deficit view of children it promotes and the prevalent expectation of Western notions of play and play development (Fleer, 1998). The complexity of play, assumptions that all children engage with play in similar ways and the social and cultural relevance of play are all omitted from such views.

While not reported in this chapter, it is important to note that the data generated throughout this phase of the project were intended to provide a snapshot of teacher perspectives, as the basis for instigating pedagogical change. Not only were these teachers willing to engage in this initial process, many have also continued involvement with the project as they have shaped inquiry questions as a basis for researching, analysing and changing their practice. Such an approach is critical to understanding the role, place and potential of play-based pedagogies in early childhood education.

New pedagogies of play

Several researchers (David, 2003; Rogers and Evans, 2008; Wood, 2007) have called for new pedagogies of play that recognise the complexity as well as the potential of play for teaching and learning. Outcomes of this project suggest that new pedagogies of play should encompass:

- awareness that such pedagogies are influenced by, and in turn have the power to influence, political, policy and practice dimensions;
- recognition of the complexity and diversity of play, rather than an expectation of the universality of play;
- awareness that play will have multiple forms and types;
- recognition that not all play is positive or desirable;
- understanding and critique of a range of theoretical dimensions;
- focus on social and cultural contexts – including power relations – and the enactment of these in play;
- increased focus on the interactive roles of adults, as they engage with children to co-construct knowledge, promote challenge and support play that is both socially and conceptually complex;
- articulation and documentation of connections between play and learning;
- generation of opportunities for teachers to reflect on their pedagogies of play, to problematise play and other pedagogies, and to engage in in-depth professional dialogue about play; and
- multiple perspectives of play – including those of children, parents, teachers and researchers.

New pedagogies of play require a reconceptualisation of play and the connections between play, teaching and learning. To be effective advocates for play, early childhood educators need comprehensive and sophisticated understandings of play, grounded in research as well as practice that reflect the relevant social and cultural contexts. Educators also need to grapple with the ambiguities of play and the realisation that play is unlikely to be universally effective or desirable as a path to promoting learning in all contexts for all children. McLane (2003: 11) urges educators to 'know enough about play to be both its advocates and sceptics . . . [to] recognise play's potential without romanticising it and reducing it to fuzzy, simplistic slogans'.

Note

1 While this project has been conducted through the South Australian Department of Education and Children's Services, the views expressed in this chapter are those of the author, rather than the Department.

References

Adams, S., Alexander, E., Drummond, M. J., and Moyles, J. (2004) *Inside the Foundation Stage: Recreating the Reception Year,* London: ATL.

Ailwood, J. (2003) 'Governing early childhood education through play', *Contemporary Issues in Early Childhood,* 4, 3: 286–99.

Ashiabi, G. S. (2007) 'Play in the preschool classroom: Its socioemotional significance and the teacher's role in play', *Early Childhood Education Journal,* 35, 2: 199–207.

Bennett, N., Wood, L., and Rogers, S. (1997) *Teaching Through Play: Teachers' Thinking and Classroom Practice,* Buckingham, UK: Open University Press.

British Educational Research Association Early Years Special Interest Group (BERA-SIG). (2003) *Early Years Research: Pedagogy, Curriculum and Adult Roles, Training and Professionalism.* Online. Available HTTP: *http://www.bera.ac.uk/publications/acreviews/php* (accessed October 10, 2008).

Broadhead, P. (2006) 'Developing an understanding of young children's learning through play: The place of observation, interaction and reflection', *British Educational Research Journal,* 32, 2:123–29.

Brooker, E. (2002) *Starting School: Young Children Learning Cultures,* Buckingham: Open University Press.

Carr, M. (2001) *Assessment in Early Childhood Settings: Learning Stories,* London: Paul Chapman.

Dahlberg, G., and Moss, P. (2005) *Ethics and Politics in Early Childhood Education,* London: RoutledgeFalmer.

David, T. (2003) *What Do We Know About Teaching Young Children?* Canterbury: Canterbury Christ Church University College. Online. Available: http://www.standards.dfes.gov.uk/eyfs/resources/downloads/eyyrsp1.pdf (accessed October 2, 2008).

Department of Education and Children's Services, South Australia (DECS). (2001) *South Australian Curriculum Standards and Accountability Framework.* Online. Available: http://www.sacsa.sa.edu.au/splash.asp (accessed October 15, 2008).

Dockett, S., and Fleer, M. (1999) *Pedagogy and Play in Early Childhood Education,* Sydney: Harcourt.

Dockett, S., Perry, B., Campbell, H., Hard, L., Kearney, E., and Taffe, R. (2007) *Reconceptualising Reception: Continuity of Learning,* Department of Education and Children's Services (DECS), South Australia. Online. Available: http://www.earlyyears.sa.edu.au/a8_publish/modules/publish/content.asp?id = 31104&navgrp = 151 (accessed October 20, 2008).

Fisher, R., (2000) 'Developmentally appropriate practice and a national literacy strategy', *British Journal of Educational Studies,* 48,1: 58–69.

Fleer, M. (1998) 'Universal fantasy: The domination of Western theories of play', in E. Dau (ed.), *Child's Play: Revisiting Play in Early Childhood Settings,* 67–80, Sydney: Maclennan & Petty.

Fromberg, D. P. (2002) *Play and Meaning in Early Childhood Education,* Boston, MA: Allyn & Bacon.

Kagan, S. L. (1990) 'Children's play: The journey from theory to practice' in E. Klugman and S. Smilansky, (eds), *Children's Play and Learning: Perspectives and Policy Implications,* 173–87, New York: Teachers College Press.

MacNaughton, G. (2004) 'Exploring critical constructivist perspectives on children's learn-
ing', in A. Anning, J. Cullen, and M. Fleer (eds), *Early Childhood Education: Society and Culture*,
45–54, London: Sage.
Marsh, J. (ed.) (2005) *Popular Culture, New Media and Digital Literacy in Early Childhood*, London:
RoutledgeFalmer.
McLane, J. B. (2003) '"Does not." "Does too."' *Thinking about Play in the Early Childhood Classroom.*,
Erikson Institute Occasional Paper Number 4. Online. Available: http://www.erikson.edu/
default/research/researchpubs/pubsbydate.aspx (accessed October 10, 2008).
Monighan-Nourot, P. (1997) 'Playing with play in four dimensions' in J. Isenberg and M.
Jalongo (eds), *Major Trends and Issues in Early Childhood Education: Challenges, Controversies, and
Insights*, 123–48, New York: Teachers College Press.
Morgan, A. E., and Kennewell, S. E. (2006) 'Initial teacher education students' views on play
as a medium for learning: A divergence of personal philosophy and practice', *Technology,
Pedagogy and Education*, 15, 3: 307–20.
Moyles, J., Adams, S., and Musgrove, A. (2002) *SPEEL: Study of Pedagogical Effectiveness in Early
Learning*, London: Department for Education and Skills. Online. Available: http://www.
dfes.gov.uk/research/data/uploadfiles/RR363.pdf (accessed October 12, 2008).
Office of Early Childhood Education and Child Care, Commonwealth of Australia (2008) *Early
Childhood Education and Care*. Online. Available: http://office.mychild.gov.au/new_agenda.
htm (accessed October 15, 2008).
Perry, B., Dockett, S., and Harley, E. (2007) 'Learning stories and children's powerful math-
ematics', *Early Childhood Research and Practice*, 9, 2 :18–35. Online. Available: http://ecrp.uiuc.
edu/v9n2/perry.html (accessed October 2, 2008).
Plowman, L., and Stephen, C. (2007) 'Guided interaction in pre-school settings', *Journal of
Computer Assisted Learning*, 23, 1: 14–26.
Pramling-Samuelsson, I., and Johansson, E. (2006) 'Play and learning – inseparable dimensions
in preschool practice', *Early Child Development and Care*, 176, 1: 47–65.
Ranz-Smith, D. J. (2007) 'Teacher perception of play: In leaving no child behind are teachers
leaving childhood behind?', *Early Education and Development*, 18, 2: 271–303.
Rogers, S., and Evans, J. (2007) 'Rethinking role play in the Reception class', *Educational Research*,
49, 2: 153–67.
—— (2008) *Inside Role Play in Early Childhood Education: Researching Young Children's Perspectives*,
London: Routledge.
Rubin, K. H., Fein, G. G., and Vandenberg, B. (1983) 'Play' in P. H. Mussen and E. M.
Hetherington (eds), *Handbook of Child Psychology*, Vol 4, 693–774, New York: Wiley.
Ryan, S. (2005) 'Freedom to choose: Examining children's experiences in choice time',
in N. Yelland, (ed.), *Critical Issues in Early Childhood*, 99–114, Maidenhead: Open University
Press.
Sharp, C. (2002) *School Starting Age: European Policy and Recent Research*, Slough: NFER.
Siraj-Blatchford, I., and Sylva, K. (2004) 'Researching pedagogy in English preschools', *British
Educational Research Journal*, 30, 5: 713–30.
Siraj-Blatchford, I., Sylva, K., Muttock, S., Gilden, R., and Bell, D. (2002). *Researching Effective
Pedagogy in the Early Years*, DfES: London.
Smilansky, S., and Shefatya, L. (1990) *Facilitating Play*, Silver Spring: Psychological and
Educational Publications.
Sylva, K., Melhuish, E., Sammons, P., Siraj-Blatchford, I., and Taggart, B. (2004) *The effective
provision of pre-school education (EPPE) Project: Final Report*, London: Institute of Education.
Walsh, G., Sproule, L., McGuiness, C., Trew, K., Rafferty, H., and Sheehy, N. (2006) 'An

appropriate curriculum for 4–5 year-old children in Northern Ireland: Comparing play-based and formal approaches', *Early Years*, 26, 2: 201–21.

Wood, E. (2004) 'Developing a pedagogy of play' in A. Anning, J. Cullen, and M. Fleer (eds), *Early Childhood Education: Society and Culture*, 19–30, London: Sage.

—— (2007) 'New directions in play: Consensus or collision?', *Education 3–13*, 35, 4: 309–20.

—— (2008) Conceptualising a pedagogy of play: International perspectives from theory, policy and practice, in D. Kurschner (ed.) *From Children to Red Hatters: Diverse Images and Issues of Play*, Play and Culture Studies volume 8, 166–90.

Chapter 4

'We are hunters and gatherers of values'

Dramatic play, early childhood pedagogy, and the formation of ethical identities

Brian Edmiston

In his speech accepting the Nobel Prize for Literature, Seamus Heaney (1995) recalls a dark hour in the history of sectarian violence in the North of Ireland when, in 1976, a minibus full of workers was stopped by a gang of marked men with guns in their hands and hatred in their hearts. The workers were forced to line up. A gun was waved in front of them as a man snarled, 'Any Catholics among you step out here'. The lone Catholic man in the group did not move when his hand was gripped by his fellow Protestant worker in a signal that said, 'we are in hell, but we are here together'. The story does not have a just ending. After hesitating, he stepped forward, only to see all his friends butchered. Yet Heaney finds hope in his belief that 'the birth of the future we desire is surely in the contraction which that terrified Catholic felt on the roadside when another hand gripped his hand'. Heaney spoke of the need to recognize and sustain,

> . . . the power to persuade that vulnerable part of our consciousness of its right-ness, in spite of the wrongness all around it, the power to remind us that we are hunters and gatherers of values, that our very solitudes and distresses are credit-able, in so far as they too are an earnest of our veritable human being.

Having grown up, like Heaney, in the divided and often violent society of Northern Ireland, for decades I have been asking myself a moral question like the one he implies: how is it that people develop 'the power to persuade themselves' of the 'rightness' of their words and deeds despite the 'wrongness' that may tempt them to act otherwize? I have explored answers to this question especially as I have reflected on my playful parenting and pedagogy in early childhood classrooms that has dramatic play at its core. In this chapter I explain how and why I have come to believe that adults' active participation in dramatic play with children, at home and in classrooms, can be highly significant in the formation of powerful morally persuasive identities.

At the core of my scholarship and teaching has been an interest in the ethical dimensions of pedagogy (Edmiston, 2008; 2005; 2000). A pedagogical use of dra-matic improvisation in both play and performance has been central to my educational career (Heathcote, 1984): as a secondary English teacher in the U.K., as an elementary teacher in the U.S., and as an academic researching my own classroom teaching with students of all ages. However, it was not until I had the opportunity over more than a decade to gather data and reflect on the moral significance of playing with my son Michael (aged 19 at the time of writing), that I began to theorize and come to understand more clearly the relationship between dramatic play and ethics.

Ethical action as answerability

Six-year-old children are laughing as they pretend to be sharks using their arms like jaws to snap at me. We are in the meeting area of a suburban classroom in central Ohio having just analyzed photographs of sharks and dolphins to compare how these creatures swim, as well as what and how they eat. The children are noisy as they circle me while I pretend to be a series of swimmers. Children take turns pretending to be Great White sharks, telling me how to react, and narrating snippets of stories: some say I escape though most want to imagine that I'm frightened and then caught; some see blood and severed limbs in the water.

The children had previously invented, and in extended dramatic play they had run with their teacher, Trish Russell, the Extreme Adventures Travel Agency; they had enacting events from a 'Swimming with Dolphins' vacation that was 'fun but safe' (Beach, *et al.* 2010). Now we imagine 'Scuba Adventures', another travel company, taking people on trips where 'others are afraid to go'. At first, the children like the idea of going 'Swimming with Sharks'. After our pretend attacks we brainstorm protective gear and invent the story of Bruce Foster who, having left the steel cage and body armour we had imagined, was lucky to survive a shark attack. We pretend to fly him by helicopter to hospital where Trish meets us as his distraught mother. Days later, meeting me as the owner of closed-down Scuba Adventures, children are adamant that the agency cannot reopen until they are clear that no more clients will be in danger.

Rather than rely solely on the dominant moral developmental framework of Piaget (1975) and Kohlberg (1984) that views young children each at a pre-adult stage on their way to becoming less egocentric, more empathetic, and able to use more abstract, objective, rational, moral rules, I turn to the Russian theorist Bakhtin. In place of a universal approach to ethics, Bakhtin (1990, 1993) conceptualizes an ethical human being as embracing an ongoing discursive, or 'dialogic', struggle among 'voices' that are competing ideological guides to what is 'right' action in particular situations. I argue that such a view can apply to people of all ages, including young children. What Bakhtin calls 'answerability' and 'addressivity' are central to his dialogic theory of ethical deeds. For Bakhtin, dialogue is more than an exchange of words. People are dialogic when they 'answer' voices that they experience as 'addressing' them; their answers are ethical when they evaluate, or assume, that one deed rather than another is the 'right' (or 'wrong') thing to do.

Like most of the children I relished pretending to be an attacking, potentially deadly, shark. Being 'addressed' by a vulnerable swimmer I 'answered' with an attack. The 'rightness' of that act, for a shark, became clear to all the children in a subsequent discussion as we considered why predators kill. Similarly, the children were in agreement about how they ought to respond to Bruce Foster's plight: all rescued him and many participated in running a hospital where he, and others in need of medical help, were cared despite many emergencies.

For Bakhtin (1990), being ethical means that any person's answer, and thus any understanding of what is right action, is never static, or 'finalized', but rather is always open to change in further dialogue in new situations. For example, whereas initially there had been little concern about vacation trips involving sharks, a developing understanding of safety was made clear as the children created drawings, stories, and models as many created the hospital and authored the story of Bruce Foster. Later, confronting me as the owner of Scuba Adventures many answered his complaint that he was losing money because he had been closed down, with a clear demand for a plan to keep clients' safe.

All of this collaborative dramatic play occurred in a classroom where children repeatedly addressed other children. They wanted to share materials or space and desired to work together or sometimes be alone. Trish, as a teacher who wanted to build a collaborative community, was consistently 'gathering' children's answers together into what they valued about their lives together in the classroom; these values were then addressed, discussed, and collaboratively agreed upon in class meetings. Dramatic play created spaces where specific questions and discourse about values like cooperation and safety could be 'hunted' for, considered, extended, and answered as they took action in very demanding particular contexts beyond the more predictable everyday contexts of schooling. For example, the need for people to collaborate in flying a helicopter or running a hospital and using medical equipment, like a blood transfusion drip represented by a drawing, or actual supplies, like bandages, were more pressing and obvious ways of addressing ongoing issues of sharing and answering in action than any classroom discussion about a need to share resources. And new understanding of the need to create and abide by rules in order to keep people safe was very apparent and obvious in the context of an imagined but very real person who had nearly died.

For Bakhtin, imagination is essential for ethical action. When a person uses what Bakhtin (1981) characterizes as the 'dialogic imagination', like the writers and readers of novels and other narratives, people imaginatively 'project' into the words and deeds of the consciousnesses of anyone whom they experience as addressing them. When we imagine ourselves as if we were other people we empathize because we view the world as they do. Additionally, imagination opens up the possibility of being addressed by those who are not actually present, adding more compelling voices and new viewpoints on actions to 'mingle' with, and affect, prior views.

Dramatic play can be an ethical portal into direct encounters with voices and viewpoints that would be sidelined or mostly silent in everyday life. As adults we develop the capacity to imagine conversations with other people and ideas without moving around as children often desire to do. For most adults, as Vygotsky (1967) put it, 'imagination is play without action' but for children 'play is imagination in action' (539).

Bakhtin's conceptualisation of an ethical dialogic struggle to answer competing imagined voices that address us about right action, was apparent one day when our son Michael was thirteen. One Saturday, the day after a Friday evening school skiing trip, Michael showed me a $20 bill that he had found on the ground near his bus. He said he didn't know whether to keep it or not having told me the story of where he had found it. I didn't tell Michael what to do but rather I raised some questions for him including what he would want someone to do if they found money he had dropped. I spoke from the perspective of a person who had lost money as I pretended to put a hand in my pocket and realize the money was gone. He didn't tell me what he would do, but on the Monday Michael gave the bill to the teacher who had been in-charge of the trip. As no one had told her that they had lost money she returned it to Michael at the end of the day.

In a subsequent conversation a week later Michael told me about his experience of what had been for him both an internal and an external ethical struggle. He was responding to the multiple voices by which he felt addressed that included mine even before he spoke with me.

I thought maybe I shouldn't have told you because at first I was thinking I could have kept it without my conscience being tested. But I was glad because if I hadn't told you I would probably have had an inner battle with my conscience over the weekend. Over the weekend I'd have been thinking should I turn it in or keep it. Personally, I think I would have decided to turn it in.

I asked Michael if what I had said had made him turn in the money. He responded, 'No. But it sort of speeded up the process and made me realize I should turn it in sooner'. Michael had experienced an inner struggle between competing inner and outer voices. He told me that when I had initially asked him what he thought he should do, and why, he was pulled in different directions.

- Other students had found money and kept it without turning it in
- Someone had lost the money
- It was impossible to know for certain who had dropped it
- He had money in his hand that he could spend.

As I had talked with him he said it was as if I had 'amplified' all of these voices. In particular, I had created a personal voice for the person who had lost the money. That voice had become more demanding than the decontextualized voice of 'finders keepers' and the dominant voices of his peers who had previously kept lost money. Finally, I had focused him on the Golden Rule question of what he would want someone else to do if he had lost the money.

Michael's actions were ethical, not because he had developed the ability to understand and follow an abstract principle like the golden rule, but because he had chosen an action in response to a struggle over how best to act when projecting into and answering all of the voices that he felt addressed him in both actual and imagined social interactions.

Authoring ethical identities

Bakhtin's (1990) relational view of consciousness provides a dynamic view of an evolving 'authoring' self that acts in everyday and imagined dialogue with other people.

An ethical self, for Bakhtin, is the acting consciousness that embraces a struggle to answer, not only those voices present in face-to-face dialogue but also those that may be sought out in encounters with others or that address us in imagination. If the self acts and answers in a conscious moment, then how a person's consciousness extends to include social, cultural, and historical relationships with other people creates 'identities'.

In their everyday and imaginative interactions over time and through their participation in social and cultural practices people continually author identities: people identify with the ongoing and past social actions and cultural practices of different groups of people. As Hall puts it, people form 'points of identification and attachment' with different cultural groups (1996, p. 5). Identities are formed in classrooms and families as much as they are, for example, within sporting, ethnic, or national groups. And, I argue, the 'pretend identities' (Dyson, 1997) taken on by children participating with others in dramatic play, at home or in school, can affect their everyday identities (Edmiston, 2008; Beach *et al.* 2010).

Especially because of my experience growing up in a sectarian society, I argue that though they overlap, people should not conflate ethical identities with socio-cultural identities; people's views of right social action should not be predetermined by the moral discourse or viewpoints of any groups with which they identify. Further, what has become clear to me over the years is that at the heart of my ethical identity is an authoring desire both to understand the viewpoints of others rather than silence them as well as being open to change my own position in any response.

For Bakhtin, discourse is more than verbal exchange between people but rather includes the ideology of the inner voices in a person's changing consciousness that underlie and guide their deeds. As Morson and Emerson put it, 'Consciousness takes shape, and never stops taking shape, as a process of interaction among authoritative and innerly persuasive discourses' (1990, p. 221). Every interaction is not only a face-to-face discourse but is also an exchange that both affects, and is affected by, a person's prior discourses. In contrast with Michael's dialogic exchange in which he showed his openness to listen and reconsider his position, the gunmen in Heaney's story had an uncompromising monologic encounter in which their rigid consciousness was unaffected by the lives of those they treated as intensely other than them: dialogue was something that they were unable to do with deadly consequences for those they annihilated.

If Michael had returned the $20 bill because I had told him to do so, or because he was following a rule or a family practice, he would have only been responding to, and acting from, an externally authoritative, or largely monologic, discourse. However, Michael's analysis of his struggle illuminated how his discourse about how to respond to found money was 'innerly persuasive': he dialogically convinced himself about how he ought to act and in doing so was authoring and extending his consciousness. This was so despite the fact that his interaction with me was clearly influential. As he noted, I had 'amplified' some voices. As his father, my discourse tended to have more authority than the discourse of, for example, a schoolmate on the bus. And in imagination by giving voice to the viewpoint of the person who had dropped the bill, that I felt he had not fully considered, I was also alluding to a powerfully authoritative discourse: the Golden Rule. His action on that day was one incident in his ongoing gathering of values that have been tested, extended, and developed over time as discourses of his ethical identity. To what extent a person's discourses are innerly persuasive or externally authoritative is apparent in their dispositions: how much, on the one hand, are they open to dialogue or, on the other hand, how much they are closed to new ideas. Put another way, people are coauthoring selves and identities when they remain open to being affected by other people's new ideas.

Though Bakhtin never wrote about education or learning, his conceptualisation of discourse and inner voices parallels Vygotsky's (1978) social constructivist educational theory: inner speech and abstract ideas develop from the interactions of external social speech. According to Vygotsky, mental concepts, that would include evaluations of what constitutes right and wrong action, must first be constructed in social interactions for them to become internalized. Bakhtin's idea that authoring requires more than acting in response to externally authoritative discourse resembles Behaviorist assumptions about the need for adult control of moral action. In contrast, both Vygotsky and Bakhtin stress that people only really understand when they socially construct, or coauthor, meaning. Meaning-making can include any shared ethical understanding or discourse that is shaped by, and in subsequent interactions shapes, an ethical identity.

Coauthoring ethical identities in dramatic play

My experience of play in schools has unavoidably been largely sporadic, even when I have been able to participate for extended periods of time, as was the case with bi-weekly visits over a year to Trish Russell's classroom. In contrast, for over five years between the time when Michael was two and seven-years-old, I played with him regularly, and for extended periods of time. Our time playing together diminished as Michael became more interested in being alone with friends and more immersed in reading literature. However, especially when he was younger, dramatic playing was a dimension of our daily life at mealtimes, in the car, and at home, as we pretended to enter the narrative of a book or video.

Playing with selves and identities

Dramatic playing with narratives allows people to try out different 'possible selves' (Marcus and Nurius, 1986) and over time author different possible identities. Michael took charge of our play. He could pretend to be any person or creature in the world of any story he liked and, moving seamlessly from one encounter to the next, he would invariably ask me to encounter him. Each imagined world became, as the Bakhtinian scholar Carl Emerson (1997) puts it in reference to adults' reading of novels, 'a test site for moral behavior' (242).

Though Michael engaged in some domestic or everyday play e.g. pretending to cook or use the telephone, he was more captivated by what I call mythic play. As Warner

(2003: vi) puts it, myths are 'stories that inquire into everyday realities, projected unto an eternal and supernatural horizon'. Doniger O'Flaherty (1995: 1) adds that myths are 'are about the human experiences we all share – birth, love, hate, death'.

In Trish Russell's classroom the everyday medical and travel agency play was closer to the sort of pro-social 'rehearsals for life' that Erikson (1963) championed. At the same time, shark attacks and the fantastic medical symptoms children invented provided a mythic dimension that many children, especially boys relished experiencing.

Some of the mythic landscapes where Michael eagerly and repeatedly encountered the power of love and hate and questions of life and death included the following: Peter Rabbit; Jack and the Beanstalk; Perseus and Medusa; St George and the Dragon; Beauty and the Beast; Dr Jekyll and Mr Hyde; Star Wars; Frankenstein and the Wolfman; and Dracula. Michael, pretending to be different possible selves (e.g. a knight, a Jedi warrior, or a human) would evaluate deeds as wrong when he commanded giants, dragons, vampires, werewolves, or people (all represented by me) to cease their monstrous deeds: attacking, killing, hurting, and not stopping when confronted. At other times he pretended to be monsters on his own or as he encountered me. As we revisited and broadly repeated the same narratives sometimes Michael most often wanted me to be one character e.g. when he had to sit still in the car he was often the Beast about to die with me, as Beauty, telling him how I loved him and what we would do if he did not die. When we could move around, Michael most often wanted us to switch back-and-forth between positions, in what I came to call positioning-play; sometimes within seconds or across days he could experience the same encounters from different perspectives. For example, he loved to be a terrorizing dragon, the heroic knight, St George, and the lady, Una, who nurtures George back to health. I was repeatedly put by Michael in a position of evaluating whatever actions he pretended to do e.g. as the knight I would try to stop the dragon using my words or my deeds if attacked me. Using Wenger's (1998) distinction, I argue that over time Michael authored a positive identification with all those deeds, that in our discourse we evaluated as 'good' or 'right' (e.g. saving people, stopping killing, tricking attackers, talking monsters into not killing, reaching win-win solutions, being kind, nurturing victims), and a negative identification with those hateful or hurtful deeds, that we evaluated as 'bad' or 'wrong'.

Self-control

Bodrova and Leong (this volume) have empirically shown what Vygotsky (1967) theorized: extended play develops children's self-control. Shifting between the positions of the perpetrators, victims, and bystanders of violent or other hateful acts not only develops children's capacity for moral action but also for restraint. Michael's developing self-control was very apparent once when I would not allow Michael, aged four, to do something. He was so annoyed that he was shaking as he said, 'I feel like hitting you'. When he added, 'Shall I cut your head off?' I responded by saying, 'You could, but you won't will you?' He was transfixed. I helped him diffuse his anger by redirecting it into a narrative where he could use a sword for good ends. 'Quick, if we don't stop the dragon it will attack the people'. Michael soon was pretending to wield a sword, moving as if he was a knight in pursuit of me as the dragon.

Michael revealed his ability to control his self by answering inner voices of restraint when he was six-and-a-half. After school he regularly went to the family of his school friend, Ben. One day I discovered that Ben had punched Michael in the stomach in an argument over which television program to watch. I asked if he'd punched back. He replied with a tone that implied that he would never considering doing that: 'Dad, I know what it feels like'. When I asked if he had wanted to hurt Ben he responded, 'Part of me does but I just say firmly, No, I don't like this'.

Dialogizing discourses in position-play

Though he reenacted some episodes from stories with little variation, Michael mostly transformed narratives to create new encounters that, using Bakhtin's (1981) term, repeatedly 'dialogized' a prior discourse. In other words, an ethical evaluation from one episode that I had stated or had implied was placed in dialogue with another evaluation so that a more nuanced answer could be tested out. This occurred both across and within narratives. For example, whereas for Michael (aged just four) Medusa always turned people to stone but would not attack if left alone, a few months later he wanted to explore how the terrorizing dragon who confronted St George could sometimes be convinced to use his power for good e.g. to burn trash. At other times as the dragon he would not stop and with a discourse of warning and then regret I would use my sword to kill the dragon. Michael would repeat the encounter with him as the knight.

Aged four-and-a-half he loved to pretend to take a potion to transform from Dr Jekyll into his shadow side, Mr Hyde. Michael positioned me to answer the deeds of Hyde whom he did not want to transform into a person who would stop.

Michael:	You're Mr Hyde and I'm Dr Jekyll. We're the same person.
	[In quick succession he imagines he is a werewolf who tries to attack Mr Hyde/me, a little boy asking me/Hyde for money, and an adult sitting in front of Hyde/me. Michael tells me/ Hyde to push him out of the way. As the werewolf he tries to wrestle me. As the boy and the adult he falls over.]
Brian/Hyde:	Get out of my way.
Michael:	Now I'm Mr Hyde and you're a person.
Michael/Hyde:	Get out of my way [pretending to push me and repeating the words I've just said as Hyde]
Brian/person 1:	Please help me.
Michael/Hyde:	Get out of my way. I'm a monster.
	Michael – You're another person who helps him [i.e. the victim].
Brian/person 2:	Can you help me?
	[He changes to imagine he is my wife and we talk about what to do. He tells me to phone the police. He imagines we are police

	officers and wants to write in a book what has happened. He wants us to look for Hyde and imagines that we go into a house. He looks up and points.]
Michael/police officer:	It's Mr Hyde. Come on. Shoot. Shoot
Brian:	Wait a minute. You have to be very careful it's the right person.
Michael/police officer:	Yea. Come on. Shoot.
Brian:	Wait a minute. You have to be very careful it's the right person.
Michael/police officer:	Oh dear. It's him his claws (inaudible).
Brian:	Shall we have it that he's up on the roof tops and you . . .
Michael:	and I (inaudible) yes
	[He changes to pretend to be Dr Jekyll.]

I resisted shooting Hyde, in contrast to killing a dragon, because I regarded him as a human. In the ten minutes between the first and second extracts, Michael turns from Jekyll back into Hyde and positioning me as a series of victims he attacks and leaves one for dead. Then we return to a similar encounter as the previous one as Michael dialogizes my earlier answer by placing me in the position of a man who had killed who refuses to surrender.

Michael:	Now I'm the little boy. OK, daddy?
Brian:	OK.
Michael/boy:	Police. There's a monster who's killed some people.
Brian/police officer:	Yea we know. Have you seen him? Do you know where he is? We've been looking for him.
Michael/boy:	Yea. He tried to kill me.
Brian/police officer:	Are you all right?
Michael/boy:	Yea.
	[He tells the police officer/me that Hyde is on the roof of a building]
Michael:	Daddy, you be Mr Hyde up on the rooftop.
	[I climb half way up the stairs.]
Michael/police officer:	Get down from that rooftop.
Brian:	No. Who are you?
Michael/police officer:	I'm a police.
Brian/Hyde:	What do you want?
Michael/police officer:	Stop doing all those mean things.
Brian/Hyde:	Why should I?
Michael/police officer:	Because they're all mean.
Brian/Hyde:	Huh. What will you do to me if I do come down?
Michael/police officer:	Well if you don't come down I'll shoot you.
Brian/Hyde:	And if I do? What will you do to me?
Michael/police officer:	I'll send you away to jail.

Brian/Hyde:	Jail? Why should I go to jail?
Michael/police officer:	Because you know. Because you're mean that's why. Huh. [We talk back-and-forth about rules until Michael refocuses us.]
Michael/police officer:	Just no talk about it. Now get down or I'll shoot you.
Brian:	How do you want it to end? Do you want to shoot him or do you want him to come down?
Michael:	I want to shoot you.
Brian/Hyde:	No [laughing]. I can get away, I'm too clever for you. [Michael shoots and I pretend to die]
Michael:	Now change back into the Shadow. [I lie down and transform my body into Hyde's. Michael stands over me pretending to hold the gun. His mother, Pat, enters the room]
Pat:	Are you going to use that gun to shoot other people?
Michael/police officer:	I only use my gun to shoot monsters [said with a tone of this being obvious].

In a subsequent conversation with Michael, his ethical disposition was clear, one that through our play I too had come to accept:

Brian:	'Would you kill all monsters?'
Michael:	'Oh no, only those that have done many, many, many mean things. . . . killing people mostly'
Brian:	'And what would you do before deciding you had to kill it?'
Michael:	'I'd teach it to stop doing those mean things'.

Conclusion

As I have argued in this chapter, when adults regularly play with children in worlds of imagination their moral explorations of difficult, dangerous, and often deadly encounters can significantly affect the development of ethical identities that are apparent in children's dispositions toward others. Playing with children makes us partners in the moral task of developing a power to persuade oneself of the rightness of acting well despite the choice to act otherwize. Vygotsky (1978: 10) stresses the connection between play and future action: 'a child's greatest achievements are possible in play, achievements that tomorrow will become her basic level of real action and morality'.

When Michael was fourteen, I asked if he remembered times in daily life when he had acted, or thought about acting, to help others. This question came after a decade of him imagining, via dramatic play and reading, countless people in problematic situations more demanding than anything Michael likely encountered in everyday life. Two of the examples he gave illustrated his ethical disposition to identify with, and help, others in need: 'I do "random acts of kindness" helping people with their homework; whenever I see someone obviously struggling with something that I can help them with I always go and try to help them'. A further example illustrated the prosaic struggle of answerability he was aware of even when he wanted to do the right thing:

When kids are making fun of another kid, you have to imagine from the point of view of the person who's being horrible and you feel sorry for the person who's being ridiculed. If you intervene and you stick up for them sometimes you don't because you're afraid others will laugh at you.

In Trish Russell's classroom she recognized how playing with children throughout the year had affected students' social and ethical identities. When I asked her why she valued playing with her students she was emphatic: 'Not only do you teach them how to be creative, but also how to be real people and to feel like they're going to be somebody in the world'. Extended collaborative play promoted more kindness in daily collaborative relationships among children; laughing at others, for example, was not tolerated. In particular, one boy, Ansel, who had begun the year isolated and angry with a highly oppositional identity, had ended the year more settled, happier, and more open to reaching out to work with others. Through dramatic play he had been able to explore different possible selves and identify differently with his classmates as he participated over extended periods of time in playful classroom social practices: as a bus driver, as a gatherer of other people's opinions, as a creator of images for whole class use, as a sharer of information with others from books, and as a person fielding class questions. Some of the other children, who had ignored or rejected Ansel at the beginning of the year, by the close of the year chose to play and work with him.

Bakhtin believes that 'ethics is a matter not of knowledge, but of wisdom' (Morson and Emerson, 1990, p. 27). Like Bakhtin, the novelist Ursula Le Guin (1979) understands that entering worlds of literature can promote the growth of wisdom in children. Adults who play with children can do more. By entering into imagined worlds alongside children, adults can extend and deepen their own as well as the children's ethical identifications when they too encounter people faced with ethical challenges and choices.

I believe that maturity is not an outgrowing but a growing up: that an adult is not a dead child but a child who survived. I believe that all the best faculties of a mature human being exist in the child, and that if these faculties are encouraged in youth they will act well and wisely in the adult, but that if they are repressed and denied in the child they will stunt and cripple the adult personality. And finally, I believe that one of the most deeply human, and humane, of these faculties is the power of imagination (Le Guin, 1979, p. 44).

References

Bakhtin, M. M. (1993) Holquist, M. and Liapunov, V. (eds). Liapunov, V. (trans.) *Toward a Philosophy of the Act*. Austin, TX: Texas University Press.

—— (1990) Holquist, M. and Liapunov, V. (eds). Liapunov, V. (trans.) *Art and Answerability: Early Philosophical Essays*. Austin, TX: Texas University Press.

—— (1981) Holquist, M. (ed.) Emerson, C. and Hoiquist, M. (trans.) *The Dialogic Imagination*. Austin, TX: Texas University Press.

Beach, R., Campano, G., Edmiston, B., and Borgman, M. (2010) 'Dramatic inquiry: imagining and enacting multiple perspectives on life', *Literacy Tools in the Classroom: Teaching through Critical Inquiry, Grades 5–12*. New York: Teachers College Press.

Doniger O'Flaherty, W. (1995) *Other People's Myths: The Cave of Echoes*. Chicago, IL: University of Chicago Press.

Dyson, A. Haas. (1997) *Writing Superheroes: Contemporary Childhood, Popular Culture, and Classroom Literacy*. New York: Teachers College Press.

Edmiston, B. (2008). *Forming Ethical Identities in Early Childhood Play*. London & New York: Routledge.

—— (2005) 'Coming home to research'. In L. D. Soto and B. Blue, *Power and Voice in Research with Children*. New York: Peter Lang.

—— (2000) 'Drama as ethical education'. *Research in Drama Education*, 5(1), 63–84.

Emerson, C. (1997) *The First Hundred Years of Mikhal Bakhtin*. Princeton, New Jersey: Princeton New Jersey Press.

Erikson, E. (1963) *Childhood and Society*. London: Routledge and KeganPaul.

Hall, S. (1996) Introduction: Who Needs Identity? In S. Hall, and P. du Gay, (eds) *Questions of Cultural Identity*. London, England: Sage Publications, pp. 1–17.

Heathcote, D. (1984) L. Johnson and C. O'Neill (eds) *Collected Writings on Education and Drama*. Melbourne: Hutchingson.

Heaney, S. (1995) *Crediting Poetry*. New York: Farrar Strauss Giroux.

Kohlberg, L. (1984) *The Psychology of Moral Development: The Nature and Validity of Moral Stages*. San Francisco, CA: Harper & Row.

Le Guin, U. (1979) 'Why Americans are afraid of dragons'. In *The Language of the Night: Essays on Fantasy and Science Fiction*. New York: Berkley.

Marcus, H. and Nurius, P. (1986) 'Possible Selves: The interface between motivation and the self-concept'. In K. Yardley and T. Holness (eds) *Self and Identity: Psychosocial Perspectives*, Chichester: Wiley, pp. 157–72.

Morson, G.S. and Emerson, C. (1990) *Mikhail Bakhtin: Creation of a Prosaics*. Stanford, CA: Stanford University Press.

Piaget, J. (1975) [1932] *The Equilibration of Cognitive Structures: The Central Problem of Intellectual Development*. Chicago, IL: Chicago University Press.

Vygotsky, L. (1978) Cole, M., John-Steiner, V., Scribner, S. and Souberman, E., (eds) (trans.) *Mind in Society*. Cambridge, MA: Harvard University Press.

—— (1967) Play and its role in the mental development of the child. *Soviet Psychology*, 5, 6–18.

Wenger, E. (1998) *Communities of Practice: Learning, Meaning, and Identity*. New York: NY: Cambridge University Press.

Warner, M. (2003) Introduction. *World of Myths*. Austin, TX: University of Texas.

Chapter 5

Revisiting Vygotskian perspectives on play and pedagogy

Elena Bodrova and Deborah J. Leong

Play has always been considered an essential part of childhood. Philosophers and educators alike have used such terms as 'spontaneous', 'inevitable' or 'natural' when describing the playful activities of young children which implies that play is something that all children do in one form or another (Isenberg and Quisenberry, 2002; Elkind, 2007). However, with increasing pressure for formal pedagogies in early childhood classrooms, it is opportunities for the most elaborate forms of play, the ones that take longer for children to develop that are most at risk. For example, while most toddlers still engage in playful exploration of objects, in some cultural contexts it is increasingly hard to find preschool and school-aged children creating fantasy worlds together and enacting these self-generated elaborate scenarios without adult participation (Levin, 2008; Rogers and Evans, 2008). This heterogeneity of play as well as differential effects of different types of play on child development and learning means that questions about the pedagogy of play should be answered differently for different types of play. Here we will focus on only one kind of play – make-believe play also known as role-play or dramatic play – and the role of adults in scaffolding this play in preschool- and kindergarten-aged children. We will view this kind of play from the perspective of Cultural-Historical Psychology by first revisiting Vygotskian insights into the nature of play and then by discussing post-Vygotskian contributions to research on play and their implications for Early Childhood Education.

Make-believe play: the Vygotskian perspective

Vygotsky's interest in make-believe play grew out of his earlier studies in psychology of art (Vygotsky, 1971) as well as from his work on the theory of development of higher mental functions (Vygotsky, 1997). In play, Vygotsky saw one of the earliest contexts where children learn to use objects and actions in their symbolic function. Since mastery of cultural signs and symbols constitutes the basic mechanism for the development of higher mental functions – symbolically mediated intentional behaviours – play was considered by Vygotsky to be the leading activity of modern day preschoolers, the activity that creates their Zone of Proximal Development:

> The play-development relationship can be compared with the instruction-development relationship, but play provides a background for changes in needs

and in consciousness of a much wider nature. Play is the source of development and creates the zone of proximal development. Action in the imaginative sphere, in an imaginary situation, the creation of voluntary intentions and the formation of real-life plans and volitional motives – all appear in play and make it the highest level of preschool development.

(Vygotsky, 1967)

While another – and better known – quote by Vygotsky about how play creates a Zone of Proximal Development by having a child behave 'beyond his age . . . a head above himself' is often used by educators to advocate for play in Early Childhood settings, it is not always made clear what kind of play provides such unique opportunities for child development. It is important to emphasize that Vygotsky's definition of play only applies to make-believe play and does not include many kinds of other activities such as movement activities, object manipulations, and explorations that were (and still are) referred to as 'play' by most educators as well as non-educators (e.g., Miller and Almon, 2009). Unlike other playful activities, 'real' play, according to Vygotsky, has three major features: children create an imaginary situation, take on and act out roles, and follow a set of rules determined by specific roles (Vygotsky, 1978).

Each of these features play an important role in the formation of a child's mind, in the development of higher mental functions. Role-playing in an imaginary situation requires children to carry on two types of actions – external and internal. In play, these internal actions – Vygotsky called these 'operations with meanings severed from objects' – are still dependent on external operations on the objects. However, the very emergence of the internal actions signals the beginning of a child's transition from the earlier forms of thought processes – sensory-motor and visual-representational – to more advanced symbolic thought. Thus, make believe play prepares the foundation for two higher mental functions – symbolic thinking and imagination. Contrary to popular views, Vygotsky saw imagination not as a pre-requisite of play but rather as its outgrowth:

> The old adage that children's play is imagination in action can be reversed: we can say that imagination in adolescents and school children is play without action.
>
> (Vygotsky, 1978, p.93)

Another way make-believe play contributes to the development of higher mental functions is by promoting intentional, self-regulated behaviour. Self-regulation becomes possible because of the inherent relationship that exists between the roles children play and the rules they need to follow when playing these roles. For preschoolers, play becomes the first activity where children are driven not by the need for instant gratification, prevalent at this age, but instead by more long-term goals, even when these goals require them to suppress their immediate impulses. At first, the notion of play being the most restrictive context for child's actions may sound completely counterintuitive. However, Vygotsky argues that this rule-based nature is an essential characteristic of children's make-believe play:

... whenever there is an imaginary situation in play, there are rules – not rules that are formulated in advance and change during the course of the game, but rules stemming from the imaginary situation. Therefore, to imagine that a child can behave in an imaginary situation without rules, i.e., as he behaves in a real situation, is simply impossible. If the child is playing the role of a mother, then she has rules of maternal behavior. The role the child plays, and her relationship to the object if the object has changed its meaning, will always stem from the rules, i.e., the imaginary situation will always contain rules. In play the child is free. But this is an illusory freedom.

(Vygotsky, 1967 p. 10)

Vygotsky himself has not created a complete theory of play; this theory was created later by his student Daniel Elkonin and further expanded by the subsequent generations of post-Vygotskians (Karpov, 2007).

Post-Vygotskian developments in the study of play

Consistent with the founding principles of Cultural-Historical Theory, Post-Vygotskians viewed play in a broader social-cultural context concluding that make-believe play as we understand it is a relatively late development in the history of humankind (Elkonin, 2005b). Based on numerous accounts of anthropologists, Elkonin concludes that in the non-literate societies of hunters and gatherers, play existed as preparation for grown-up activities as children practiced with scaled-down versions of grown-up tools. In modern societies however play cannot serve this pragmatic function because grown-up activities and the tools they require are sometimes too complex for young children and may change significantly by the time children grow up making practice useless. Instead, according to Elkonin play helps today's children develop general competencies that will allow them to master the use of any tools of the future – even ones not yet invented.

Extending the idea of play as preparation for future tool use beyond physical tools and the competencies associated with their use (such as fine motor skills, hand-eye coordination, etc), Elkonin (1978) viewed play as the leading activity–the activity where children master a variety of mental tools (such as symbols) necessary for them to function successfully in a post-industrial society. Speaking of play as 'the leading source of development' Vygotsky used the term 'leading activity' more as a metaphor than as a theoretical construct. The Vygotskian idea that a leading activity may be used as an indicator of a specific age was later extended and refined in the work of Alexei Leont'ev (1978) and Daniel Elkonin (1977, 1978) who described leading activities throughout childhood and identified their role in bringing about the main developmental accomplishments of each age period (Leont'ev, 1978). In Elkonin's theory of periods of child development, play is placed on the continuum of leading activities following adult-mediated object-oriented activity of toddlers and followed by the learning activities of primary grade children (Elkonin, 1977).

In a thorough analysis of play, Elkonin identified the unique characteristics that make play the leading activity of preschoolers. He particularly emphasized the symbolic nature of play that allows children to model real-life objects, actions, and relationships: since children act out not the exact actions of a firefighter or a doctor but rather synopses of these actions, they, in fact, generate a model of reality. This modelling, according to Elkonin requires children to isolate and abstract the essential features of these objects, actions, and relationships that lay the foundation for the further development of abstract thinking and imagination. Elkonin described play as the 'giant treasure chest of creativity' available to a growing individual. Specifically, Elkonin has identified four principal ways for play to facilitate the mastery of mental tools and the development of higher mental functions:

1.   Play impacts the child's motivation. In play, children develop a more complex hierarchical system of immediate and long-term goals, where immediate goals can be occasionally forgone in order to reach long-term goals. Through the process of coordinating these short-term and long-term goals, children become aware of their own actions, which make it possible for them to move from reactive behaviours to intentional ones. In order to play 'shops' children have to stop and make signs and price tags and stock the shelves with boxes. They have to postpone the shop play to make props and set up the environment.

2.   Play facilitates cognitive 'de-centering'. The ability to take other people's perspectives is critical for coordinating multiple roles and negotiating play scenarios. In addition, in play, children learn to look at objects 'through the eyes' of their play partners, a form of cognitive de-centering. Think of a child playing passenger who is being 'examined' with a ruler: to act according to his role, this child needs to put himself in the shoes of the child playing the airport security officer for whom this ruler is a pretend wand. Later, this ability to coordinate multiple perspectives and to de-center will be turned inward leading to the development of reflective thinking.

3.   Play advances the development of mental representations. This occurs when children separate the meaning of objects from their physical form. First, children use replicas to substitute for real objects (for example, the doctor's kit), then proceed to use objects that are different in appearance but that can perform the same function as the object-prototype (a pencil held as a syringe), and finally, most of the substitution takes place in child's speech or gestures with no physical objects present (gesture indicates that a doctor is giving his patient a 'shot'). Learning to operate not with real objects but with their symbolic substitutes contributes to the development of abstract thinking and imagination. It is important to note again that for Vygotskians, imagination is not a prerequisite for play but an expected outcome.

4.   Play fosters the development of deliberate behaviours – physical and mental voluntary actions. The development of deliberateness in play becomes possible due to the child's need to follow the rules of the play. In addition, as children constantly monitor each other's following of these rules, they engage in

'other-regulation' – a process, that involves comparing observed behaviors with the 'planned' ones. Planning and monitoring are essential features of deliberate behaviors. Practicing other- and self-regulation in play prepares the foundation for more advanced deliberate behaviors including planning and monitoring of one's mental processes – that is metacognition.

Elkonin also identified the main structural elements of play including roles, pretend actions, the use of props, and the relationships children enter as they play. According to Elkonin, the centre of make-believe play is the role that a child acts out. This role determines which pretend actions the child will carry out, which props he or she will use and how the relationships between play partners will be formed. Pretend actions are different from real actions even if they involve the use of same objects because pretend actions are more abbreviated and present more of an outline of an action than its exact imitation. The way props are used in play is also different from how the same objects are used in real life because children use these props to perform pretend and not real actions. Finally, the specific feature of the relationships between players is that they engage in play-specific communication that allows children to maintain the flow of play by setting the rules and monitoring how these rules are being followed.

The concept of 'fully developed' or 'mature' play

Elaborating on Vygotsky's insights on the nature of play, Elkonin (1978, 2005b) introduced the idea of 'mature' or 'fully developed' play; emphasizing that only this kind of play can be a source of development in early childhood. With this in mind, Elkonin (1978) has identified four levels of play:

Level one: The main content of play is *actions with objects* directed at the play partner. The roles exist, but they are determined by the nature of the actions instead of determining the actions. As a rule, children do not name the roles they play, neither do they assign themselves the names of people whose role they are playing. The actions themselves are stereotypical and consist of repetitive motions: e.g., when playing 'dinner', children follow the same routine as they serve salad, main dish, and dessert. The entire script of 'eating dinner' is limited to the actions of serving and eating with no other actions preceding or following these (e.g., setting the table, washing hands, etc). There seems to be no logical order in how the actions are performed. If one child acts inconsistently with how this script unfolds in real life (e.g., serves dessert first) other children do not object.

Level two: Actions with objects remain the main content of play similar to the Level One. However, at this level, it is important for the play action to accurately reflect the real action. Children label the roles they play. For a child, to play a role means to perform actions associated with this role. The structure and sequence of play actions is determined by how these actions unfold in real life. When one of the players does not follow the 'real life' sequence of the actions (e.g., a 'doctor' first puts the 'patient's' arm in cast and then makes an x-ray), the other players do not accept these actions but do not argue with them, neither do they explain what was done wrong.

Level three: The main focus of play is now *the role* and the actions determined by this role; special actions emerge that signal the relationships between the players. The roles are distinct and well defined. Children name the roles they will play before they the play starts. The roles determine and direct the children's behaviour. A special kind of 'role speech' emerges when one player talks to another one using vocabulary, intonation, and register in accordance with the specific roles both of them are playing. The nature of actions and their logic are determined by the role the child plays. The actions become more varied: for example, the 'mother' does not just put her baby to bed, but also gives him a bath, reads a bedtime story, etc. If a child acts in a way inconsistent with the real-life logic of actions, other children object by saying 'you are not supposed to do it'. When corrected, children treat their mistake seriously and try to fix it and to explain why they broke the rule.

Level four: The main content of play is now carrying out actions associated with the *relationships* between the roles children play. For example, the relationship between a 'father' and a 'child' are associated with the 'father' being in charge which is manifested in the way he addresses the 'child'. The roles are well defined. A child playing a role acts in the manner consistent with this role throughout the entire duration of play. The 'role-related speech' is consistent with the role playing by the child who uses it as well as with the role of the child to whom this speech is addressed. The sequence of play actions is well defined and consistent with the logic of these actions in real life. Children object when someone does not follow the logic of actions or breaks the rule. Children go beyond stating that 'you are not supposed to do this' but refer to the reason for this rule in real life.

Thus play according to Elkonin starts with the 'object-centred' role-play of two- and three-year-olds (level one) where object-oriented actions determine their choice of roles evolves gradually to become the elaborate 'relationship-centred' play of kin-dergarten-aged children (level four) characterized by well-defined roles as well as children's awareness of the reasons behind the rules they adopt. The ability to follow rules in play rather than submit to one's immediate desires seems to start appearing at level two but is not fully developed until level four. Combined with the changes in the use of play props and in the relationships between play roles and play actions, this evolution of play rules allows us to consider level four the stage of 'well-developed' or 'mature' play.

One of the ways post-Vygotskian researchers were able to demonstrate the unique role of play in the development of higher mental functions was through a series of experiments that compared children's performance on various tasks in play and non-play situations (Manuilenko, 1975; Istomina, 1977). A common pattern emerging from these studies indicated an age-related change in the way play supports children's cognitive (e.g., memory) and social-emotional (e.g., self-regulation) competencies: the gap between play and non-play performance was most dramatic in 5-year-old children who were assumed to be at the peak of mature play. At the same time, this gap was vir-tually non-existent both for 3-year-old children who had not yet developed advanced forms of play and in 7-year-old children who no longer needed the support of play to regulate their behaviours.

These findings support Vygotsky's view that play 'is the source of development and creates the Zone of Proximal Development [ZPD]', further demonstrating that new developmental accomplishments are apparent in play far earlier than in other activities. The findings also indicate that in order to produce these new developmental accomplishments, children need to reach the stage of 'well-developed' and 'mature' play.

Play in today's preschoolers and kindergartners: is it mature enough to create the ZPD?

Recently, researchers and practitioners working with young children began to notice that the play observed in many of today's early childhood classrooms does not fit the definition of mature play (Gudareva, 2005; Levin, 2008). Even 5-and 6-year-old children who according to Vygotsky and Elkonin should be at the peak of their play performance often display signs of immature play that is more typical for toddlers and younger preschoolers: playing only with realistic props, enacting play scenarios that are stereotypical and immature, and displaying a limited repertoire of themes and roles.

With the main elements – imaginary situation, roles and rules – underdeveloped, this 'immature' play cannot, according to Vygotskians, serve as a source of child development or create a ZPD. Evidence for this was demonstrated in a Russian study replicating Manujlenko's experiment (Elkonin, 1978) described earlier. The original study compared preschoolers' and kindergartners' ability to follow directions in play and non-play settings. The preschoolers of the 1940s followed directions better in play situations than in non-play settings; however, the play of preschoolers today did not generate that difference until the children were much older. Demonstrating superior self-regulation in play, a common characteristic of past generations of preschool children, seemed to be less prevalent in contemporary classrooms (Smirnova and Gudareva, 2004). In addition, the ability to follow directions at all ages and in all conditions appeared to have declined in comparison to the 1940s study. These researchers found that the 7-year-olds of today have self-regulation levels more like those of the preschool children of the 1940s. The researchers attributed this phenomenon to the changes in the culture of childhood in general including the changes in the way children play both at home and in the classroom. This conclusion was supported by the fact that only 10 per cent of observed 6-year-olds demonstrated a mature level of play and 48 per cent of the 5-year-olds demonstrated the lowest ('toddler') level of play (Gudareva, 2005).

Similar findings were obtained in another study in the United States, where the correlations between play and self-regulation were found for children playing at a high level but not for the ones playing at a low level (Berk et al., 2006). Researchers from other countries agree that make-believe play of today's children is not simply different from the play of the past, but is less complex and mature than in previous generations (for review, see Johnson et al., 2005; Karpov, 2006). This decline of play is even more troubling in light of declining self-regulation in young children that may put them at risk of later cognitive and social-emotional difficulties (Blair, 2002; Blair and Razza, 2007; Raver and Knitzer, 2002; Rimm- Kaufman *et al.* 2000).

Changes in children's social situation of development and the need for new pedagogies of play

Vygotsky's and Elkonin's views of play as a cultural-historical phenomenon call for a detailed analysis of the changes in today's preschoolers' social development and the effects of these changes on their make-believe play. This analysis even when not performed from the Vygotskian perspective (e.g., Chudacoff, 2007; Golinkoff *et al.*, 2006; Zigler and Bishop-Josef, 2006) might provide us with valuable insights into the factors responsible for the seeming decline in quantity and quality of play in today's preschoolers and kindergartners. It is suggested that the factors preventing young children from developing the most mature forms of make-believe play include, but are not limited to an increase in adult-directed forms of children's learning and recreation, the proliferation of toys and games that limit children's imagination, and safety limits set by parents and teachers on where and how children are allowed to play. According to Karpov (2006) the most important factor, however, may be the decrease in adult mediation of make-believe play affecting not one but all of its components.

The idea that we need to teach some young children how to play is not a new one; until recently, however, it has been primarily discussed in terms of enhancing or facilitating play that has already reached a certain level of development (see Wood, 2009 for a review) with explicit play instruction limited to the context of special education. While children with language delays or emotional disorders are thought to benefit from play interventions, typically developing children are usually expected to develop play skills on their own. This approach, while valid in the past, may no longer be appropriate if we want all young children to develop mature forms of play.

For many children, early childhood settings may be the only place where they have the opportunity to learn how to play. It is important to note, however, that learning how to play in the classroom will not look the same as learning to play within informal neighbourhood peer groups. First of all, in the past, most play occurred in multi-aged groups where children had an opportunity to learn from older 'play experts', practice their play skills with the peers of the same age, and then pass their knowledge on to other 'play novices'. In today's early childhood settings, children are almost always segregated by age and have to interact with play partners that are as inexperienced as they are. As a result, many of the play skills that children were able to learn in the past by observing and imitating their older playmates may now need support from knowledgeable adults.

In addition, unlike the unstructured play of the past that often lasted for hours and days, play time in today's early childhood classroom is limited and rarely exceeds one or two hours and it may be subject to many interruptions (Rogers and Evans, 2008).

Applying new pedagogies of play in an early childhood classroom: tools of the mind curriculum

Tools of the Mind is an attempt to apply Vygotsky's and post-Vygotskian approaches to scaffolding play in an American early childhood classroom. While sharing most pedagogies with the approach used by current generation of Vygotskians in Russia (see e.g., Michailenko and Korotkova, 2000), *Tools of the Mind* has been designed to address the needs of children growing up in different sociocultural contexts which require the development of alternative instructional strategies that would fit this particular context. Further development of pedagogies based on Vygotsky's cultural-historical approach would need to take into account changes in children's 'social situation of development' (Vygotsky, 1998).

Tools of the Mind is a comprehensive early childhood curriculum for children in preschool and kindergarten that explicitly focuses on the role of self-regulation in learning and academic ability by using specific activities that promote self-regulation and by embedding self-regulation promoting activities in instruction designed to build foundational skills in literacy, mathematics and social-emotional competence (Bodrova and Leong, 2001; Bodrova *et al.*, 2003). An essential part of the curriculum is a systemic play intervention designed to provide play scaffolding to preschool- and kindergarten-aged children. It is based on Vygotsky and Elkonin's theories of make-believe play and uses specific strategies to scaffold such critical play components as using toys and props in a symbolic way; developing consistent and extended play scenarios; being able to take on and to stay in a pretend role for an extended play episode or a series of play episodes; and being able to consistently follow the rules determining what each pretend character can or cannot do.

Using toys and props in a symbolic way. Many young children today grow up using mostly realistic toys and have limited or no experience with using low-structure materials for play, which makes it difficult for them to develop a broad range of symbolic substitutions associated with higher levels of make-believe play (Linn, 2008). For these children, early childhood teachers might model how to use props in a symbolic way gradually expanding the repertoire of different uses for the same object. Over the period of several months, the teachers need to introduce more unstructured and multi-functional props at the same time removing some of overly realistic ones, such as plastic fried eggs. Older preschoolers and kindergartners can start making their own props while younger preschoolers can be shown how to make minimal changes in the existing props to change their purpose. An important part of adult scaffolding is observing and recording children's language use to make sure that changes in the prop use are accompanied by the changes in prop labelling.

Developing consistent and extended play scenarios Scaffolding play scenarios has several components. First, children sometimes lack contextual knowledge to build play scenarios. Even to play 'house' or 'hospital' requires knowledge of the setting, roles, and actions associated with these roles. To build this knowledge, teachers use field trips, guest speakers, as well as books and videos. The choice of places to take children on a field trip as well as the choice of books and videos is guided by Elkonin's ideas of role being the core unit of play. In other words, when field trips or books center on objects or animals, very little of their content gets re-enacted in make-believe play. Discussing the use of books as a source for make-believe play, Elkonin (2005b) commented that 'Only those works that clearly and understandably described people, their activities, and how they interacted caused the children to want to reproduce the content of the story in play' (p. 41). Positive impact of explicit modelling of play scenarios on children's engagement in play was found in several studies that involved demographically varied groups of children (see Karpov, 2006 for a review). It indicates that in today's context not only at-risk children but all preschoolers benefit from in-classroom scaffolding of pretend scenarios.

Developing and maintaining play roles and rules As Elkonin (1978) pointed out, the focus of mature play are the social roles and relationship between people – something that children cannot learn by simply observing adult behaviours. Therefore, to promote mature play, teachers need to explain the purpose of these behaviours, their sequence, the cause and effect relationships between different behaviours, etc. The rules that hold make-believe play together are not arbitrary but are based on the logic of real-life situations (Elkonin, 1978), so not knowing how these life scripts unfold will keep children from practicing self-regulated behaviours by following these rules. This calls for greater involvement of ECE teachers in children's play. However, for most children this involvement needs to last for a relatively short time: soon they would be able to use models provided by the teachers to build their own roles and rules thus requiring only occasional support of the adult.

Elkonin identified planning as one of the features of highly developed play describing play of older children as consisting mostly of lengthy discussions of who is going to do what and how followed by brief periods of acting out (Elkonin, 1978). As with other components of play, role planning can benefit from adult scaffolding, supporting children what they want to play or what they want to be and encouraging them to discuss the choice of the roles with their peers. Later, the teacher can ask children about more specific details of their future play scenarios including what props they might need or whether they need to assume a different role. By making planning a necessary step in play, the teacher directs children's attention to the specifics of their roles and to the existence of rules associated with them. The planning process can take place orally, but if children are encouraged to represent their plans in drawing or pretend writing this process produces even greater benefits (Bodrova and Leong, 2005, 2007).

Efficacy studies of the *Tools of the Mind* curriculum demonstrated that it has positive impact on children's emergent academic skills as well as their self-regulation skills (Bodrova and Leong, 2001; Diamond *et al.*, 2007; Barnett *et al.*, 2008). These results as well as the results of other interventions that involved intentional scaffolding of make-believe play in ECE classrooms (see, e.g., Karpov, 2006) indicate that in current social context in play scaffolding in the ECE classroom can and should be provided in order to support mature play. When this scaffolding does address the most critical components of play, not only the quantity and quality of play improves, but so do many other competencies – language, cognitive, social, and emotional – for which mature play creates Zone of Proximal Development (Bodrova and Leong, 2001, 2003b; Barnett *et al.*, 2008).

Vygotskian and post-Vygotskian research on play has serious implications for today's early childhood pedagogy. The lesson learned from the Vygotskians is that dramatic play should be considered a major, central activity for preschool children and that it deserves the same level of adult support and scaffolding as other more formal activities. Dramatic play is an important and unique context providing opportunities to learn not afforded by other classroom activities. It should not be considered something extra that can be cut to accommodate more time for academic skills nor should it be used as a means of adding mere 'entertainment value' for inherently boring and decontextualized drills. Instead, play should be preserved and nurtured as one of 'uniquely preschool' – in the words of Vygotsky's colleague and student Alexander Zaporozhets – activities that provide the most beneficial context for children's development:

> Optimal educational opportunities for a young child to reach his or her potential and to develop in a harmonious fashion are not created by accelerated ultra – early instruction aimed at shortening the childhood period – that would prematurely turn a toddler into a preschooler and a preschooler into a first-grader. What is needed is just the opposite – expansion and enrichment of the content in the activities that are uniquely 'preschool': from play to painting to interactions with peers and adults.
>
> (Zaporozhets, 1986, p.88)

References

Barnett, W., Jung, K., Yarosz, D., Thomas, J., Hornbeck, A., Stechuk, R., and Burns, S. (2008). Educational effects of the tools of the mind curriculum: A randomized trial. *Early Childhood Research Quarterly*, 23 (3), 299–313.

Berk, L. E., Mann, T. D., and Ogan, A. T. (2006). Make-believe play: Wellspring for development of self-regulation. In D. G. Singer, R. M. Golinkoff, and K. A. Hirsh-Pasek (Eds) *Play = Learning: How Play Motivates and Enhances Cognitive and Social- Emotional Growth*. New York, NY: Oxford University Press, 74–100.

Blair, C. (2002). School readiness: Integrating cognition and emotion in a neurobiological conceptualization of child functioning at school entry. *American Psychologist*, 57(2), 111– 27.

Blair, C., and Razza, R. P. (2007). Relating effortful control, executive function, and false felief understanding to emerging math and literacy ability in kindergarten. *Child Development*, 78 (2), 647–63.

Bodrova, E., and Leong, D. J. (2001). *The Tools of the Mind Project: A case study of implementing the Vygotskian approach in American Early Childhood and Primary Classrooms*. Geneva, Switzerland: International Bureau of Education, UNESCO.

—— (2003a). Chopsticks and counting chips: Do play and foundational skills need to compete for the teacher's attention in an Early Childhood classroom? *Young Children, May*, 10–17.

—— (2003b). Learning and development of preschool children from the Vygotskian perspective. In A. Kozulin, B. Gindis, V. Ageyev and S. Miller (Eds), *Vygotsky's Educational Theory in Cultural Context*, New York, NY: Cambridge University Press, 156–76.

Bodrova, E., Leong, D., Norford, J., and Paynter, D. (2003). It only looks like child's play. *Journal of Staff Development*, 24 (2), 47–51.

Bodrova, E., and Leong, D. (2005). Vygotskian perspectives on teaching and learning early literacy. In D. Dickinson and S. Neuman (Eds), *Handbook of Early Literacy Research* (Vol. 2). New York, NY: Guilford Publications, 243–56.

Bodrova, E., and Leong, D. (2007). Play and early literacy: A Vygotskian approach. In K.A. Roskos and J.F. Christie (Eds) *Play and Literacy in Early Childhood* (2nd edition). Mahwah, NJ: Lawrence Erlbaum Associates, 185–200.

Chudacoff, H. P. (2007). *Children at Play: An American history*. New York, NY: New York University Press.

Diamond, A., Barnett, S., Thomas, J., and Munro, S. (2007). Preschool program improves cognitive control. *Science,* 3(18) 30 November.

Elkind, D. (2007). *The Power of Play: Learning What Comes Naturally*. Cambridge, MA: Da Capo Press.

Elkonin, D. B. (1977). Toward the problem of stages in the mental development of the child. In M. Cole (Ed.), *Soviet Developmental Psychology*. White Plains, NY: M. E. Sharpe.

—— (1978). *Psychologija igry* [The psychology of play]. Moscow, Russia: Pedagogika.

—— (2005a). The psychology of play: Preface. *Journal of Russian and East European Psychology*, 43 (1), 11–21. (Original work published 1978)

—— (2005b). The psychology of play: Chapter I. *Journal of Russian and East European Psychology,* 43 (1), 22–48. (Original work published 1978)

Golinkoff, R. M., Hirsh-Pasek, K. A., and Singer, D. G. (2006). Play = learning: A challenge for parents and educators. In D. G. Singer, R. M. Golinkoff, and K. A. Hirsh Pasek (Eds), *Play = Learning: How Play Motivates and Enhances Cognitive and Social Emotional Growth*. New York, NY: Oxford University Press.

Gudareva, O. V. (2005). Psikhologicheskie osobennosti suzhetno-rolevoy igry sovremennykh doshkol'nikov [Psychological features of make-believe play in today's preschoolers] Unpublished doctoral dissertation. Moscow, Russia: Moscow City University for Psychology and Education.

Isenberg, J. P., and Quisenberry, N. (2002). Play: essential for all children. (A Position Paper of the Association for Childhood Education International). *Childhood Education,* 17 (1), 33–9.

Istomina, Z. M. (1977). The developmental of voluntary memory in preschool-age children. In M. Cole (Ed.), *Soviet Developmental Psychology*. New York: M. E. Sharpe.

Johnson, J. E., Christie, J. F., and Wardle, F. (2005). *Play, Development, and Early Education*. Boston, MA: Allyn and Bacon.

Karpov, Y. V. (2006). *The Neo-Vygotskian Approach to Child Development*, Cambridge, New York: Cambridge University Press.

Leont'ev, A. N. (1978). *Activity, Consciousness, Personality*. Englewood Cliffs, NJ, Prentice Hall.

Levin, D. E. (2008). Problem solving deficit disorder: The dangers of remote controlled versus creative play. In E. Goodenough (Ed.) *Where Do Children Play?* Detroit, MI: Wayne University Press, 137–40.

Linn, S. (2008). *The Case for Make-Believe: Saving Play in a Commercialized World*. New York: The New Press.

Manuilenko, Z. V. (1975) The development of voluntary behavior by preschool-age children. *Soviet Psychology* 13, 65–116.

Michailenko, N. Y., and Korotkova, N. A. (2000). Organizatsiya suzhetnoj igry v detskom sadu [Pedagogies of make-believe play in early childhood classrooms]. Moscow: Gnom Press.

Miller, E., and Almon, J. (2009). *Crisis in Kindergarten: Why Children Need to Play in School*. College Park, MD: Alliance for Childhood.

Raver, C., and Knitzer, J. (2002). *Ready to Enter: What Research Tells Policymakers about Strategies to Promote Social and Emotional School Readiness Among Three- and Four-Year Old Children*. New York, NY: National Center for Children in Poverty.

Rimm-Kaufman, S., Pianta, R. C., and Cox. M. (2001). Teachers' judgments of problems in the transition to school. *Early Childhood Research Quarterly* 15(2): 147–66.

Smirnova, E. O., and Gudareva, O. V. (2004). Igra i proizvol'nost u sovremennykh doshkol'nikov [Play and intentionality in modern preschoolers]. *Vopprosy Psychologii*, 1, 91–103.

Rogers, S., and Evans, J. (2008). *Inside Role Play in Early Childhood Education: Researching Children's Perspectives*, London: Routledge.

Vygotsky, L. S. (1971). *The Psychology of Art*, Cambridge: MIT Press.

—— (1978). *Mind in Society: The Development of Higher Mental Processes*. Cambridge, MA: Harvard University Press.

—— (1997). *The History of the Development of Higher Mental Functions* (M. J. Hall, Trans.) (Vol. 4). New York, NY: Plenum Press.

—— (1998). *Child Psychology* (Vol. 5). New York, NY: Plenum Press.

Wood, E. (2009) Conceptualizing a pedagogy of play: International perspectives from theory, policy, and practice. In D. Kuschner (Ed.), *From Children to Red Hatters: Diverse Images and Issues of Play*. Lanham, MD: University Press of America. 166–89.

Zaporozhets, A. (1986). *Izbrannye psychologicheskie trudy* [Selected works]. Moscow, Russia: Pedagogika.

Zigler, E. F., and Bishop-Josef, S. J. (2006). The cognitive child vs. the whole child: lessons from 40 years of head start. In D. G. Singer, R. M. Golinkoff, and K. A. Hirsh-Pasek (Eds) *Play = Learning: How Play Motivates and Enhances Cognitive and Social Emotional Growth*. New York, NY: Oxford University Press. 13–35.

Chapter 6

Exploring culture, play, and early childhood education practice in African contexts

Kofi Marfo and Linda Biersteker

Introduction

In Africa, as in many other parts of the non-Western world,[1] Western-style schooling has become the institutionalized medium of organized or formal education since the era of colonization. The ubiquity of Western-style schooling in Africa is problematic when measured by the criteria that education must 1) be locally relevant and 2) transmit a society's enduring values and best traditions across generations. Today, the alienating effects of schooling in Africa are a major theme in discourse on education. Cole has remarked on the large amounts of time children spend in formal schools 'where their activity is separated from the daily life of the rest of the community' (2005: 195). Serpell (2005) has lamented the absence of a connection between the Western theories that inform teaching and learning in African classrooms and the perspectives and everyday life circumstances and experiences of students, teachers, and parents in their local contexts. In the area of early childhood development (ECD), Nsamenang (2008: 142) has expressed the concern that 'western ECD services initiate Africa's children into an educational process by which children . . . increasingly gain unfamiliar knowledge and skills but sink disturbingly into alienation and ignorance of their cultural circumstances.'

In brief, there is a widely acknowledged gulf between the culture of schooling (read as the content and processes of formal, Western-style education) and the local cultures and life experiences of Africa's numerous constituent societies across its 54 nations. Schooling, in these diverse societies, is generally perceived to be dysfunctional because it fails to guarantee the cultural identities of Africa's children, breaks intergenerational continuity in the core values and traditions that define the uniqueness of Africans as members of the family of human cultures, and denies newer generations the competencies and values necessary to function productively within their own local contexts and realities. When children are denied meaningful education that is grounded in local realities their ability to be productive adults in the local context is compromised.

We welcomed the invitation to contribute to this volume as an opportunity to bring a cultural-historical, contextualist perspective to the discourse on play pedagogy and early childhood education (ECE). The chapter is organized around several themes. We begin with an examination of the relationship between culture and play. Bearing in mind the predominantly Euro-American knowledge bases that currently inform ECE theory and practice, we discuss the perennial *problem of relevance* – the degree to which exclusively Euro-American models of ECE practice are appropriate for Africa. Even as we acknowledge Africa's new realities in the face of inevitable social change, we make a case for serious consideration of cultural differences and local realities in curriculum design. To capture the thrust toward play-based pedagogy on the continent, we present a case study of ECE policy and practice trends in South Africa. Finally, we explore ways in which understandings about play and learning mechanisms in local contexts might contribute to the formulation of curricular and pedagogical frameworks that could complement Western-style schooling's predominantly didactic instructional models.

Play as a culturally embedded concept

Play is held widely as a universal phenomenon, one that is not even unique to humans (Hughes 1991; Lancy, 1980a). Scholars examining play from an evolutionary perspective (e.g., Power 2000) have been inspired by the desire to understand the mediating role of different aspects of play in brain development as well as cross-species similarities and differences in play forms. Universal conceptions of the role of play in children's acquisition of developmental competencies have part of their foundations in this view of play as a dimension of the shared biological heritage of humans across cultures (Hughes 1991). However, play is also seen widely as a culturally defined construct, as exemplified by wide variations in the nature of play across cultures. These variations, in turn, emanate from the different mores, value systems, and traditions that define play within cultures and from characteristics of the material environments that determine the forms of objects and routines associated with play.

As a culturally mediated activity, play serves a variety of functions, prominent among which is as a mechanism for enculturation (Schwartzman 1978). Across cultures, children model substantial aspects of their play on adult activities (Kamp 2001) and, in so doing, learn not only the social roles and cultural values and norms typical in the culture but also the skills and competencies necessary for survival and productive community membership. Kamp (2001) has underscored the circular relationship between culture and play. On one hand, cultures structure the pastimes of children through the games, songs, and other play activities transmitted from one generation to another. On the other hand, cultures benefit ultimately from the play-engendered creativity that prepares newer generations of citizens for innovative problem solving and new contributions to society.

Play and enculturation in African contexts: Selective research overview

With developmental psychology so preoccupied with issues pertaining to the ontology of play and its reciprocal relationship with cognition in particular, insights on the enculturation functions of play come predominantly from anthropology and cultural psychology. From anthropological studies of play in African societies in the 1930s, much has been gleaned not only about the overall socializing role of play but also the richness of play interactions as sources of insights on children's cognitive, linguistic, and social competence. Detailed descriptions of prolonged play episodes among Tallensi children of Northern Ghana (Fortes, cited by Schwartzman 1978) revealed the interweaving of recreational and imaginative play with practical activities. The texture and routines of play demonstrated the children's adept knowledge of nature, the religious rituals of their ethnic group, and remarkable creativity in their use of materials in their environment to construct make-believe worlds.

Similar to Fortes' findings on Tellensi children, observations of Tanzanian Chagga children's play in the 1930s by Otto Raum (the son of a missionary born and raised in Tanzania) countered the prevailing conception of play in Africa and other non-Western societies as consisting predominantly of simple imitations (Schwartzman 1978). Raum's work underscored the presence of such higher-level representational and linguistically rich play as the satirical caricaturing of ridiculous adult behaviours and habits, including parodies of schooling's rote memorization and recitation culture (Schwartzman 1978). Beyond the 'playful exercise of sensory and motor activities' and competitive games, Raum also documented dimensions of the social organization of play, such as the selection of leaders, allocation of resources, the adoption of secret languages, and the ingenious invention of new games and play objects (Schwartzman 1978: 105).

In more recent ethnographic research, Lancy's work on Kpelle children in the West African country of Liberia (see for example Lancy 1980b, 1996) particularly stands out in terms of the insights it sheds on play as an agent of enculturation in African societies. Lancy's goal in much of his research was 'to provide a portrait of Kpelle society that emphasized the kinds of things a typical child needed to learn in order to succeed as an adult member and . . . to identify the practices that were implicated during this developmental process' (Lancy 1996: 2). He used interviews of adult informants to make inferences about antecedents of adult skills, while also analyzing children's play forms for evidence of skills that might be used later in adult life. His analyses underscore the intricate interplay of play and work in children's socialization. While 'preparation for work takes up the largest proportion of the child's education' (Lancy 1996: 8), the 'same open spaces throughout the village and on the farm that serve as the locus of adult work also serve, on other occasions, as playgrounds' (p. 9).

Through observation, participation, apprenticeship, and other forms of exposure to the values and traditions of their social group, Kpelle children develop a clear sense of character and identity and gain specific skills and competencies necessary to carry out their responsibilities as children and later as adults. Particularly relevant to this chapter's focus is the manner in which participation in play and games serves as a gateway to children's acquisition of the complex range of social, linguistic, cognitive, and ethical functions that are valued in adult life. Lancy illustrates this with a discussion of an important feature of Kpelle life referred to as 'talking matter', a type of court appearance routine that Kpelle adults and youth were likely to experience in any one of several roles: as defendant, witness, elder, or judge (see Lancy 1980c 1996; Schwartzman 1978). 'Talking matter' required a high level of wit, spontaneity, verbal agility, and memory for proverbs. Lancy saw evidence of informal preparation for 'talking matter' in a variety of older children's play activities and routines during which children were often interrupted and challenged by peers to defend the meaning and validity of their utterances. These challenges and the ensuing interchanges required astute demonstration of linguistic and dramatization skills on the part of the challenged and the challenger alike. Observing mixed-aged groups of children in informal settlements around Cape Town, South Africa, Reynolds (1989) has similarly reported on the richness of unsupervised cooperative play drawing on and rehearsing local cultural practices in the course of building a village in the sand dunes using scraps, leaves, and household items.

Several striking themes emerge from the research on children's play in Africa. First, play is often not schemed and directed by adults. Indeed, Lancy (2007) has argued that the dominant narrative within developmental psychology that mother-child play is critically important for children's linguistic and cognitive development is very much a Western white middle-class value that is often imposed on other cultures. In African contexts, peers and older siblings are perhaps more significant in the socialization of play. A literature review of indigenous play practices within Southern African cultural groups (Sedite 2009) underscores the important role that older children play in young children's learning of traditional games, where play helps with the development of physical agility, concepts, and cultural and social learning. In relation to Shona games, Nyota and Mapara (2008) note that older children are instrumental in adapting games for younger children. Swart *et al.* (1996) describes an Ndebele practice in which children are encouraged to go around in fairly stable mixed-age groups called *ubungani*, within which a lot of learning takes place. Roughly translated, *ubungani* means friendship, comradeship, or playing together. Similar groups were known in Sotho communities.

Second, work and play are not two separate activities. From her research on environmental learning in a small village in central-eastern Sudan, Katz (1986: 47) noted that 'one of the most striking aspects of the children's lives was the fusion between the activities of work, play, and learning in time, space and meaning.' Katz described children's work and play as a 'rich unity' that 'overshadowed formal means as the way in which children acquired, experimented with, and consolidated environmental knowledge' (p. 47). A great deal of children's play occurs in the context of work and chores. For example, rural Ghanaian children were known to turn the daily morning chore of fetching water from the river into play by building a simple 'vehicle' with two wooden wheels and a long wooden pole connected to the rod that held the wheels together. On the other end of the pole that rested on the '*driver's*' shoulder there was also a steering device. Big nails hammered partway through the pole at points closer to the steering device were used as anchors to hold buckets of water. The joy of driving and outracing siblings or peers with this make-believe transporter could not escape the attention of onlookers. Thus, children construct their own play objects from whatever they can find in their environment. Indeed, one way to assess the impact of social change on any given society is to analyze changes in the types of toys and play materials children create over time. The objects children create often reflect what is new and exciting in their environment. In his boyhood years in the Ashanti region of Ghana, the first author remembers fondly the many peer group-launched competitions for best talent in the design of toy cars and trucks from raffia palm material. Finally, young children learn to play not through direct instruction but through observation and participation. Play is a key socializing force independent of the intentional enculturation activities of primary caregivers, extended families members, and communities (Lancy 1996). From these observations, children's play should be seen as an important source of insights on organized instruction for young children.

One of the strongest cases for grounding ECE pedagogy in knowledge of African play forms and routines was made a quarter of a century ago by Belgian socio-cultural anthropologist Jean-Pierre Rossie. In his report on a UNESCO-sponsored project on children's play and games in Tunisia, Rossie expressed the hope that:

> the school system of developing countries will take into account the immense value of the cultural heritage of games and toys and that in the Saharan North African states common games, and the toys used with them, will receive pedagogical application in order to replace many of the typical European educational games that have been adopted through teacher training programmes based on French or Anglo-Saxon models and so have been imposed as alien cultural items on the children from those countries.
>
> (1984: 2).

Rossie's recommendations followed an analysis of 180 games and the toys and other objects used in those games. To Rossie, not only are the games and toys in children's play a rich source of knowledge and insight into the individual child and his/her society, but they have 'an immense developmental value' both as 'an instrument of informal socialization' and a method of formal socialization or education' (Rossie, 1984: 3).

Play and ECE in Africa

Largely because of the poorly developed status of ECE on the continent, there is very little systematic documentation on its history, policy trends, or curricular approaches – although this situation has begun to change through the attention ECD is receiving under the influence of private foundations (e.g., Aga Khan and Bernard van Leer) and international multilateral organizations (see Garcia *et al.* 2008). In this section, we draw on the second author's experience in South Africa to highlight the relationship between play and ECE programmes. While the policy elements and the historical timing of specific developments may be unique to South Africa, the overall picture of a disjuncture between pedagogy and local realities may not be all that different from what is happening elsewhere on the continent.

ECE in South Africa developed through efforts within the private sector, parent and community groups, and non-governmental organizations (NGOs). Play was introduced into pedagogy for nursery-age children (ages 2–6 years) through the nursery school movement which emerged in the 1930s largely for white children. Standards for certification by the Nursery School Association of South Africa explicitly stated that 'the nursery school excludes instruction in the three Rs' (Webber 1978: 101). This orientation within the emerging nursery education system reflected the influence of the more informal British nursery movement, which had the greatest influence on African ECD in general (Prochner and Kabiru, 2008).

When projects for disadvantaged children were started in the late 1960s and early 1970s under the influence of the Head Start movement, nursery education in South Africa was described as following the 'traditional' (i.e. British nursery) approach. Nursery school programmes of the time emphasized free play, free expression and socialization with little attention given to intellectual and linguistic development based on the needs of the urban middle class children who up until then were the major beneficiaries of nursery programmes and whose homes provided the required stimulation (Short 1985).

Interventions for children from disadvantaged circumstances which gained momentum from this time also drew on models that were established or being tested in North America and Europe. Examples included the Montessori movement and various curricula which developed as part of the Head Start movement. Most were adapted in some way to local circumstances. For example, the High Scope approach was adapted for use in rural areas, while others followed a more eclectic approach informed by Western child development models but with modifications for local contexts. Without exception, there was an emphasis on children's learning through exploration and play. 'Play is children's work', was a common expression heard from early childhood educators, whether trained by the official colleges or by NGOs.

Reflecting the strong influence of Piagetian theory on ECE curriculum, a text widely used to train the paraprofessionals providing the majority of early childhood services stated one of its basic beliefs about children is as follows: 'young children learn by playing – play is very important for young children because they learn by playing by themselves and with each other' (Van der Merwe 1988: 3). Such a play-based approach was considered essential for long-term development and scholastic success. A recent review of training provision found that all of the curriculum approaches included in NGO training and courses offered by vocational colleges continue to have a strong focus on learning informally through play activities considered appropriate to the developmental stage of the child (Biersteker 2008).

Nevertheless the importation of an approach from one context to another often leads to differences in interpretation and implementation. As a recent report on ECE curriculum implementation in South Africa notes, 'the exact nature of play and what practitioners mean by a play-based approach is an area of debate and differing interpretation' (Wits School of Education 2009: 138). In South Africa, this applies both to the way that the Western play-based ECE curriculum is often implemented in community-based ECE programmes and in more formal school-based programmes. Regarding the first, an early education specialist who had worked in the United Kingdom noted, on her return to South Africa in 1991, that play was much more structured and the daily programme much more rigidly followed than the play-based pedagogy practised in the UK.

Another construction of play-based pedagogy is found in the apartheid education system's 'Bridging Period Programme' for 5-to 7-year-old African children. The programme focused on perceptual development and on language and gross and fine motor skills (Grove and Hauptfleisch 1989). While a free choice philosophy and learning through play were emphasized, activities were too teacher-directed and group-based to be consistent with the claimed orientation (Padayachie *et al.* 1994). The Bridging Period Programme was based in primary schools and to a great extent a more formal approach persists in the school-based Reception Classes of today. The ECD directorate in the National Department of Education has emphasized that learning activities should be 'through play, play and more play – outdoor as well as indoor play,'[2] suggesting that children need sufficient time to play on their own rather than specific play activities related to the acquisition of particular learning outcomes. Nevertheless, teachers have very different notions of what play is, and for many, the completion of worksheets and teacher-directed group activities constitute play activity.

These examples illustrate the extent to which constructions of play vary according to context and orientation. It seems likely that aspects of the formalization of the play approach in South Africa have been influenced by indigenous ways of instructing children as well as by schooling. A danger of introducing play into such settings is that the learnings that are gained from free play in mixed age groups are lost as play is reconstructed into something entirely different and takes up the time and space once used for those purposes.

Despite the fact that black children constitute the overwhelming majority of children in ECE programmes in South Africa, very little can be gleaned from the available literature about the cultural appropriateness of the various ECE models. One consultancy report noted that much of the literature on ECE curricula stressed the importance of play in promoting cognitive development (Penn 1996). This is perhaps a signal that the cognitive aims of preschooling took precedence over a broad range of other developmental outcomes with practical relevance for day-to-day life in Black African communities. According to Penn, while curriculum materials were adapted, the 'Anglo-American tenets which inform them are generally assumed to be universal' (p. 12). Penn noted further:

> Most of the articulated pedagogy therefore relied on a watered down version of the theory and practice of what was available in the white nurseries. Some ingenious efforts had been made to incorporate relevant materials but there was no articulated view of a black culture which might in significant ways be different from the standard pedagogy.
>
> (1996: 14)

Summary and implications

With cultural considerations as the backdrop, we have tried in this chapter to stimulate interest in explorations of the linkage between knowledge of children's play and development in local contexts and ECE practice within Africa's diverse eco-cultural landscape. Such explorations should contribute to the necessary dialogue that must take place on how best to think about, plan for, and implement programmes for young children within educational systems that continue to draw heavily from Euro-American curriculum traditions. As the South African case presentation illustrates, imported programme models and curricular approaches are hardly implemented without local adaptations. However, it does also appear that whatever adaptations are made to adopted programmes may not necessarily be driven by explicit guidelines emanating from formalized policies on contextual or cultural relevance. In this final section, we highlight some of the central issues raised earlier in the chapter and discuss two broad sets of implications: those pertaining to philosophical and socio-political values that inform educational policy and those with direct bearing on curriculum and pedagogy.

Policy Implications

We opened this chapter with observations about the alienating effects of Western-style schooling in Africa and went on to identify the problem of relevance as a key concern. The related policy implication we draw here is based on the premise that both the Euro-centric traditions that have governed educational practice on the continent and the history of colonial domination behind those traditions have possibly exacted a lasting impact on Africa's cultural psyche in ways that have profound implications for African children's sense of worth and identity. Children in contemporary Africa are certainly far removed, historically, from the pervasive and explicit pressure for cultural dissociation experienced by their great grandparents during the era of colonization. However, in many ways, the vestiges and legacies of that era can be said to be well preserved in modern times by a culture of schooling in which the African child finds very little of him/herself. The continent's rich values and social mores (e.g., the primacy of collectivist existence and the moral obligations flowing from it), performing arts (e.g., oratory, music, and dance forms), and forms of learning (e.g., observation, active participation, and apprenticeship in life skills) were, for the longest time, relegated to the status of relics of the past to be studied academically or admired by connoisseurs of historical artifacts and practices. Cycles of school reform in post-independence Africa have done little to either restore the legitimacy and validity of core values and traditions or lay the foundations for authentically African institutional structures that can confidently place primary responsibility for the solution of Africa's problems in the hands of well-educated, contextually grounded Africans. Today, many African children grow up primed to see in their own culture and traditions the antithesis of what schooling promotes as the path to civilization.

Underlying the widely acknowledged failure of schools to provide culturally appropriate and contextually relevant education are at least two core problems: 1) failure on the part of the colonial establishments which presented the continent with a de-contextualized system of education and 2) failure on the part of post-independence African societies to appropriately domesticate the institution of schooling for their own purposes. The first problem is in the past but the second can and should be confronted. If thoughtful domestication of schooling is a desirable goal, there is no better place to initiate that process than in the context of education in the earliest years of life. ECE may very well present the ideal opportunity for African educationists to 're-engineer' basic education to better integrate Western-style schooling into a 'modernized' African education system. The goal of such a system will be to make schooling meaningful and relevant in the local context and simultaneously generative enough of the kinds of competencies and dispositions necessary for survival and productive membership in a global context. Discussion of the specific mechanisms for attaining this outcome falls outside the purview of this chapter, but the starting point lies, perhaps, in systems-level policy instruments that set the stage for serious and sustained pursuit of substantive curriculum reorientation and design. It is not sufficient to merely include local games, songs, activities, and play materials in the existing ECE curriculum. Systematic developmental and pedagogical analysis of the kinds of local assets and knowledge reviewed in this chapter must receive priority attention in African curriculum research and serve as the foundation for designing contextually sensitive curricula.

Pedagogical Implications

As Alexander (2000) notes, pedagogy entails not just the 'act' of teaching but also the connection between teaching, culture, organization, and mechanisms of social control. Pedagogy evokes the inevitable interplay of values, priorities, and purposes that determine the content and methods of instruction. Thus, pedagogy is by definition context-bound and value-laden. This effectively means that teaching requires not just knowledge of how children acquire competencies but also an understanding of the contexts within which children develop, learn, and apply their competencies. Our review of the literature on culture and play in the African context underscored some of the child- and context-level understandings that should inform pedagogy.

Briefly, children are active rather than passive 'drivers' of their own learning and development, as reflected in the observation that children's play is often self-propelled or co-constructed with peers rather than schemed or directed by adults. Indeed, the socialization processes that accompany children's play and games are imbued with mechanisms of learning that are the antithesis of the didactic, assembly-line instruction found typically in school-based academic instruction (Rogoff *et al.* 2003). Young children learn spontaneously and incidentally by attending, observing, imitating, creating, co-constructing, and participating in a self-driven or guided manner. Rogoff and her associates have classified this collection of learning mechanisms under the construct of *intent participation*, noting their significance as the primary or natural learning mechanisms by which children gain knowledge of their world. By taking advantage of the learning mechanisms children employ spontaneously in their 'natural' developmental ecologies, ECE programmes provide a smooth bridge from the unstructured learning that takes place at home and in the community to the structured, formalized learning in school contexts.

It is important to highlight the way our analysis of the play and general learning behaviours of African children in their local contexts yields pedagogical insights and principles compatible with constructivism and discovery learning, both bedrocks of Euro-American play-based pedagogy. Stated simply, embedded within the practical life experiences of young children in their local contexts are the core ingredients of pedagogical principles associated with activity-based, cooperative, problem-based, and self-regulated as well as socially-guided learning. This convergence of pedagogical implications from theory and research in the Western and African contexts should serve to drive home the critical point that careful theory-driven analysis of learning and development in African contexts can provide valid guidance for the design of locally relevant instructional practice.

Another salient theme with relevance to pedagogy pertains to the linkage between play and learning. It is important to highlight this theme here because some of the barriers to play-based pedagogy emanate from misconceptions and attitudes about the place of play in school-based learning. Some of the resistance to play-based pedagogy at the level of parents and teachers appears to be linked to the conception that play is not learning. Even in the South African context, where we have noted significant policy support and training for play-based pedagogy by NGO and government teacher training programmes, the notion that play is not learning remains entrenched among teachers and parents. There is a large constituency of teachers in early schooling who appear to tolerate play only in so far as it is a bridge into 'real work.' This attitude manifests itself in statements like 'everything we do must be based on play, although as a teacher you want them to learn' or 'curriculum should be applied to the child but in a play way/method that the child is not able to recognize.'[3] We found further support for attitudinal barriers on the part of parents in a dissertation study conducted in 20 ECE settings in Sierra Leone (Dabor 2008).Within a sample of 83 parents, 87 per cent agreed with the concern that in preschools *'Children play most of the time and do not learn much.'* Parents and teachers may not be alone in their apparent attitudes regarding play. Phatudi (2007) found in a transition-to-school study that some children leaving preschool for grade school showed excitement because, for them, 'preschool was associated with playing and not with serious work' (p. 144).

These attitudes are not likely to disappear as long as ECE programmes are seen, even in the African context, as the place for young children to gain competitive advantage in the narrow-band academic and cognitive competencies that are privileged in school over indicators of more holistic development. However, it is important to underscore that the more fundamental challenge, perhaps, is that play-based pedagogy has itself neither been sufficiently articulated nor validated practically enough in model demonstration programmes for teachers, parents, and children to develop an informed understanding and appreciation of its educational value. As noted in our South African case presentation, there is no consensus on play-based approaches or how to implement them in ECE or formal school settings. Thus, there is a pressing need for educational establishments to move beyond sheer advocacy of play-based learning to build model play-based programmes that can then be used to provide both pre-service and in-service training for ECE teachers. Consistent with the thrust of this chapter, such model programmes, while borrowing from the outside world, must adhere to the fundamental principle of drawing on knowledge of local conditions and realities to ensure the utmost degree of continuity between home- and community-level learning and learning in school.

Conclusion

In this chapter we have argued for consideration of culture and local contexts in the design of ECE programmes, and we have suggested that ECE provision may, indeed, be an ideal starting point for educational thinkers in Africa to explore ways to 'domesticate' Western-style schooling. Reorienting ECE curriculum development research and practice to draw relevantly from knowledge of children's learning and development in local contexts is central to this domestication process. We have also identified a significant gap between recognition and advocacy of play-based pedagogy and the readiness on the part of educational establishments to prepare teachers substantively in the use of play-based approaches. Hopefully, countries, such as South Africa, with a history of demonstrated commitment to ECE policy and practice advances – and the fiscal resources to back them – will begin to bridge this gap and serve as a learning laboratory for other countries on the continent.

We end the chapter with two caveats. The first, a cautionary note, is that Africa is a large continent with over 900 million people across 54 constituent countries. There are so many points of diversity that sweeping generalizations are often untenable. Africa's educational systems vary widely in their historical roots, their levels of post-independence advancement, and the magnitude of budgetary allocations to the sector. The attention ECE provision receives varies across the continent, and in many countries it is even unrealistic to expect that curricular and pedagogical innovations, such as play-based approaches to early learning, will be a priority. Where the priority exists, however, it is imperative that both play-based pedagogy and the ECE system in general be grounded in local conditions and experiences and promoted through appropriate training and demonstration.

Second, African nations are at different stages of transition, with cultural values and traditions in a constant state of flux. The continent will continue to witness dramatic changes in its social, economic, and political systems, as illustrated by its status as the most rapidly urbanizing region of the world. These changes will, in turn, condition corresponding changes not only in the goals and processes of socialization but also in how children develop, learn, and respond to their changing worlds. Thus the structures and goals of education systems will vary from country to country, depending on variations in the rate and stage of social change. However, the inevitability of these forces of change will not alter the imperative for the proposed domestication of the Western-style schooling system inherited during the era of colonization. After all, domestication itself is a dynamic process requiring continuous fine-tuning of exogenous systems and technologies to respond meaningfully to local contexts and changing realities.

Acknowledgment

We are grateful to Lisa Deters who, while a Columbia University graduate student, assisted with initial explorations into play-based instruction in African ECE contexts.

Notes

1 'Western,' 'Euro-Western', and 'Euro-American' are used interchangeably in relation to ideas originating from nations with Western European cultural heritage.
2 ACESS conference presentation 24 July 2008.
3 Email communication in relation to Grade 1 teacher statements U. Hoadley, University of Cape Town.

References

Alexander, R. J. (2000) *Culture and pedagogy: International comparisons in primary education*. Oxford, UK: Blackwell Publishing.

Biersteker, L. (2008) A review of qualifications, training provision and training delivery in relation to the needs of the National Integrated Plan for ECD and the ECD component of the Expanded Public Works Programme. Working paper for the scaling up ECD 0–4 years project. Cape Town, South Africa: Human Sciences Research Council.

Cole, M. (2005) Cross-cultural and historical perspectives on the developmental consequences of education. *Human Development*, 48(4), 195–216.

Dabor, M. C. (2008) *Parents', preschool teachers' and instructors of tertiary institutions' perceptions of early childhood education; and curriculum proposal for training preschool teachers/educators*. Unpublished doctoral thesis, University of Sierra Leone.

Garcia, M., Pence, A., and Evans, J. J. (eds) (2008) *Africa's future, Africa's challenge: Early childhood care and development in Sub-Saharan Africa*. Washington, DC: World Bank.

Grove, M. C. and Hauptfleisch, H. (1989) *Learning through play. A school readiness programme*, Pretoria: De Jager – HAUM,.

Hughes, F. P. (1991) *Children, play, and development*, Boston: Allyn and Bacon,.

Kamp, K. A. (2001) Where have all the children gone? The archeology of childhood. *Journal of Archeological Method and Theory*, 8(1), 1–34.

Katz, C. (1986) Children and the environment: Work, play and learning in rural Sudan. *Children's Environments Quarterly*, 3(4), 43–51.

Lancy, D. F. (1980a) Play in species adaptation. *Annual Review of Anthropology*, 9, 471–95.

—— (1980b) Work as play: The Kpelle case. In H. Schwartzman (ed.), *Play and culture* (pp. 295–304) West Point, NY: Leisure Press.

—— (1980c) Speech events in a West African court. *Communication and Cognition*, 13, 397–412.

—— (1996) *Playing on the mother-ground: Cultural routines and children's development*, New York: The Guilford Press.

—— (2007) Accounting for variability in mother-child play. *American Anthropologist*, 109(2), 273–84.

Nyota, S. and Mapara, J. (2008) Shona traditional children's games and play: songs as indigenous ways of knowledge. *Journal of PanAfrican Studies*, 2(4), 189–202.

Nsamenang, A. B. (2008) (Mis)Understanding ECD in Africa: The force of local and global motives. In M. Garcia, A. Pence, and J. J. Evans (eds) *Africa's future, Africa's challenge: Early childhood care and development in Sub-Saharan Africa* (pp. 135–49) Washington, DC: World Bank.

Padayachie, R., Atmore, E., Biersteker, L., King, R., Matube, J., Muthayan, S., Naidoo, K., Plaatjies, D., and Evans, J. (1994) *Report of the South African Study on Early Childhood Development*, Johannesburg/Washington DC: Centre for Education Policy Development/World Bank.

Penn, H. (1996) *Early childhood services in South Africa. Consultancy report for Save the Children Fund*, UK., unpublished report for Save the Children Fund, UK.

Phatudi, N. C. (2007) A study of transition from preschool and home contexts to Grade 1 in a developing country. Doctoral thesis Education Policy Studies, University of Pretoria. Etd 09192007–134056 Accessible at http://upetd.up.ac.za/UPeTD.htm, (accessed July 2009).

Power, T. G. (2000) *Play and exploration in children and animals*. Mahwah, N.J.: Erlbaum.

Prochner, L., and Kabiru, M. (2008) ECD in Africa: A historical perspective. In M. Garcia, A. Pence, and J. J. Evans (eds) *Africa's future, Africa's challenge: Early childhood care and development in Sub-Saharan Africa* (pp. 117–43) Washington, DC: World Bank.

Reynolds, P. (1989) *Childhood in crossroads. Cognition and society in South Africa*, Cape Town: David Philip.

Rogoff, B., Paradise, R., Arauz, R. M., Correa-Chavez, M., and Angelillo, C. (2003) Firsthand learning through intent participation. *Annual Review of Psychology*, 54, 175–203.

Rossie, J-P. (1984) *Games and toys: Anthropological research on their practical contribution to child development*. Paris: UNESCO (Document No. ED—84/WS/55). Online. Available http://unesdoc.unesco.org/images/0006/000621/062190eb.pdf (accessed 15 August 2008).

Schwartzman, H.B. (1978) *Transformation: The anthropology of children's play*. New York: Plenum Press.

Sedite, D. (2009) *Indigenous play of children from 0–8 years with older children and grandmothers as caregivers*. A literature review produced for the South African ECD Learning Community. Unpublished, Save the Children, South Africa.

Serpell, R. (2005) Optimizing the developmental consequences of education: Reflections on issues by Michael Cole. *Human Development*, 48, 217–22.

Short, A. (1985) *Seeking Change: Early childhood education for the disadvantaged in South Africa*. Ypsilanti Michigan: Bernard van Leer Foundation International Series on Education and High/Scope Press.

Swart, T., Berman, L., Mahahlela, M., Mlonzi, L., Phakhati, L., and Sixako, L. (1996) Mothers' ideas of model offspring inform training, *Recovery* (September), 22–26.

Van der Merwe, K. (1988) *How children develop and learn*. Cape Town: Early Learning Resource Unit.

Webber, V. K. (1978) *An outline of the development of preschool children in South Africa: 1930–1977*. Pretoria: South African Association for Early Childhood Education.

Wits School of Education (2009) Implementation of the National Curriculum Statement in the Foundation Phase. Report submitted by Wits School of Education, University of the Witwatersrand to Directorate: Curriculum Development – General Education and Training, Gauteng Department of Education. Johannesburg: Wits School of Education.

Chapter 7

Play and pedagogy framed within India's historical, socio-cultural, pedagogical and postcolonial context

Amita Gupta

In Western discourses of early childhood education, play has occupied a central and defining position. However, more recently it is recognized that cultural differences across nations and communities make it difficult to construct a single definition of play that can be universally applied. For example, Genishi and Goodwin (2007) present a strong argument against the mono-cultural specificity of the guidelines for developmentally appropriate practices (DAP) promoted widely in the USA, since they cannot be applied to the complex lives of children in diverse cultural contexts. A growing international body of work critically examines dominant ways of explaining play in early childhood arguing that there are different manifestations of play within different socio-cultural groups (Rogoff, 2003; Haight *et al.*, 1999; Brooker; 2003; Long *et al.*, 2007); and preferred forms of play look different in diverse cultural contexts (Roopnarine *et al.*, 1998, Haight *et al.*, 1999).

The purpose of this chapter is to examine how play and pedagogy is conceptualized within the Indian cultural context. Drawing on postcolonial theory, I will consider ideas which appear to have shaped the relationship between play and pedagogy within the Indian context. I also draw examples from a study of early childhood teachers' perceptions of play in India. Critically, I will consider the extent to which it is possible or desirable to import a child-centred, play-based pedagogy to the Indian context, without causing other rifts, inequities, and impediments to social justice.

An interplay between the global and the local: postcolonial theory as a conceptual framework

The term 'postcolonial' may literally refer to an historical period that marks the end of colonization and the beginning of political autonomy in a former colony such as India. However, it may be of more use to include also the period of influence from the start of colonization. The idea of colonialism can be viewed as an imposition of an ideological standard of a privileged power against which other less powerful ideologies are measured and found wanting (Macedo, 1999). It is generally quite clear as to what is socially and intellectually appropriate according to these standards: mostly behaviours that are valued by the socially, racially, and linguistically privileged sections of Western colonizing societies. Thus there is an implicit recognition that if it does not conform to Western standards then it is inappropriate. This has led to frenzied attempts in the developing non-West to deploy adaptations of Western curricula and approaches in systems of education. Colonialism also implies the idea that the 'truth' exists in a place that is inaccessible to the natives of the colonized developing world and within the reach of only a privileged few (Viruru, 2005), thus leaving little scope for understanding the diversity of human thought and consciousness.

Postcolonial theory is concerned with how knowledge is produced, the nature of relationships between the dominant and marginalized, and between the colonizer and the colonized. It allows the examination of the interplay between the colonial and central discourses of education, and the peripheral, more local voices of education. It helps frame contemporary educational issues within the context of underlying colonial experiences, and provides a platform for non-Western critics located in the West to present their cultural inheritance as knowledge. Further, postcolonial theory allows a critical examination of the past in an attempt to reveal 'marginalized' experiences and facilitates an openness to multiple perspectives (Viruru, 2001); as well as a revision of the past to better examine and understand the present (Kaomea, 2003).

The particular ideas that have shaped my own engagement with this theoretical framework includes perceptions of the colonized condition such as it being the inter-cultural negotiation between the ideas of the colonizer and the colonized (Pratt, 1992); a transaction, a two-way dialogue between the philosophies of the colonized and the colonizer (Trivedi, 1993); a phenomenon of cultural hybridity (Bhabha, 1994); a continuing contest between the dominance of the colonizers and the consequent legacies that were created (Alva, 1995); and a powerful interdependence between the colonized and the colonizer (Gandhi, 1998). In earlier work, I applied these ideas to the field of education in a discussion of the interactions between Indian educational ideas and Euro/American educational ideas, the assumption being that the two educational views are located within two different worldviews, each making sense of the world in a different way. A postcolonial framework enabled the understanding of alternative perspectives by lending an ear to the intrinsic 'other' voice of early childhood in a non-western culture (Gupta, 2006). In postcolonial India, two competing discourses of play co-exist in early childhood education. The first derives from historical perspectives of play and childhood. The second derives from dominant Western discourses of play, development and learning contrast sharply with the formal, academic approaches that became prevalent during colonial rule. Further, a discourse of play is re-emerging in India today not only through the influence of Western progressive education ideas but also from pre-colonial local perspectives on childhood and children. This creates an interesting matrix of postcolonial dynamics, as what is today Western or global reflects also what in the past might have been Indian and local, although the cultural textures of the two are very different.

The Indian context: theory and policy influencing play and pedagogy

Historically, play and young children in India have been inextricably linked in mythological, philosophical, religious, educational and literary texts. Extending back more than 5000 years to the Indus Valley civilization when marbles, balls, dice, hunting were popular games among children. Later, during the Vedic period (2500–600 BC) there is mention of chariot racing, swinging, ball games, 'hide and seek' and run and catch. In the Hindu epics, the *Ramayana* and *Mahabharata*, sports and games such as chariot racing, horse riding, *Chaturang* or chess, wrestling, ball games, hide and seek, *gulli danda*[1], and water sports are described. In other texts such as the *Puranas* discus, *pasi yuddha* (rope fighting), archery wrestling, *udyana krida* (garden sports), and *salila krida* (water sports) are mentioned (Srivastava, 2008).

Several Indian historical texts, folk tales and epics place the child at play at its centre. The common Hindi word for play is '*khel*' and is applied to activities variously conceptualized to include fun and frolic; games and sports; gambling; participating in fairs and celebrations; dramatization of stories; dance, music and rhythm; fierce competition of skills and abilities; and so forth, activities that are structured or unstructured, player centred or externally controlled. Play in its various benevolent and malevolent forms appears to encompass not only preferred skills such as cooperation, sharing, taking turns, following rules, but also survival skills such as harassment, deception, teasing and trickery which are certainly not encouraged in classrooms by any teachers but which are inherent in successfully navigating the world and human relationships.

Today children in India are certainly not deprived of opportunities for play but the degree to which it occurs may vary from urban metropolizes to smaller towns and rural villages across the nation. In large urban centres, where children have access to new technologies, childhood increasingly reflects a lifestyle that is typical of the urban West where children's play is marked by long hours of sitting indoors in front of televisions, computer screens and video games. However, in the smaller Indian towns and villages, and within extended family systems in big cities, children from India's massive middle class are reared along a prolonged child-adult continuum with almost constant human contact and interaction within the home environment: the mother or grandmother or aunt – one of the several mother figures a child in India has – massages the infant, sings rhymes, plays games that stimulate the baby to distinguish the familiar face from the stranger's face. Babies are held, spoken to, rocked and cuddled. Young children are often found with their mother or grandmother in the kitchen playing with pots and pans while the adult is cooking. Young children are always in the company of family members, friends and neighbours. Children play with each other in the neighborhood, visiting each other's homes freely and within mixed-age groups, using materials they find in the home and in the yard. They sing and dance to folk songs and Bollywood music. Most children are familiar with frequently retold stories from India's great epics, the *Ramayana* and the *Mahabharata,* enacting popular scenes in their pretend play. This picture of play *outside* school is vastly different from the academic rigor typical of most Indian classrooms. During British colonial rule there was a shift from an emphasis on cognitive and intellectual development to academic proficiency. The imposition of a formal academic pedagogy created a textbook culture tightly controlled by colonial administrators. In turn this served to deny teachers' voice and autonomy (which was prevalent until the mid-1800s), (Kumar, 1992/ 1997). The colonial curriculum was alien to the socio-cultural contexts of both teachers and children and widened the gulf between children's lives inside and outside the classroom. Classroom life became increasingly defined by 'work' whereas 'play' was relegated to children's activities outside the classroom.

In response to this imposed educational system, several nineteenth and twentieth century Indian philosophers and educators argued for a classroom pedagogy based on 'the play-way method' or 'learning by doing'; for young children in particular and went on to establish their own versions of ideal schools. Notable examples include, Sri Aurobindo (1872–1950) a prominent Indian philosopher and Vedic scholar who believed that education based on academic performance which ignored the study of the human mind would impair intellectual growth. Every child was viewed as being unique, a lover of narrative, an investigator, intellectually curious, with the gift of imagination and every teacher a 'guide', whose role it was to provide an appropriate environment for learning by doing. His ideas formed the basis of the International Center of Education in Pondicherry in southern India (National Council for Teacher Education [NCTE], 1998).

Rabindranath Tagore (1861–1941), a prominent philosopher, educator and Nobel Laureate, started his own school, Shanti Niketan near Kolkata, and believed that good education was based on the arts for developing empathy and sensitivity, and the importance of nurturing a profound relationship with one's cultural and natural environment. Tagore envisioned education as being deeply rooted in one's immediate surroundings but connected to the cultures of the wider world. His classes were held outdoors under the trees, with nature walks, study of the life cycles of insects, birds and plants and flexibility to allow for shifts in the weather, natural phenomenon and seasonal festivals: all indicative of nurturing an interconnectedness and harmony between the individual and the surrounding world (O'Connell, 2003).

Similarly, philosopher and educator Krishnamurti (1895–1986) also believed that education should work toward the fullest development of a human being. Educating the person as a whole (and not in parts), as well as educating a person within a whole (as part of society, humanity and nature) was the true essence of education, drawing on three principles 1) aesthetics, not only for its pleasing quality but a sensitivity to beauty; 2) special areas of silence so that children could experience a quiet mind and reflection; and 3) an atmosphere deliberately created to foster spiritual growth rather than consumerism and material growth (Forbes, 1997). India's political and spiritual leader, Mahatma Gandhi, also had a distinct educational philosophy called the Basic Education approach. Gandhi outlined his educational ideas for each stage of development, from infancy through secondary education. Gandhi held the belief that for the very young child education should be constructive, creative and in the form of play because for a child everything is play (a speech addressed to teachers at

Sevagram Ashram on February 17, 1946, translated from Hindi). He believed that an infant starts learning from the moment of conception. The first teacher is the mother, the 'mother-teacher'. A teacher should be like a mother to the child, her responsibility is to teach the child about cleanliness, stories from Hindu mythology and epics, history and geography of where they live, geometrical figures, sing and recite verses in the native language, to handspin yarn on the wheel and physical exercises (Gandhi, 1929).

The early childhood educators, Gijubahi Badheka and Tarabai Modak, recognized the need for children to be educated in an environment that would nurture their independence and self-reliance. Both these educators were deeply influenced by Maria Montessori's educational philosophy and worked on implementing her ideas within the Indian cultural context. Badheka established the Bal Mandir in Gujarat in 1920 and demonstrated how to teach subject matter through stories and rhyme that appealed to children. Tarabai Modak started Shishu Vihar Kendra in 1936 in Bombay, utilizing play way methods that could be used by weaving knowledge into stories and games for primary school children (Vittachi, *et al.*, 2007).

In spite of this long history of child-centred educational philosophy, the colonial school system in India firmly established schools as purely academic institutions. Children had access to plenty of unstructured play at home whereas schools were places of formal instruction. With these changes came changes in the expectations of parents and society which persist today. It is only recently that early childhood classrooms in mainstream education are viewed as extensions of the home offering a play-based experience. For educators and policy makes today, re-thinking the early childhood curriculum is influenced in two major ways:

1) renewed interest in the work of Indian educators on the importance of play in childhood by educators and
2) exposure to current Western early childhood debates on the importance of play.

The 2005 version of the National Curriculum Framework (NCF-2005) for India overseen by the National Council of Educational Research and Training (NCERT) proposed a major shift away from the academic textbook culture of schools and classrooms toward a more child-centred pedagogy based on a constructivist theory of learning, recognizing that children construct their own knowledge through meaningful activities. As part of NCF-2005, research-based position papers provide a comprehensive review of existing knowledge in the field. In an attempt to move toward a more child-centred and play-based approach the Early Childhood Education Focus Group Position Paper has identified several quality indicators for ECE programmes which include an activity-based, child-centred, age-appropriate, contextualized curriculum that will lead to holistic development of children and prepare the young child for the demands of more formal teaching in later years. A special emphasis has been given to play and the arts as the basis for learning and the use of local materials, arts and knowledge, utilizing Indian dance forms and songs to teach children in early education classrooms (see for example Singh, 1999).

According to the 2001 Indian Census, about 60 million children under the age of five years are living in poverty and only about 20 million of them are getting preschool education under the Integrated Child Development Services (ICDS) provided by the government. Within the private arena, the figures are unclear due to a lack of a comprehensive survey for that domain. At the time of the 2001 Census there might have been about 10 million additional children enrolled in private settings. The ECE Position Paper (2006) details the various categories of early education, pedagogies and classroom practices that may be seen in diverse early educational settings in India. ECCE in India is currently sponsored by three distinct sectors: the government; private schools; and NGOs. Settings include spaces such as *Anganwadis, Balwadis,* crèches, slum schools, family day cares, day care centers, preschools, and nursery/kindergarten schools with huge variation between settings. Early childhood settings reflect both play-based experiences and more formal academic-based experiences. However, remembering that a primary purpose of early education in India is to provide children with basic custodial, nutritional and health services, the tendency is towards a formal pedagogy. In the next section I will illustrate practitioners' perceptions on classroom play as shared by some teachers in early childhood settings within urban private schools.

Teachers' perspectives from private early childhood and early elementary classrooms

The objective of private for-profit nursery schools and preschools is mainly custodial and a preparation for elementary schools and their management styles are hierarchical and non-transparent. The majority of private early childhood schools admit children on a competitive basis, to overcrowded classrooms. They often lack adequate supply of play materials and emphasize formal teaching methods. More time is spent on workbooks than on active learning, skills-based competency assessments are used extensively, and children are often given homework. Play materials, where they exist are used more for display than play by the children. Pedagogical approaches vary from school to school as is seen by the contrasting descriptions offered by teachers. Anjani, a Nursery-Kindergarten (N/K) teacher in New Delhi explained: 'Play may be fitted into classroom life by creating some space (removing tables and chairs/ benches), by making groups, and by providing an opportunity for each child to do something beyond the textbooks' (field notes, 2008). Surabhi, at the same school reflected: 'Children in schools today are increasingly over burdened with academics. Most parents make all efforts to get them to excel at studies. But all work and no play is not necessarily the best strategy to improve a child's performance . . . For children to grow and develop as healthy individuals there needs to be a reasonable balance between work and play' (field notes, 2008).

Both Anjani and Surabhi teach in a school which has a strong academic focus. Clearly, much effort has to be put into creating time and space for play activities in their classrooms. In contrast, Preeta, a Nursery teacher in another private nursery school, presents an early childhood classroom routine which suggests that implementing an activity-based approach was easier in her school:

In our classroom children are playing and working with materials and other children . . . have access to various activities throughout the day such as block building, pretend play, picture books, paints and other art materials, and table toys and puzzles . . . Children learn numbers and alphabets in the context of their everyday experiences. Exploring the natural world of plants and animals, cooking, taking attendance, serving snack are all meaningful activities to children.

(field notes, 2008)

All three teachers demonstrate different understanding of a play-based classroom, and their comments are indicative of the relative ease or difficulty for each of them to establish a play-based classroom environment within their own schools. The study showed that several teachers conceptualized play using terms such as 'joyful', 'enjoyable', 'interesting to children', 'free', 'freedom', 'spontaneous', 'of the children's own initiative', 'creativity' and 'imagination'. At the same time there was frequent use of the words 'learning', 'skills development' and 'growth' when referring to play. With regard to the kinds of play children engaged in outside of the school examples cited included football (soccer), jumping, sliding, swinging, cricket, hide n' seek, playing ball, free play or simply running around. Interestingly, one teacher said 'it rains because children need to play with water'. These examples fit in with the kind of play which adults hope will be confined to the playground and were in contrast to teachers' descriptions of potentially educative classroom play. In fact, one of the teachers said explicitly that 'in classroom life one should not allow play which creates noise or indiscipline'. This desire to keep 'chaos' out of the classroom is perhaps understandable in the case of India where typical class sizes range from 35–60 children.

Several teachers considered that a classroom supporting a play-based approach was one which was well-designed, offered hands-on experiences, included the use of colourful teaching aids, and had spaces where meaningful learning was taking place. Play occurred when children were working in small groups, were engaged in active games, were working with educational toys, learning numbers and alphabets in the context of everyday experiences, and 'everyone was smiling'. Rubina, who taught playgroup for very young children, believed that that a play-based classroom was one which was full of educational toys, and that play which leads to 'any kind of indiscipline, like making noise or creating any type of violence must be unacceptable'.

The idea of play being another form of learning was common because some teachers indicated explicitly that in their classrooms play appeared in the form of learning while playing, and learning while chanting rhymes and colouring. Only Bina, a Nursery/Kindergarten teacher, mentioned dramatic play as part of the curriculum but even within that there was an emphasis on the learning of values and preferred behaviours rather than on free play:

In a group of children playing 'house' for example, different children take on the role of various members of a family and play-act familiar family situations. It is acceptable for the 'grandchild' to be helpful and caring toward the 'grandparents' and it is unacceptable for the 'master of the house' to be rude to the 'domestic help' . . . It is acceptable for the children to display/enact he good moral values that the children imbibe from their families.

(2008)

In addition to learning social, emotional, physical skills, and academic content, the emphasis was definitely on the 'values' learnt by children such as cooperation, sharing, taking turns, social living, tolerance, making friends, compassion, kindness, respect, discipline, speaking the truth, working hard. This was very much in keeping with my earlier research (Gupta, 2006). Although in Western discourse educators would categorize all of these as skills within separate but overlapping developmental domains, teachers in India almost universally referred to them as 'values'. To me it was an important indication of the value or importance that was given to human behaviours that were most prioritized within the Indian worldview.

That free and spontaneous play was important for the healthy development of young children was acknowledged by most teachers. But in their classrooms play almost always took the form of individual and discrete activities rather than a comprehensive pedagogy. An activity-based curriculum was usually understood to be a play-based curriculum. Typically children's spontaneous play was tempered within the classroom because it was linked to the learning of developmental and academic skills and subject to teacher planning and direction.

Postcolonial perspectives on play

As we have seen the policy recommendations in India are drawn from a mix of Indian and Euro-American educational ideas and philosophies: from the emphasis given sensory and practical experiences by Rousseau, Froebel, Montessori and Dewey to the use of play, rhyme, rhythm and different materials promoted by Gandhi, Tagore, Badheka, and others. We are left with the challenge of articulating how a play pedagogy can be defined for the multi-layered complexities of diverse cultural contexts. It is interesting to note that educational settings which offer play-way methods or holistic experiences leading to self-discovery and explorations are categorized as 'alternative' schools because they do not fit into the academic mainstream educational system of India. These include the pioneering institutions of the great Indian educational philosophers Krishnamurty, Sri Aurobindo, Tagore and Gandhi, as well as the hundreds of smaller early childhood centres that are found across India today (Vittachi, et al., 2007).

Nowadays, the terms 'play school', 'play-way methods' and 'play-based teaching' are seen on signboards of the countless private nursery schools appearing across India. These terms are also being used to describe appropriate early education philosophy by school principals and teacher educators in schools and colleges across India. However, implementation of a play-based pedagogy as defined by 'Western' parameters into Indian classrooms is problematic in a system that continues to prioritize textbook knowledge, and where examination scores are used to measure students' success in schools and their admission into higher education. The pressure to strive towards academic excellence filters down through grade levels to determine pedagogical approaches in early childhood settings. Dominant definitions of play pedagogy, from European and North American perspectives raise important questions about its applicability to socio-cultural-political-economically diverse classrooms and can often be at odds with culturally different worldviews and seem remote and disconnected to non-Westerners.

The views of teachers expressed here seemed to echo western discourses with regard to the value of play in their classrooms. However, in practice their approach clearly reflected an activity-based curriculum that would lead to the learning of required developmental skills and subject knowledge. The teachers nevertheless believed that play was important and most found no problem coupling play with pedagogy. However, this should be contextualized within the private schools they worked in and which prioritized academic excellence. Although there certainly seems to be general agreement about the value of play for young children, teachers are unable to synthesize the dialectic of play and work into a comprehensive pedagogy of play within their schools which continues to prioritize academic excellence. Their teaching, instead, offers a parallel curriculum of discrete activities comprized of either 'play' or 'work' experiences.

Further, the complexities of classrooms in India in general pose a different challenge. There are problems with the expectation that the play pedagogy can be implemented in all classrooms. The core ideals of this pedagogy are rooted in the central tenets of progressive education emphasizing child-centricity and choice in the classroom – each child being able to choose whom and with what to engage, usually within large blocks of free play time, and having the freedom to waive any adult involvement in their activities. There are several assumptions underlying this child-centric approach which may be viewed as prerequisites for the successful implementation of a true play-based pedagogy. These assumptions include:

1)   young children in schools are receiving basic requirements of health and nutrition, and that schools are adequately equipped with running water, electricity and sanitation facilities;

2)   there are adequate resources in the classroom including materials, time and space: a wide selection of *materials* that enables choice; large blocks of available *time* wherein children can engage in free play and wherein teachers can encourage free play without the constraints of completing a prescribed curriculum; and ample *space* in classrooms to house the material resources and for children to move about freely from one activity to another of their own will;

3)   teachers have been adequately trained and prepared in the philosophy and pedagogy of play and child-centred classroom approaches; current teacher training in India is based on the idea of teachers being technical experts and not decision makers. Child-centred teaching with a play-based pedagogy requires teachers to be able to make classroom decisions on a regular basis with regard to the use of classroom materials, nature of experiences provided to children, and the use of classroom time. This would imply that teachers need to be trained under a new

system that would foster more teacher autonomy and increased local control within schools, ideas which do not sit comfortably alongside a predominantly examination and textbook culture;

4) teachers are adequately equipped with the tools and time within their classrooms to document children's voices and activities to create the comprehensive assessment portfolio for each child that is a critical tool to assess growth and learning in a play-based and learner-centred classroom. Some assessment techniques recommended for classroom teachers by western proponents of a play-based pedagogy include documentation such as capturing moments of children's play using tools like cameras and camcorders; anecdotal reports; observing and documenting play in all classroom centers such as the block area, book corner, writing center, dramatic play, art center; creating documentation panels to display children's work samples, stories, quotes, photos, and so forth;

5) classrooms have low teacher-child ratios because a play-based pedagogy is grounded in the belief that children choose to voluntarily engage with activities related to their interests and liking; but how the individual interests of 50 children in one classroom can be addressed, how their work can be displayed, and how assessment portfolios can be maintained for each child would be a formidable challenge;

6) children are entitled and able to make choices with regard to their engagement with classroom life and come to school already comfortable with the decision-making skills that are essential to successfully navigate a choice-based classroom. This last one is, perhaps, the most challenging in terms of cultural differences and the nature of the young child-adult relationship within Indian society. The right to choose is based on the individual-oriented view of society which often finds itself out of place in Indian homes and classrooms that are based on a more group-oriented view of society.

Universalizing the expectation that all classrooms must adhere to a play-based pedagogy also raises issues of equity and social justice. In many settings, the primary concern is to provide basic levels of hygiene, care and nutrition to children who come from low socio-economic backgrounds; these are schools where the average teacher-child ratio may be even higher than 50 children per classroom; where the size of a classroom may be as small as seven feet by seven feet; where teachers may have little or no formal training; which have a high level of teacher absenteeism; and which may lack basic furniture, running water and toilet facilities.

Postcolonial perspectives: interplay between the dominant and the marginalized

A child-centred play pedagogy could be viewed as a colonizing condition imposed on early childhood settings that are not based upon western middle-class values or have middle-class resources (Canella, 1997). Child-centred and developmental pedagogy draws on discourses that profess to understand the 'nature' of children but fail to address the cultural or developmental differences in the 'nature' of children living in different socio-cultural contexts. Further, the nature of children's development itself can be viewed as a 'creation of certain adult minds who were concerned with producing self-regulated citizens within a particular governmental framework . . . children remained un-free as ever and logical reasoning came to occupy its present, almost sacred, place in Western society' (Viruru, 2001, p. 27–28). In other words, even in play-based classrooms of the West, do children truly have the choice to make their own decisions in the classroom? (see for example, Rogers, 2010).

Even though a pedagogy of play might find some support and consideration in the classrooms of the more resourceful private schools in India, can it be implemented as a true pedagogy of play wherein children are engaged in classroom activities voluntarily, spontaneously, and without necessarily working toward an end product? Or will the pedagogy become what it already is in some schools – the prescribed parallel curriculum presented to the children in the guise of activities and play that teachers direct in terms of time, materials and goals. Would this be an imposition of yet another western pedagogical approach on children in India? Can there be a pedagogy of play that synthesizes the dialectics of play and work, one that grows out of the traditions of India and that would also reflect dominant early childhood education and play pedagogy discourse of the West?

Much depends on how the definition of a play pedagogy has been constructed and by whom. One could argue that early childhood classrooms in India are already employing such a pedagogy even if academic teaching occurs in classrooms. Viruru describes her ethnographic study of an urban early childhood center in South India and admits that although learning the alphabet was the obvious and visible focus for the year:

> The daily lived experiences of the children were about many other things such as creating friendships and exploring what school was about. Real life was a part of their classroom: playing, exploring, eating lunch and learning the alphabet as well. Thus the alphabet did not replace anything in their lives: life continued with it as one interesting part of it.
>
> (2001: p. 36)

In my own study of urban early childhood teaching in India, children seemed to enjoy academic work:

> As I entered Vasudha's Nursery classroom of four year olds there was a noisy buzz with sounds of talking, laughing and eating . . . It was break time . . . Forty children were sitting at four large tables . . . ten children at each table . . . After break time, they had a Language class. The letter for that day was 'S'.
>
> Two bowls of crayons in different colours were placed on each table. . . . Vasudha encouraged them to think of things that begin with the sound of 's'. The students responded in different ways – 'sea water', one child said. Vasudha responded, 'very good'. Another child said 'sipper'. Once again the teacher

responded by saying 'very good'. The students were talking to each other excitedly, but they were also intently choosing colours and colouring their work sheets. Both teachers walked around the room offering comments and instructions, 'Very good. I want to see nice and neat colouring'. One little boy said – 'Ma'am, look!' and Vasudha affirmed his efforts. There were clear boundaries, with no confusion or chaos . . .

(Gupta, 2006: p.166)

Acknowledging, first and foremost, that there is no typical early childhood school in India, the common defining characteristic of education in India has been its colonial pedagogy which prevails long after the end of colonial rule in India. Would a play-based pedagogy as defined by the West be another instance of educational imperialism? Or could a play-based pedagogy emerge from the Indian context?

Across the globe, early childhood education has been deeply influenced by Western discourses about young children, play and child-centred pedagogy (Canella and Viruru, 2004). The uncritical global application of these ideas essentially ignores multiple ways of being and thinking in diverse cultures. Perhaps we need to educate ourselves about how these terms are conceptualized within societies that are built on different sets of beliefs and world views. My thoughts go back to the teacher who indicated in the survey that 'it rains so that children can play in the water'. To me this was a very telling comment and shed some light on another way of approaching child-centeredness. In her own cosmic understanding she was placing the child at the centre of a universe which revolved around the needs of children. This teacher was not voicing an idea that she had learnt in school or college or in seminars on play. Her perspective stemmed from socio-cultural influences, the culmination of her experiences within a society where spirituality dominates thoughts and actions, where the scarcity of water is a harsh reality, and where the monsoon season is welcomed as a gift from the gods to provide pleasure and relief from the hot scorching heat of the long summer season. The first rains are welcomed joyously and deliriously by children and adults across India. I recall an image of my own sons standing in the monsoon rain one day – faces upturned, exuding delight and wonder, and taking in this very sensory experience of feeling the wet rain, tasting it as the clean raindrops drizzled into their open mouths and onto their tongues, seeing the rainwater wash away the summer dust in little rivulets that formed on the dusty streets, hearing the raindrops beat a pattern against the leaves, and smelling the freshness of rainwater as it mingled with the dry earth. Could this delightful and engaging play experience also be providing a deeper spiritual experience? And was it any surprise that the teacher brought a more cosmic understanding to the meaning of child-centric that was certainly more spiritual than scientific? Would a spiritual conceptualization of play in schools be acceptable as a play pedagogy within global educational discourses?

I urge researchers to work toward comparative studies on early childhood education and play-based pedagogies across the global South, paying special attention to realities such as child-centric, colonialism, citizenship, identity, choice, and subjectivity. A South-South comparison, as opposed to a North-South comparison, will work toward problematizing the standard use of these terms, and will contribute new dimensions to their usage beyond dominant Western perspectives, to change the frame of reference so that the 'West' does not remain the sole norm against which educational systems measure each other. Educators need to challenge the very way dominant early child-hood discourses have been constructed and imposed, and rebuild them 'differently by understanding difference in a different way' (McLaren, 1998: p.230). This would provide a healthy counterpoint to the ethnocentrism ingrained in the widespread belief that scientific knowledge about education is typically Western. Stressing that the Western 'minority' perspective cannot hold true for the 'majority' of the world population situated outside Western Europe and North America, future research on traditional educational theories and practices developed in the majority world is critically important in order to study how they can improve children's schooling globally.

Notes

1   *Gulli Danda* is a popular street game played by children in India. The sport is a variation of the bat and ball game where the *danda*, a sturdy stick about 12–18 inches long serves as the bat, and the *gulli*, about 3–6 inches long and tapered on both ends, serves as the ball.

References

Alva, J. J. K. de (1995). The Postcolonization of the Latin American experience: A reconsideration of 'Colonialism', 'Postcolonialism' and 'Mestijaze'. In G. Prakash (ed.), *After colonialism, imperial histories, and postcolonial displacements*. Princeton, NJ: Princeton University Press.

Bhabha, H. (1994). *The location of culture*. London, U.K.: Routledge.

Brooker, L. (2003). Learning How to Learn: Parental Ethnotheories and Young Children's Preparation for School, *The International Journal of Early Years Education*, 11(1), 117–128.

Canella, G. S. (1997). *Deconstructing early childhood education: Social justice and revolution*. New York, NY: Peter Lang Publishing.

Canella, G. S. and Viruru, R. (2004). *Childhood and postcolonization: power, education and contemporary practice*. London and New York: Routledge.

Forbes, S. H. (1997). Jiddu Krishnamurti and his insights into education. Paper presented at the first Holistic Education Conference, Toronto. Available online: www.infed.org/thinkers/et-krish.htm (accessed December 2009).

Gandhi, L. (1998). *Postcolonial theory: a critical introduction*. New York, NY: Columbia University Press.

Gandhi, M. K. (1929). Navjivan, CW pp.5–9. Available online: http://www.ncte-in.org/pub/gandhi/chap5.htm. (accessed December 2009).

Genishi, C. and Goodwin, L. (2007). *Diversities in early childhood education: Rethinking and doing*. New York, NY: Routledge.

Gupta, A. (2006). *Early childhood education, postcolonial theory, and teaching practices in India: Balancing Vygotsky and the Veda*. New York, NY: Palgrave Macmillan.

Haight, W.L., Wang, X., Fung, H. H., Williams, K. and Mintz, J. (1999). Universal, developmental, and variable aspects of young children's play: a cross-cultural comparison of pretending at home. *Child Development*, 70(6), 1477–88.

Kaomea, J. (2003). Reading erasures and making the familiar strange: defamiliarizng methods in formerly colonized and historically oppressed communities. *Educational Researcher*, 32 (2), 14–25.

Kumar, K. (1992/1997). *What is worth teaching?* New Delhi, India: Orient Longman Limited.

Long, S., Volk, D. and Gregory, E. (2007). Intentionality and expertize: learning from observations of children at play in multilingual, multicultural contexts. *Anthropology and Education Quarterly*, 38(3), 239–59.

Macedo, D. (1999). Decolonizing indigenous knowledge. In L.Semali and J. L. Kincheloe (eds), *What is indigenous knowledge: voices from the academy?* New York and London: Falmer Press.

McLaren, P. (1998). *Revolutionary multiculturalism*. Boulder, CO: Westview Books.

National Council for Teacher Education (1998) Curriculum Framework for Quality Teacher Education, New Delhi: NCTE.

O'Connell, K. M. (2003). Rabindranath Tagore on education in The Encycolpedia of Informal Education. http://www.infed.org/thinkers/tagore/htm (accessed December 2009).

Pratt, M. L. (1992). *Imperial eyes: Travel writing and transculturation*. New York and London: Routledge.

Rogers, S. (2010) Powerful pedagogies and playful resistance: children's experience of role play in early childhood education. In E. Brooker and S. Edwards, (eds), *Engaging Play*. Maidenhead: Open University Press.

Rogoff, B. (2003). *The cultural nature of human development*. Oxford, UK: Oxford University Press.

Roopnarine, J. L., Lasker, J., Sacks, M., and Stores, M. (1998). The cultural contexts of children's play. In Saracho, O. and Spodek, B. (eds), *Multiple perspectives on play in early childhood education*. Albany, NY: SUNY Press.

Singh, A. (1999). The appeal of rhythm and movement. Special issue with the Sunday Magazine, The Hindu Folio. http://www.hinduonnet.com/folio/fo9902/99020200.htm (accessed August 2009).

Srivastava, P. (2008). Exploring children's understanding of play and games. Unpublished Masters Thesis, Lady Irwin College, New Delhi, India.

Trivedi, H. (1993). *Colonial transactions: English literature and India*. Calcutta: Papyrus.

Viruru, R. (2001). *Early childhood education: Postcolonial perspectives from India*. Delhi, India: Sage Publications.

—— (2005). The impact of postcolonial theory on early childhood education. *Journal of Education* (35), pp. 7–29.

Vittachi, S., Raghavan, N., and Raj, K. (2007). *Alternative schooling in India*. New Delhi, India: Sage Publications.

Chapter 8

Learning through play in Hong Kong

Policy or practice?

Doris Cheng Pui-wah

Introduction

The significance of play as a vehicle for young children's development and learning is widely recognized, exemplified in a long history of ideas from pioneer educators and theorists such as Froebel, Freud, Erikson and Piaget alongside a vast research literature. More recently, the significance of play has been endorsed in a number of influential reports, including one issued by the American Academy of Paediatrics which concluded that play helps children develop new competencies that lead to enhanced confidence and the resilience they will need to face future challenges (Ginsburg, K. R., the Committee on Communications, and the Committee on Psychosocial Aspects of Child and Family Health, 2007). In addition, a cross-national study of more than 1,500 young children in ten countries found that children's language performance at age seven improved when teachers let children choose their activities, rather than adopt a purely didactic approach (Miller and Almon, 2009). Play pedagogy is further endorsed in a number of international official reports for the education of young children; for example, Developmental Appropriate Practice (DAP) (Bredekamp and Copple, 1997), the English *Early Years Foundation Stage* framework (Department for Education and Skills, [DfES], 2007), the *Japanese Ministry of Education Preschool Guidelines* (Lewis, 1995), and the guidelines issued by the Swedish Ministry of Education and Science (1998). Moreover, a review of early childhood curriculum and pedagogy carried out by the Organisation for Economic Co-operation and Development (OECD, 2002) noted that play is widely perceived to be the central pedagogy for young children's learning and teaching in many Western countries. In 1982, in Hong Kong an overseas group called the Llewellyn Visiting Panel, made strong recommendations to the government to adopt the central tenet of 'learning through play' in pre-primary pedagogy which had traditionally been based on formal and highly didactic methods of teaching and learning (Llewellyn *et al.*, 1982).

Against a background of such growing endorsements globally for play-based learning in early childhood, this chapter will address the following questions: Has the official policy recommendation to introduce a play-based pedagogy in the Hong Kong early childhood curriculum led to a paradigm shift in how teachers teach and young children learn? In the process of pedagogical innovation, what are the challenges and key issues for Hong Kong early childhood educators? To this end, I will examine the implementation of the pedagogical innovations that have taken place in recent years in Hong Kong, drawing upon national and local policy and research reports and the extent to which the implementation of play-based pedagogy in Hong Kong early childhood settings is evident in contemporary practice. I will also consider issues surrounding the concept of a play based pedagogy from within the specific socio-political and cultural perspective of Hong Kong.

The Hong Kong early childhood context

Hong Kong is a densely populated city in South East China with 6.9 million citizens. In 1997, 150 years of British rule ended when it reverted to the People's Republic of China. Over 90 per cent of Hong Kong's population is Chinese (Census and Statistics Department, 2006). During the years of colonialism, there was some blending of Western influences with the Chinese cultural inheritance. Many aspects of Chinese culture have changed and are changing, but one of its enduring features is the importance placed on children's academic achievements (Chao, 1994; Mok, *et al.* 2008). Education is valued highly as a means of raising the status of the family, and children are imbued with the importance of success from their earliest years. It is common for parents to accept responsibility for teaching their children, and studies have found that much of the interaction between parent and child is related to teaching academic skills (Mok *et al.* 2008).

Early childhood education in Hong Kong refers to the education of children from aged two to six. The Hong Kong Government did not have direct responsibility for ECE, until the late 1980s, when it accepted the suggestions of the Llewellyn Visiting Panel, by adopting 'learning through play' as a central tenet for pre-primary pedagogy (Education Commission, 1986). The government's intention was to improve the quality of education for young children, which had been described by the Llewellyn Visiting Panel as didactic and overly structured. Since then, the tenet 'learning through play' has been reiterated in numerous curriculum documents issued by the Hong Kong government, as the central pedagogy recommended for early childhood education (see for example, Education Department, 1993, 1996; Education and Manpower Bureau, 2006). In the latest *Guide to the Pre-primary Curriculum* (Education and Manpower Bureau, 2006), the government stresses that 'the child-centred concept is a key element of the learning and teaching strategies in early childhood education . . . play is an indispensable and important tool for facilitating children's learning' (p.51).

In summary, the Hong Kong Government explicitly welcomed the importation of Western theories and associated pedagogy of play-based learning and, since 1986, has shown its willingness to adopt 'learning through play' as its core principle, with a view to promoting a paradigm shift in the learning and teaching of young children. However, in reality minimal resources have been allocated to early childhood education. Though the government has increased its intervention, in the form of quality assurance mechanisms and teacher training, it is still reluctant to take direct responsibility for the pre-school sector and at the time of writing, kindergartens in Hong Kong are primarily operated as private and market-driven enterprises.

The quality of 'play' implementation in Hong Kong

Beginning in the early 2000s, the Hong Kong Government introduced an appraisal system for early childhood institutions' self and external evaluation. The seven Quality Assurance Inspection (QAI) annual reports published between the years 2000/2001 and 2006/2007 all describe a general picture in which the learning and teaching performance of most of the kindergartens inspected was less than satisfactory. The annual reports show that most teachers were seen playing a role of directing, instructing, lecturing and even controlling the learning and teaching flow in classrooms, and reveal that almost 60 per cent of the kindergartens performed merely at the 'acceptable' and 'unsatisfactory' levels in the 'curriculum design' aspect in the first few years from 2001/2002 to 2003/2004, increasing to over 70 per cent by 2005/2006 and 2006/2007 (Cheng *et al.* 2008). Similarly disappointing percentages were also recorded for the aspect of 'teaching strategies and skills', showing that 65per cent of kindergartens performed in the range of 'acceptable' and 'unsatisfactory' levels in 2004/2005, and 72 per cent in 2006/2007 (Education and Manpower Bureau, 2004/2005; Education Bureau 2006/2007). The QAI Annual Report of 2002/2003 points out plainly that,

> 80% of kindergartens still put much emphasis on writing skill training, giving excessive drilling and copying assignments to children. Some kindergartens even required children to memorize and dictate words. Children did not have much chance to use the language in authentic situations.
>
> (Education and Manpower Bureau, 2002/2003, p. 4)

The aforementioned comment shows that, even after the turn of the century, early childhood education in Hong Kong still focuses on the teaching of academic knowledge in a formal manner. A teacher-oriented and knowledge-transmitted mode of pedagogy is identified from the government's inspection reports, showing that most kindergartens were inclined to place undue emphasis on the intellectual aspect, without taking full account of children's needs, interests and levels of development.

With regard to the quality of 'play' provision in Hong Kong early childhood educational settings, Opper (1992) tracked the quality of teaching and learning in early childhood education services across the territory. Her study showed that early childhood teachers had failed to alter their pedagogies and that teaching methods remained predominantly didactic, stressing rote learning, conformity and uniformity. Rather than promoting a play-based pedagogy, in line with government recommendations, her data showed that early childhood programmes still focused on learning of academic skills necessary in later schooling, especially the so-called 'three Rs' of reading, writing and arithmetic.

A decade after Opper, Cheng (2001) examined the quality of play enactment by conducting research among six kindergarten teachers who were undergoing professional training. The results showed that while all teachers acknowledged 'play' to be the best pedagogy in the teaching and learning of young children, their practices were found to be rigid and uncreative. There was a conflict between the teachers' intentions and their actions. The findings of this study showed that the process of teaching and learning was mainly teacher–centred where the teachers focused on low-level activities, such as writing Chinese characters, English words or numbers that offered little cognitive challenge for the children. 'Chalk and talk' was the only teaching method observed during this process.

Yet the study found that some teachers brought a personal interpretation to the newly introduced notion of 'learning through play'. For example, in one kindergarten, a teacher brought in an Easter egg and showed it to a group of children in her class. She then explained to the children the origin of Easter and why an Easter egg is associated with it. She then passed the egg around to each of the children and allowed them to touch and look closely at the egg. In interview she described how the children were given the opportunity to 'explore' the egg and that this approach helped the children make sense of the concept of Easter. By so doing, the teacher explained that she had been helping children to 'learn through play' because she was not just lecturing them on the origin of Easter but had allowed them to understand the concept by means of exploring the egg (Cheng, 2001). Cheng found that, paradoxically, the proposed pedagogical change seemed to have given rise to a particular interpretation of 'play' reminiscent of a traditional behaviourist approach. The egg had been used as a means to transmit specific knowledge, thus the dominant pedagogy in that classroom continued to be based on a transmission model of teaching and learning.

Similarly, in her research on classroom practices in Hong Kong kindergartens, Li (2001) noted that '[there is a] clear differentiation between learning and play. They are not integrated . . .' within classroom pedagogy (p. 59). More recently still, Li (2004) points out that 'teachers appeared to concentrate on their own needs for task completion, rather than on children's needs' (p. 40).

Cheng and Stimpson (2004) went further in researching the quality of how play is enacted in early childhood by extending the study to teachers with diverse professional backgrounds. Again, a technical and instrumental pattern of 'play' enactment was identified for five out of the six kindergarten teachers, where play was used as a means of capturing the initial interest of children, and to make the children attentive for subsequent inputs of information. Guided by a technical framing and reframing, this group of teachers perpetuated a narrow, rigid, taken-for-granted belief that led to a superficial, technical level of mastery. The teachers almost exclusively focused on the pursuit of teaching aids, such as pictures and real objectives, to hold the attention of young children for knowledge transmission (Cheng, 2008). For example, one teacher noted that 'if you don't use something to hold their [the children's] attention, it is really very difficult to make them listen' (Cheng, 2008, p.89). In short, both the QAI reports and empirical studies plainly reveal that the formal pedagogy identified in the Llewellyn report (Llewellyn *et al.* 1982) has not changed significantly in the intervening decades, and that the concept of 'learning through play' has not become embedded in practice as had been anticipated and indeed encouraged by the government.

Discrepancies between policy and practice

'If a new program works, teachers get little of the credit; if it fails they get most of the blame' (Fullan and Stiegelbauer, 1991, p. 117). Perhaps we should not be surprised that policy makers, teacher trainers, parents and the public will readily blame teachers for failing to implement a play-based pedagogy in Hong Kong early education classrooms. Yet it is more complex than that. Whilst the Hong Kong Special Administrative Region (SAR) Government intends to invest a huge amount of money to enhance the quality of early education to meet the competitive demands of the twenty-first century, it is indeed sad to recognize that there continue to be many mismatches between the proposed innovation and early education in the context of real-life classroom practice. These mismatches have inevitably led to a number of structural issues in the field of early education which hinder the enhancement of the educational quality of the young children in the region. These mismatches are discussed later in the chapter.

A mismatch between the complexities of play and the assistance given in its implementation in classrooms

Several authors argue that the enactment of theory into practice is a very complex process (e.g. Calderhead and Shorrock, 1997; Connelly and Clandinin, 1994; Richardson, 1996), and the implementation of theories of 'play' is no exception (see for example Bennett, Wood and Rogers, 1997 and Rogers and Evans, 2008). The notion of 'play' is found to have pronounced difficulties with regard to its definition (Spodek and Saracho, 1991). Educators are unable to present a universally accepted criterion of play, especially when it is adopted as a teaching and learning strategy with pre-determined objectives (Anning, 1991; Wood and Bennett, 2000; OECD, 2004). Calls to examine the relationship between 'play' and 'learning' in young children's curriculum are widespread, both here and abroad (Cheng, 2001; Cheng and Stimpson, 2004; OECD, 2004). Apart from the messy nature of the theory itself, play-based pedagogy is very different from the traditional teaching and learning in Hong Kong.

As Biggs (1996) observed regarding the manner in which teaching and learning is conducted in Hong Kong, 'the curriculum, teaching methods and student study methods are focused on the next major assessment hurdles' (p.5). Owing to this 'upward preparation', the here-and-now characteristics of learning are often neglected. Children in Hong Kong are hurried throughout their schooling. Starting in the early years, children are expected to know at least 100 Chinese characters and English words, and to be able to write at least 50 of them by the time they move into primary schooling (Chow, 1993). There is great tension in kindergarten education involved in preparing for the next stage, and a highly didactic approach is seen as unavoidable (Board of Education, 1994). Though formal testing for admission to a primary school was recently abolished by the government, Hong Kong communities (namely, parents, early years' institutions operators and teachers themselves) still regard successful early education as that which assures children admittance into prestigious primary schools and allows them to excel in the primary schools' academic-oriented curriculum.

Yet the government of Hong Kong seems unaware of the complexities embedded in the practicalities involved in the implementation of play based pedagogy. Apart from speeding up the process of teacher training in this sector and the reiteration of the desired pedagogy in the government documents (Education Department, 1993, 1996; Education Commission, 2000; Education and Manpower Bureau, 2006), few resources are available to support or monitor the implementation of a play-based pedagogy at the local level.

A mismatch between policy innovation and the beliefs of parents

The introduction of the voucher system for early years' education in 2007 in Hong Kong clearly demonstrates the government's intention to adopt a market-driven mode of operation in this sector. To this end, the demands and satisfaction of the customers (parents) are of vital importance to the kindergarten operators. In Hong Kong, as in other Chinese societies, education is considered a highly important means to a good job and economic prosperity (Llewellyn, *et al.* 1982), 'Education is seen as a main vehicle for social mobility, especially with those who fled to Hong Kong from the mainland after WWII' (Pong and Chow, 2002 p. 140). Pong and Chow (2002) further point out that Hong Kong parents paid more attention to their children's achievement-oriented activities and school work than to their social and cultural activities. Added to this basic belief, the limited places in higher education (with 18.9 per cent of high school students going to universities in Hong Kong[1]) have led to competitive examinations and pressure on students to achieve good results.

Moreover, some argue that the curriculum in Hong Kong has been designed around an unreasonably high standard; thus, there is great pressure on children from parents and teachers to complete homework, often at the expense of the child's social life (Salili, 1996). Cases where, for instance, a three-year-old was consistently beaten for not doing enough homework, and where the guilt and shame of not being able to cope academically has led to depression and suicide in some pre-teenage children, are unfortunately not isolated (Biggs and Walkins, 1996; Nian You, 2008).

A well-known Chinese proverb about education and teaching says that 'rearing without upbringing is the fault of the father; teaching without disciplining is the flaw of the teacher'. In Chinese culture, teachers are expected to be stern and strict (Cheng, 1994; Hayhoe, 2008). Allowing children to play and teachers to take a non-directive role would likely be regarded as a form of negligence by much of the Chinese community, as well as by the teachers themselves. According to Confucianism, which has its deep rooted popularity amongst the Chinese community, education and learning are always associated with effort, and there is an old Chinese saying;

if another man succeeds by one effort, he will use a hundred efforts. If another man succeeds by ten efforts, he will use a thousand. Let a man proceed in this way, and, though dull, he will surely become intelligent; though weak, he will surely become strong.

(The Mean, XX. 20–21; cited from Lee, 1996, p. 31).

Thus, we can see that self-determination or will power is the driving force of effort, which is highly valued in many parts of the Chinese community (Lee, 1996). Though Hong Kong has been westernized under British sovereignty for more than a century, the concept that 'diligence yields rewards, while play gets nowhere' is embedded in the Chinese psyche (Cheng, 2001). With such a marked clash of cultures, between the ideologies of the people on the one hand and the notion of 'play as learning' as stated by the government on the other, it is perhaps no surprise that implementation of a play-based pedagogy has been difficult to establish in Hong Kong.

A mismatch between the teachers' professional autonomy in theory and practice

Hargreaves and Fullan (2000) note that teachers face considerable contradictory tensions between rhetoric and reality in the age of postmodernism. They need to take charge of their own professional learning and carry out life-long retraining as needed, so as to excel in their profession. Zeichner (1993) argues that teachers should play the most important role in educational reform. They should not be regarded as mere technicians who simply carry out mandated policies. Calls for teachers to be autonomous agents of change are repeatedly heard, both locally and internationally, and was included as one of the target objectives in the local educational reform (Hong Kong Special Administrative Region Government, 2000).

Theoretically, this call for teachers to be autonomous agents of change is in line with the reform in teaching, as flexibility is essential in a play-based curriculum. Yet it is not. Driven by market forces, the kindergarten operators have to meet the expectations of the parents who (as mentioned earlier) see academic excellence as the most significant achievement in early schooling.

Local research reveals that in Hong Kong early childhood teachers see themselves as powerless to change all these parental as well as societal demands, even if they disagree with them (Cheng, 2001; Cheng and Stimpson, 2004). The situation is worsened by the fact that kindergarten education takes place outside the nine-year official educational system. Teachers in this sector do not enjoy equal financial benefits to their counterparts in primary and secondary schools. This affects their social image and status as they often regard themselves as inferior to other teachers. Working under such conflicting demands and expectations, most kindergarten teachers exercise autonomy by selecting a rigid epistemology in place of uncertainty and an endless succession of pedagogical innovations. It is not surprising that they fall back on a more familiar, secure and traditional conformity where they are safely embraced by authoritarian simplicities (Cheng, 2008).

A mismatch between the required competence of teachers and their preparation

Due to the complex nature of play pedagogy, studies show that in order to implement play-based pedagogy in the Hong Kong curriculum, teachers needs to have the professional confidence to frame puzzles in their teaching so as to identify and challenge taken-for-granted practices (Cheng and Stimpson, 2004; Cheng, 2008), to face the uncertainties and challenges involved, and cope with the anxiety caused by the contradictions between government rhetoric and contextual reality. Moreover, the teacher has to be knowledgeable enough to utilize multiple knowledge bases rooted in the context of the children and which are subject to critical scrutiny and adaptation. In addition, s/he has to be open enough to collaborate with the surrounding community (parents, kindergarten owner, etc.), and to have the ability to be self-critical in an ongoing assessment of his/her own performance in a work place which allow certain autonomy in curriculum decisions.

Constrained by the fact that kindergarten teacher education in Hong Kong is still mainly offered as an in-service mode,[2] most kindergarten teachers have learnt to teach solely through practical apprenticeship in their work place. The teacher then refines his/her expertise on the job within the classroom or through part-time, in-service courses after several years of teaching. In other words, novice teachers are immersed in the traditional teaching culture when they begin their teaching career. It is likely that these novices pick up on the ways and means of teaching without fully understanding the principles which inform practice. Without external support, new teachers are unlikely to develop the professional confidence and expertise required and may instead be satisfied by the acquisition of a 'quick fix' in teaching, and not with the potential to continue growing (Dewey, 1965). The recent popularity of 'curriculum kits' (Li, 2005) in local kindergartens to support teaching practice is an example of this. It would seem, then, that the current training provision available to early childhood teachers cannot yet meet the authentic needs of teaching professionals and enable them to face the challenges of educational change within an environment and culture with long-held beliefs about education and deeply embedded structural issues (Hargreaves and Lo, 2000).

To add to these difficulties, kindergarten education still operates in an entrepreneurial fashion in Hong Kong. For example, it is not uncommon for kindergartens to employ secondary school leavers with basic qualifications in order to save on costs (Education and Manpower Bureau, 2003). Until 2001, only two passes in the HKCEE[3] were needed in order to register as a kindergarten teacher; it was only after this time that the regulations changed to requiring five subjects. Hence, kindergarten teachers are usually secondary school leavers with low academic achievement and thus it is very likely that they themselves have adopted rote learning and have acquired ineffective learning strategies during schooling. In a recent study of early childhood teachers, Cheng (2008) has identified that the teaching approach of a teacher is similar to his/her own learning pattern. With such a background, it is not surprising that these teachers find it difficult to understand the complexities surrounding the concept of 'play as learning' and be confident enough to face the implementation of a play based pedagogy. To what extent could this group of teachers find courage to confront the tensions and contradictions between government policy and centuries of tradition, and between the rhetoric and reality of policy and classroom practice? Without significant changes in how teaching and learning are viewed more widely in relation to academic achievement alongside changes in teacher training approaches, will they have the skills to offer meaningful play experiences and understand their role in it? (Cheng, 2001)

Conclusion

In many ways it is disappointing (but perhaps unsurprising), to note that the introduction of play-based pedagogy in Hong Kong has highlighted a range of the conflicting dilemmas and tensions. Many of these are due to the existing socio-political and cultural situation in Hong Kong, traditional and long-held beliefs about the nature and purposes of education and a lack of training for teachers that would match the aspirations of the government's recommendations. Unfortunately, the traditional practices of early education that had been deemed inappropriate by the Llewellyn panel in 1982 prevail some two decades later, suggesting that the teaching reforms that were introduced then resulted only in a 'façade' of change in this region. Meanwhile other issues have arisen, as a result of the enforcement of the teaching reforms, which have demanded due attention. Gore and Zeichner (1995) state that 'greater intentionality by teachers may help, in some cases, further to solidify and justify teaching practices that are harmful to students' (p. 204). Their concerns have been confirmed by local research that has identified an obsessive focus on the 'technicality' of teaching amongst early years' teachers. Instead of improving the quality of learning for young children, the teaching reforms seem to have brought forth a behaviourist interpretation of 'learning through play' and the perpetuation of a cycle of behaviour that is undesirable for the development of an appropriate early childhood pedagogy.

Comparing teaching reforms across several countries, Calderhead notes that:

> . . . clearly care needs to be taken to recognize the different social and political contexts in which reforms are being proposed, the different stages of development of educational systems, and the diverse histories that have preceded them. The same educational reform can have different meanings and effects in different countries, cultures and contexts.
>
> (2001: p. 797)

This seems particularly relevant to the Hong Kong experience. Without a thoughtful, comprehensive and systematic inquiry into the socio-cultural context, educational reformers seem destined to propose simple solutions to complex problems, with little appreciation of their real effect on the lives and learning of the teachers and children in schools.

Notes

1 According to the Hong Kong Special Administrative Region Government statistics, there were a total 80,043 students in form 5 (senior secondary) in the year 2005/06; and the student enrolments of First-Year-Undergraduates of the UGC-funded Universities in 2008 was 15,147. Thus, it is 18.9 per cent.

2 The first cohort of the three-year full-time preservice Certificate in Early Childhood Education Programme for kindergarten teachers graduated in 2001. A one year full-time preservice Qualified Kindergarten Teacher Programme started in 2001. The majority of the kindergarten courses within the School of Early Childhood Education at the Hong Kong Institute of Education are still operating on an in-service mode.

3 Hong Kong Certificate of Education Examination for School leavers is a kind of public examination for secondary school students in Hong Kong. A pass in this examination is equivalent to a pass in the General Certificate of Secondary Examination in the UK.

References

Anning, A. (1991). *The First Years at School*. Milton Keynes: Open University Press.

Bennett, N., Wood, L., and Rogers, S. (1997). *Teaching through Play*, Bucks: Open University Press.

Biggs, J. (1996). The assessment scene in Hong Kong. In J. B. Biggs (Ed.), *Testing: To Educate or to Select: Education in Hong Kong at a Crossroads* (pp. 3–12). Hong Kong: Hong Kong Educational Publishing Co.

Biggs, J., and Walkins D. (1996). The Chinese learner in retrospect. In D. Watkins and J. Biggs (Eds), *The Chinese Learner: Cultural, Psychological, and Contextual Influences* (pp. 269–85). Melbourne: Australia Council for Educational Research.

Board of Education (1994). *Report of the Ad Hoc Sub-Committee on Pre-primary Education*. Hong Kong: Hong Kong Government Printer.

Bredekamp, S., and Copple, C. (Eds) (1997). *Developmentally Appropriate Practice in Early Childhood Programs*. Washington, DC: National Association for the Education of Young Children.

Calderhead, J. (2001). International experiences of teaching reform. In V. Richardson (Ed.), *Handbook of Research on Teaching* (pp. 777–802). Washington, DC: AERA.

Calderhead, J., and Shorrock, S. B. (1997). *Understanding Teacher Education*. London: The Falmer Press.

Census and Statistics Department (2006). *Women and Men in Hong Kong: Key Statistics* (2007 Ed.). Hong Kong: Hong Kong Special Administrative Region Government Printer.

Chao, R. K. (1994). Beyond parental control and authoritarian parenting style: Understanding Chinese parenting through the cultural notion of training. *Child Development, 65*(1), 111–19.

Cheng, D. P. W. (2001). Difficulties of Hong Kong teachers' understanding and implementation of 'play' in the curriculum. *Teaching and Teacher Education, 17*(7), 857–69.

—— (2008). Meta-learning ability: A crucial component for the professional development of teachers in a changing context. *Teacher Development, 12*(1), 85–95.

Cheng, D. P. W., and Stimpson, P. (2004). Articulating contrasts in kindergarten teachers' implicit knowledge on play-based learning. *International Journal of Educational Research, 41*(4-5), 339–52.

Cheng, D. P. W., Fung, C. K. H., Lau, G., and Benson, P. (2008). *The Implementation of Play-Based Pedagogy: Views from Hong Kong and International Perspectives*. Public policy research project: Enhancing the quality of learning and teaching in Hong Kong early childhood education:

Meeting the challenges of the new policy. (Rep. No.1). Hong Kong: Hong Kong Institute of Education, Department of Early Childhood Education.

Cheng, K. M. (1994). Quality of education as perceived in Chinese culture. Paper presented at the Quality of Education in the Context of Culture in Developing Countries, Finland.

Chow, H. Y. M. (1993). Kindergarten and primary school teachers' expectations of school readiness in young children. In S. Opper (Ed.), *Educational Paper 16: Early Childhood Education in Hong Kong* (pp. 67–90). Hong Kong: The University of Hong Kong.

Connelly, F. M., and Clandinin, J. (1994). Telling teaching stories. *Teacher Education Quarterly,* 21(2), 145–58.

Department for Education and Skills (2007). The Early Years Foundation Stage Retrieved 15 September, 2008, from http://www.standards.dfes.gov.uk/primary/foundation_stage/eyfs/

Dewey, J. (1965). The relation of theory and practice in education. In M. Borrowman (Ed.), *Teacher Education in America: A Documentary History* (pp. 140–71). New York:Teachers College press. (Original work published 1904).

Education and Manpower Bureau (2002/03). Quality assurance inspection (QAI) annual report. Retrieved July 15, 2008, from http://www.edb.gov.hk/ FileManager/TC/Content_756/KG_AnnualReport_0203.pdf

—— (2003) *LegCo panel on education: Progress on the harmonisation of pre-primary services – Way forward for harmonisation of kindergartens and child care centres.* LC Paper No. CB(2)1125/02–03(01). Retrieved September 15, 2008, from http://www.edb.gov.hk/FileManager/EN/content_713/ed0217cb2-1125-1e.pdf

—— (2004/05). Quality assurance inspection (QAI) annual report. Retrieved July 15, 2008, from http://www.edb.gov.hk/FileManager/TC/Content_756/kg_annualreport_0405.pdf

—— (2006). *Guide to the Pre-primary Curriculum.* Hong Kong: Hong Kong Special Administrative Region Government Printer.

Education Bureau. (2006/07). Quality assurance inspection (QAI) annual report. Retrieved July 15, 2008, from http://www.edb.gov.hk/FileManager/TC/Content_2325/kg_annual-report0607.pdf

Education Commission (1986). *Education Commission Report no. 2.* Hong Kong: Hong Kong Government Printer.

—— (2000). Review of education system: Reform Proposal Retrieved July 20, 2008, from http://www.e-c.edu.hk/eng/online/annex/e_ABR.pdf

Education Department (1993). *Guide to the Kindergarten Curriculum.* Hong Kong: Hong Kong Government Printer.

—— (1996). *Guide to the Pre-primary Curriculum.* Hong Kong: Hong Kong Government Printer.

Fullan, M., and Stiegelbauer, S. (1991). *The New Meaning of Educational Change* (2nd Ed.). New York: Teachers College Press.

Ginsburg, K. R., the Committee on Communications, & the Committee on Psychosocial Aspects of Child and Family Health (2007). The importance of play in promoting healthy child development and maintaining strong parent-child bonds. *Pediatrics,* 119(1), 182–91.

Gore, J. M., and Zeichner, K. M. (1995). Connecting action research to genuine teacher development. In J. Smith (Ed.), *Critical Discourses on Teacher Development* (pp. 203–14). London: Cassell.

Hargreaves, A., and Fullan, M. (2000). Mentoring in the new millennium. *Theory Into Practice,* 39(1), 50–57.

Hargreaves, A., and Lo, L. N. K. (2000). Professionalism in teaching. The paradoxical profession: Teaching at the turn of the century. *Prospects,* 30(2), 167–80.

Hayhoe, R. (2008). Philosophy and comparative education: What can we learn from East Asia? In K. Mundy, K. Bickmore, R. Hayhoe, M. Madden and K. Madjidi (Eds), *Comparative and International Education: Issues for Teachers* (pp. 23–48). Canada: Canadian Scholars' Press Inc.

Hong Kong Special Administrative Region Government (2000). *2000 Policy Address: Quality Education-Policy Objective for Education and Manpower Bureau*. Hong Kong: Hong Kong Special Administrative Region Government Printer.

Lee, W. O. (1996). The cultural context for Chinese learner: Conceptions of learning in the Confucian tradition. In D. A. Watkins and J. B. Biggs (Eds), *The Chinese Learner: Cultural, Psychological and Contextual Influences*. (pp. 25–41). Hong Kong: Comparative Education Research Centre.

Lewis, C. C. (1995). *Educating Hearts and Minds: Reflections on Japanese Preschool and Elementary Education*. Cambridge: Cambridge University Press.

Li, H. (2005). *Developing School-based Curriculum in Hong Kong Kindergartens: Insights, Challenges and Solutions*. Hong Kong: Hong Kong Institute of Education.

Li, Y. L. (2001). Curriculum management and classroom practice in kindergartens in Hong Kong. *Education 3–13,* 29(1), 56–61.

—— (2004). Pupil-teacher interactions in Hong Kong kindergarten classrooms – its implications for teachers' professional development. *Learning Environments Research,* 7(1), 23–42.

Llewellyn, J., Hancock, G., Kirst, M., and Roeloffs, K. (1982). *Llewellyn Report: A Perspective on Education in Hong Kong: Report by a Visiting Panel*. Hong Kong: Hong Kong Government Printer.

Miller, E. and Almon, J. (2009). *Crisis in the Kindergarten: Why Children Need to Play in School*. Maryland: Alliance for Childhood publication. Retrieved on September 15, 2009 from www.allianceforchildren.org

Ministry of Education and Science in Sweden. (1998). *Curriculum for Pre-school, Lpfo* 98. Stockholm: Fritzes.

Mok, M. M., Kennedy, K. J., Moore, P. J., Shan, P. W., and Leung, S. (2008). The use of help-seeking by Chinese secondary school students: Challenging the myth of 'the Chinese learner'. *Evaluation & Research in Education,* 21(3), 188–213.

Nian You (2008) Xue Tong Zi Sha 3 Nian 4 Zong 1 Ren Si. [Young Children suicide four cases one died in three years]. *MingPao Daily,* February 28 p. A17.

OECD. (2002). *Starting strong: Early Childhood Education and Care*. France: OECD.

—— (2004). *Five Curriculum Outlines*. Paris, France: OECD.

Opper, S. (1992). *Hong Kong's Young Children: Their Preschools and Families*. Hong Kong: Hong Kong University Press.

Pong, W. P., and Chow, J. C. S. (2002). On the pedagogy of examinations in Hong Kong. *Teaching and Teacher Education,* 18(2), 139–49.

Richardson, V. (1996). The role of attitudes and beliefs in learning to teach. In J. Sikula (Ed.), *Handbook of Research on Teacher Education* (pp. 102–19). New York: Macmillan.

Rogers, S., and Evans, J. (2008). *Inside role play in Early Childhood Education: researching children's perspectives*. London: Routledge.

Salili, F. (1996). Accepting personal responsibility for learning. In D. Walkins and J. Biggs (Eds), *The Chinese Learner: Cultural, Psychological, and Contextual Influences* (pp. 85–106). Melbourne: Australia Council for Educational Research.

Spodek, B., and Saracho, O. N. (Eds) (1991). *Issues in Early Childhood Curriculum*. New York: Teachers College Press.

Wood, E., and Bennett, N. (2000). Changing theories, changing practice: Exploring early childhood teachers' professional learning. *Teaching and Teacher Education,* 16(5–6), 635–47.

Zeichner, K. M. (1993). Connecting genuine teacher development to the struggle of social justice. *Journal of Education for Teaching,* 19(1), 5–20.

Chapter 9

Meeting at the crossroads

Postmodern pedagogy greets children's aesthetic play-culture

Faith Gabrielle Guss

Introduction

Considered from the perspective of postmodern pedagogy, how should we meet and relate to young children's collaborative dramatic playing (pretend play, socio-dramatic play, role-play)? In the field of children's peer culture, there has been a lack of studies of the significance the aesthetic dimension in children's play. From an arts point of view, the political-pedagogical agenda for my research has, therefore, been to make visible the aesthetic and child-cultural significance of self-initiated, inventive fantasy playing. I will discuss theory and implications stemming from a three year ethnography of fourteen children aged from birth to seven and their three teachers in an early childhood daycare setting in Norway. To contribute towards an aesthetic pedagogy of play, I studied what *kind* of dramatic form-language constitutes the children's communication in the drama medium of play; and what *kind* of reflection, interpretation, meaning seeking and meaning construction can take place and the significance of dramatic playing for the formation of an autonomous child-cultural arena.

In order to make these aspects visible in my analyses, I have activated theoretical perspectives from the academic disciplines of social anthropology, aesthetics, theatre/dramaturgy, performance studies, and cultural studies. The results have led to a reconceptualization of play, with such concepts as play*ing*, *paidia, ludus, the* aesthetic dimension, form-languages, mimesis, and the dialogic imagination. I offer an aesthetic reconceptualization of dramatic playing as a supplement to, and an implicit resistance to, play theories and instrumental politico-educational agendas found in developmental psychology and sociology. For many decades their theories and perspectives have dominated the curriculum in early childhood studies and shaped our ways of perceiving and relating to play in educational institutions. My findings join explicit critical theory of the past decade (see Dahlberg *et al.*, 1999; Ryan and Grieshaber, 2005; Guss, 2005a; 2005b; Rogers and Evans, 2008; Wood, 2004; Guss, 2008).

Through this research the teachers and assistants gained new awareness about the complexity of children's symbolic form-making and reflection, and the vitality and agency in their autonomous play-culture. They learned to observe, deconstruct and reconceptualize play with an aesthetic vocabulary. This led to allowing more time for free play, for symbolic play-modeling and a two-way, acting-in concert-with the children. In short, toward a co-learning participation and mutuality (Ryan and Grieshaber, 2005); and to what Rogers and Evans (2008) conceptualize as a co-construction of a pedagogy of play. Therefore, I argue for a pedagogy of play that is inspired by insight into the ways in which children express themselves, interpret experience, and construct knowledge in their autonomous play-culture. First, I will introduce some key concepts from my research; second, I will present an example of a dramatic play sequence; and third, I will activate the key concepts in analyses that illustrate *how* the children interpret the meanings of their experience in dramatic form, question and construct meanings, and thereby expand their subjectivities/identities.

Playing

In our theoretical discourse about play, it is important to define how we understand the play concept. The philosopher Mihai Spariosu posits that we cannot create a universal definition, but can best understand the play phenomenon by describing '*how and under what conditions* an action is performed /. . ./. One can define play by what it *does*' (1989: 3, my emphasis) specifically, in its context; rather than by what it could mean as a general phenomenon. In my research I set out to describe what dramatic playing does, and *how* it is done by the players. This is valuable knowledge for teachers about children's autonomous life forms, whether or not the intention is to harness play to subject learning or, rather, to inspire/stimulate it.

'Play' is a generic substantive that denotes an activity sphere. 'Play*ing*' on the other hand is a verbal form that suggests an active player. In order to increase my *aesthetic* play vocabulary, I turned to the philosophy of art. According to Hans-Georg Gadamer play is not just freedom from particular ends, it is free impulse. Gadamer conceives of play as repetitive back and forth movement by which the player is moved, and in which 'neither pole of the movement represents the goal in which it would come to rest' (1960/96: 22). To concretize this abstract idea, I use an analogy from ball playing: If two people play a game of catch, the ball is the 'raw material' (see Mouritsen, 1996; Schechner, 1988) that is played, but that also plays the players. The ball is thrown and is set in movement. We say: The ball is in play. For the players, playing consists of responding to the back and forth movement impulses from the ball. The movement of the ball cannot be fully controlled so that, in playing, the aspects of chance and coincidence and, therefore, risk, figure largely. The players play along with coincidence and the risks of chance. Therefore, I would say that the ability for playing has to do with the ability to abandon oneself to the chance happenings and impulses that emerge, *ad hoc*, in the back-and-forth movement. The players are caught up in the play-movement. *They* are played/moved. Gadamer observed that in the acts of play, the player is also a spectator who plays along with the movement of the play. 'The structure of play absorbs the player into itself' (1977/1991: 105). In my analysis later, I attempt to make visible the play movement and the aesthetic, sensory structure that absorbs the players, in a way that illustrates Gadamer's *aesthetic* view of play.

Paidia and ludus

The cultural theorist Roger Callois (1961) differentiates, with Plato's Greek vocabulary, between free, unbounded playing, *paidia*, and rule-bound playing, *ludus* – game. In dramaturgical terms, we would say that the difference between *paidia* and *ludus* is that the first is open for the players to develop new directions, rules/frames/structures, whilst the second generally operates within a predetermined frame/structure and has, thus, a closed outcome, win or lose. In light of Gadamer's understanding of play as open-ended, no-goal movement, we could rightly ask to what extent *ludus* allows for the play of free impulse of *paidia* within its closed structure. To be sure, in a rule bound ballgame, there are unplanned actions and co-incidences of chance, but the goal is to maintain the rules of the game. In pedagogical settings it is, of course, an ethical responsibility to teach children to understand and uphold rules, to take turns, to cooperate for the common good, and *ludus* works towards fulfilling these responsibilities. Certainly there are examples of 'closed' *ludus* that simultaneously produce inspiring aesthetic experiences and aesthetic models that also can inspire dramatic play expressions for instance, nursery rhymes and song-and-dance games. However, in *paidia*'s unbound playing the players can create their *own* rules/structures, with which to investigate their own life experiences. I differentiate between social realistic playing and inventive fantasy playing. In the first instance, the motivation seems to be to *reproduce* fascinating actions and forms; whereas, in the second instance, the motivation seems to come from the desire to follow impulses from the imagination and to *create* actions and forms with which to express these. Viewed from an aesthetic perspective, what babies (see Stern, 1985), toddlers and young children learn from direct mimicry or from delayed, reproductive, imitation of others, gives them the necessary *action vocabularies* for symbolic expression and communication in their social realistic playing. Subsequently, as they gain experience in symbolic playing, they can free themselves from constricted scripts, and eventually perform transformative actions in inventive fantasy playing, where they experiment with staging their imaginations.

Callois (1961) also identifies four dynamic aspects of play: *agon* (competition), mimicry (imitation), *alea* (chance) and *ilinx* (vertigo, – a destabilization of one's perception). Although *alea* can be present both in *paidia* playing and *ludus* games, it would seem that *alea* is a prerequisite for the unknown to emerge and, therefore, for discoveries to emerge. Therefore, openness for both *alea* and *ilinx* would seem to be prerequisites for learning – in the movement to new experience. As I will show in the analysis of my research material, it is the children who abandon themselves to the chance movement of their imaginations, who become momentarily destabilized in the excitement and tensions they create in their enactments, who can discover themselves anew and expand their experiences.

Play-drama, play-culture, and dramatic form-language

Because I have come to understand children's inventive socio-dramatic playing as spontaneous drama that they create and perform in the cultural context of their play, I refer to it as play-drama. In play-drama children create sensory-symbolic reproductions or transformative re-presentations of their experience, through the enactment of roles and situations, in dramatic form. In this dramatic medium they can explore, interpret and communicate the workings of their minds-emotions-imaginations. As in dramatic art, when children tell or invent a story in dramatic form, they symbolize/personify/present the characters' actions – including verbal text. The same story can be told dramatically in innumerable forms. However, it is always necessary to establish symbolically four basic elements: where we are (symbolic place), who we are (symbolic role-figure), when the action takes place (symbolic time), and what happens (symbolic action).

In their symbolic use of the body, voice, sound, verbal language, space, objects, and time, both play-drama and dramatic art combine the expressive languages belonging to the whole fan of art forms: visual arts, movement/dance, music, and literature/verbal art. In my research, children's functions in play-drama can be fruitfully compared to those of a dramatist, actor, director, stage designer, light-designer, props-person, costume designer, dresser, choreographer – dancer, sound designer, composer – musician. Whereas in traditional theatre production, these functions are filled by artists who are specialists in each their field, and are preplanned and produced prior to a performance for spectators; in play-drama, children fill these functions in the moment, albeit in less refined form. In their spontaneous composition, they perform two kinds of actions simultaneously: the dramatic actions within the fiction, and the production actions which make it possible to perform the dramatic actions (for instance, constructing the fictive space, finding props, etc.) The children are simultaneously performers, producers and spectators – who perceive and respond to their own and each other's actions (see Sutton-Smith, 1979).

The aesthetic dimension and knowing

In the inventive fantasy play that I will discuss later, the children dwell largely in a sensual, pre-lingual, or pre-rational, state of interpretation and experience. Rather than with the precision of verbal language alone, it is with the intuitive poetry of the symbolic form-language that they converse with each other. Therefore, I tie the concept of aesthetics to children's cultural expressions. The philosophical field of aesthetics emerged in the early eighteenth century, at which time there was a heightened concern with understanding the particularity of sensuous experience (Gadamer, 1977/1991). The term aesthetic is derived from the Greek 'aisthanomai', to perceive, and refers to sensory perception and sensory knowledge – knowledge that we gain through sensory experience. Baumgarten ([1758]1961), who coined the concept, considered aesthetics as one of the two branches of the study of knowledge – namely the study of sensory experience coupled with emotion – as opposed to the study of rational logic and abstract ideas. He saw the unique potential for apprehending truth in sensory representation, in contrast to conceptual representation.

I illustrate later *how*, in the process of play, reflection and aesthetic knowing are constituted by the children. The players are fully present with all their senses and being, which means that they are receptive to the chance happenings that emerge, and that they follow these impulses. We can call these qualities presence, immediacy, and spontaneity. Theirs is not a rational, logical process. It is a process that grows out of the illogic of the investigating imagination, which necessitates their finding a form (language) in which to investigate it. This form does not have to do with 'beauty' and harmony for an outside spectator, as in a classical aesthetic ideal, but, rather, with the *players'* experience of verisimilitude: to express the imagination in a way that feels true for them, and grips their senses.

In the physiological – psychological dimension of perceiving with the senses, there is no split between mind, body and emotion. What is experienced with the body is directly connected with the workings of the mind-imagination-affect, and the converse. However, instead of employing the term sensory 'knowledge', which means the act of already knowing a thing; I prefer to use sensory 'knowing', which means the action of getting to understand. The process of getting to understand implies active, moving reflection.

In children's play-drama, I identify a transcendent, non-classical aesthetic. Early in the twentieth century, the Russian philosopher and literary theorist Mikhail Bakhtin set forth an interpretation of the spirit of Carnival in the middle ages, in terms of a popular aesthetic that I often recognize in children's play-drama. He writes of *incomplete form* and ambiguous meanings, in 'a boundless world of humorous forms and manifestations opposed to the official and serious tone of the culture' (Bakhtin, 1984: 4); '[. . .] a temporary liberation from the prevailing truth and from the established order' (ibid: 10) with 'numerous parodies and travesties, humiliations, profanations. . . . a second life' (ibid: 11). 'Carnival is a rebellious practice, characterized by the material bodily principle'. The following qualities describe this aesthetic: '[. . .] all that is bodily becomes grandiose, exaggerated, and immeasurable' (ibid: 18). Bakhtin shows *how* the aesthetic expressions of Carnival constitute a reflection of the imbalance of power and how the power relationships of everyday reality are turned upside down and inside out.

Mimesis

In a cultural-historical perspective (Diamond, 1997) developed in feminist theatre theory, there are two meanings of mimicry. The first is copy or imitation, as Callois (1961) understands it, which involves a striving to reproduce an image of an original: the Same. This we find in social-realistic play. The second meaning of mimicry is 'mimesis', which suggests a *re*-presentation of an 'object' (an experience), which is filtered through the perception and sensibility of the form-maker. I understand this as a seeking of the Other, as I have observed in examples of children's inventive fantasy playing. Therefore, in the concept of mimesis, I have found a term for conceptualizing the transformative, critical potential that lies in playful *re*-presentations of experience. According to feminist theatre theory (ibid.), mimesis in artistic representation is, historically, a sensual, critical receptivity to, and transformation of, the object. It implies a sensuous moment of discovery, rather than a rational reproduction of an original; a critical movement away from accepted ideals and norms. Historically, mimesis has been a political practice, inseparable from interpretation and contestation (ibid: viii). In this practice, one reaches only temporary truths. And truths change with the change of context, as in the context of children's playing.

A play-drama illustration: capture the wolf, we shall!

In my examples later, I wish to illustrate that when children play dramatically, the stuff of their imaginations/thoughts are raw materials, impulses that keep the play in motion. The players continually cast impulses back and forth between each other, catch them, and build a drama, which moves in unpredictable directions. As 'expert players' (Gardner, 1983), they commit themselves to following the free impulses that move back and forth, sparking associations, tension, risk-taking and excitement.

When I begin to film two girls playing on a sunny morning in kindergarten, Tessa (three years and eight months) and Hilde (five years and two months) are taking care of some babies and chickens (dolls and wooden eggs) which lie in a cradle hanging from the ceiling. Tessa goes to fetch a book from the bookshelf to read for the babies and selects *Little Red Riding Hood*. The illustration on the book cover is a watercolour where the wolf is portrayed in the foreground with an exaggeratedly large head and gaping jaw. Dwarfed in the background are the other characters. The cover illustration gives a visual, aesthetic impulse to Tessa, causing her to change the course of their social-realistic theme ('playing house') to inventive fantasy play drama. Tessa stalks over to Hilde and announces: 'Capture Red Riding Hood and the Wolf, we shall!' I note the poetic phrasing.

From this moment, the children create and perform, for themselves and for one another, a forty-minute, non-linear drama in which they move from performing the myth of good mothering to performing the myth of good murdering. They transform themselves from Nurturing Mothers to Wolf-slaying Mothers, who protect their babies from a frightening and omnipotent Wolf. The drama is divided into two major parts, with several side-actions. In the first part, the Mothers/Wolf-slayers protect their babies by shooting, capturing and repetitively hopping on/torturing/slaying The Wolf. He dies but returns time after time. Tessa also enacts/*re*-presents fragments of The Wolf's actions in the original fairytales, where she invents alternative solutions to his fate there. In the second part of the drama, the Mothers/Wolf-slayers cut open his stomach to release the innocent victims he has devoured. He dies finally-finally, but revives again. The Wolf-slayers also die because they have touched the dead wolf, but they are 'really only pretending to sleep'. In the end, they finally bury the wolf, but he howls again, not dead after all?

Analytical interpretations

In order to provide an overview for readers, I will first summarize my overall interpretation of the play-drama: I have found it to be predominantly *Tessa's* search for, and construction of, meanings. It is her interpretive, critical investigation and performance of the culturally inherited myth of The Wolf, whom she has experienced in various tales, in various media. The drama seems to circle around Tessa's search for the meanings of The Wolf as a mythical figure. Her main impression of the tales seems to be that the *same* wolf dies in one fairytale, but returns again in the next and in the next, etc. She seems to enact a composite image of an indestructible and ever-present wolf-threat. She also seems to conflate her experience of him *across* the three fairytales and to intertextualize them. She stages an exploration of what actually happens to the wolf – and she invents alternative scenarios and solutions. A secondary theme lies in her enactment of dying, of trying out what it means to die – in regard to both The Wolf's death and the Wolf-slayers' deaths. *How* is dying? Is it like sleeping? Can we resurrect? This theme could reflect both Tessa's questioning of The Wolf's repeated demise and his repeated return across the fairytales.

In my analysis here I focus mostly on Tessa's process, but Hilde's collaboration, as performer and spectator, aids Tessa's enjoyment and spurs her on to her maintain her focus and to develop the drama. The following excerpts illustrate how selected parts of the performance are developed and expressed. I present the play episodes in the form of a theatre manuscript, in which I interpolate interpretive comments. Beside the players' names, I have interpreted which role-figures and which theatre functions they are performing. These are my interpretations of the mental and emotional positioning of their actions.

In the excerpt later, Tessa and Hilde have already established the wolf-theme (in lines 1–20). They have shot twice at the imagined wolf with L-formed blocks.

9.28 a.m.

(Line 20) **TESSA/MOTHER/WOLF-SLAYER/PROPS PERSON/SOUND DESIGNER:** She lays the book she has fetched from the bookcase, *Little Red Riding Hood*, in the cradle and goes to the mattress where she fetches an L-formed block. She aims and fires into the open space: *Bang, bang, bang*. The block is the same size as a small revolver and she holds it with both hands as police do on crime-series on television.

(l. 25) **TESSA/WOLF:** *Ahhhhh. Ouuuuuu.* She walks toward the cradle.

Above, Tessa begins to shift back and forth between performing the role-positions and perspectives of Mother/Wolf-slayer and Wolf. This shift is the start of *an aesthetic structuring convention* that carries the enactment and which she expands underway.

(l. 26) **TESSA/WOLF-SLAYER:** She lays the gun in the cradle.

TESSA/WOLF: She wanders aimlessly around the space, seemingly punch-drunk/injured.

The Mothers/Wolf-slayers decide to celebrate that the wolf is injured. A few minutes elapse:

(l. 45) **TESSA/MOTHER:** She goes to the book *Little Red Riding Hood* which is now lying on the floor beside the cradle. She looks at the picture of the wolf on the cover: *Why do you come back the whole time, Wolf?*

I interpret this question as a key to the full arch of the dramatic action – its driving force. In a later episode, Tessa stamps vigorously on the book illustration, which appears to be a symbolic representation of The Wolf.

9. 31 a.m.

(l. 60) **TESSA/MOTHER/WOLF-SLAYER/SINGER:** *Ha, ha, ha.* (She sings the melody from the film or cassette of Disney's *Three Little Pigs.*) She climbs up on the ladder chair beside the group of pillows where she has caged the (imagined) wolf. *Hello, you dumb old wolf! Hello you dumb old wolf! Hello, you dumb old wolf!* She directs the song, with its skipping rhythm, to her right – down behind the wall of pillows where she imagines the wolf to be held captive. *Hello!*

TESSA/WOLF: *Auuuuu!*

TESSA/MOTHER/WOLF-SLAYER: She fans her left hand toward the wolf (slapping him?).

TESSA/WOLF: She turns on the chair, lifts her head and *breaths heavily* with her tongue hanging out, dog-like (wolf-like?)

Two more minutes of Tessa's and Hilde's inventive action pass. Tessa now initiates a torture action, which she repeats many times, with variations. She stands on a ladder chair, shouts rhythmic taunts to the imagined wolf, and hops on him. She hops on a brightly covered mattress which lies under a long window, a meter from the chair.

(l. 101) **TESSA/DRAMATIST:** She returns to the ladder chair. She climbs up: *Now then, the hopping shall begin!*

TESSA/MOTHER/WOLF-SLAYER/CHOREOGRAPHER-DANCER: She hops from the highest step of the chair onto the mattress, a space that represents the imagined Wolf, then returns to the chair. *The wolf is frightened.* She hops on the wolf again.

I assign the aforementioned theatre position of Dramatist, because her plan for the next action is made explicit. However, she and Hilde are, of course, dramatists throughout, as they develop the story *in* their actions. I also assign the function of Choreographer – dancer here (l.103) because this is the beginning of what I view, aesthetically, as a repetitive, circular dance ritual: hopping down/punishing, turning over, standing up, and continuing the circular movement back to the chair. I comment upon this in greater detail later.

After the wolf-shooting episode in the beginning of the drama, Hilde returns to caring for their babies. As spectator, she becomes aesthetically involved in Tessa's ritual torture, even with her back turned, and joins in:

HILDE/MOTHER: Lays the baby in the cradle and makes it comfortable. She is standing with her back to Tessa. *The wolf was frightened, that wolf, yes indeed.*

(l. 110) She turns and walks over to the hopping-chair, determinedly – with her hands on her hips.

(9.34 a.m.)

TESSA/WOLF-SLAYER: *So – we hop, one two, three.* She hops on the wolf again.

HILDE/WOLF-SLAYER: She climbs onto the chair: *Upon the wolf I shall hop!* She hops.

Hilde is using poetic phrasing earlier. This is not the world of her timid everyday way of being. She is trying on the authoritative subjectivity/identity of a wolf-slayer, an 'Other'.

TESSA (meta-fictional commentary): To the camera: *We're playing wolves.*

This is a telling commentary regarding which 'Other' Tessa is investigating/interpreting – which subjectivity/identity she is trying on. Methodologically, in regard to the presence of the camera, we see that in the next episode she is probably performing for the outside eye. Nonetheless, this fact does not reduce the value of her aesthetic and reflective competence. She gradually forgets the camera and returns to self-forgetfulness as the drama's excitement augments.

(l. 115) TESSA/MOTHER/NARRATOR: She climbs up on the chair, and *mimes* that she rolls out an imaginary parchment scroll, in the manner of a herald in days of old. She pretends to read: *The wolf has stolen gold from our children – gold we have bought.*

In addition to shifting between the role-positions of Mother and Wolf, she now introduces a Narrator, a third role-position which supplies a third-person perspective on the dramatic events, from *outside* the dramatic action. (I am not familiar with a fairytale in which the wolf steals gold.)

(l. 120) HILDE/WOLF-SLAYER: She climbs up on the chair. *Oh no, and hop and hop!* She hops on the wolf.
TESSA/WOLF-SLAYER: *Wolf, watch out now! One, two, three, ha, ha, ha!*
She hops and comes immediately around to the chair again.
TESSA/NARRATOR: *And so the wolf comes with eyes and noses.*
TESSA/WOLF-SLAYER: *One, two, three. He's not watching out, here I come.* She hops again.

Tessa's phrase earlier, 'Ha, ha, ha', is part of the taunting theme song from the Disney version of *The Three Little Pigs*. Her phrase 'with eyes and noses' is a line fragment from Red Riding Hood's meeting with The Wolf in Grandmother's bed.

In this twelve minute sequence, Tessa has invented a hopping punishment of the wolf that is not found in the fairytales. However, she may have associated to the action of the wolf in *The Three Little Pigs*, where he enters the house of the oldest/wisest pig by hopping down the chimney, to his demise in the fireplace. Hopping from a height is a common game for young children, an exuberant non-symbolic play-form. Tessa has adopted and transformed this raw material into a symbolic instrument for wolf-torture/slaying. Together, the girls repeat and develop variations on these torture actions and taunts; but only young Tessa creates, and shifts among, the perspectives of three role-figures. The Wolf dies, but comes to life again repeatedly; he *finally* dies but comes to life once more; he *finally, finally* dies, but again comes back to life. Viewed from a child-cultural perspective, if he did not revive, the play movement would die out, and with it the children's great enjoyment together.

The aesthetic here is physically and verbally vital and wildly boisterous, as in Bakhtin's (1984) descriptions of folk-cultural aesthetics (Guss, 2000). The play-drama is seemingly chaotic, discontinuous and full of repetitions and digressions. However, with closer study I discover that Tessa, not yet four-years-old, adopts a *structural form* that enables her to have great fun while, at the same time, reflecting in all seriousness, searching for the meanings of the fairytales: After many minutes of the centrifugal, ritual hopping dance, Tessa begins intermittently to move the drama to calmer actions. In these episodes she directly intervenes in the world of three fairy tales – in which The Wolf devours innocent victims. Alone, she invents and performs short intertextualizations of narrative bits from *The Wolf and the Seven Young Goats* and *The Three Little Pigs*, with echoes of *Little Red Riding Hood*. I will present a transcription of one of these enactments below, followed by an interpretation of what her actions might represent and mean for her:

9.35 a.m.

(l. 135) Tessa is standing in the middle of the space between the mattress and the chair.

TESSA/NARRATOR: *Then someone knocks.*

TESSA/WOLF: She knocks on the floor.

TESSA/NARRATOR: *And it was the poor wolf. And so he dressed in a disguise and they* [the goats] *ask who it is and then the wolf hopped on them, but then it was only a*

(l. 140) *person. So then, the wolf became very frightened. And then the person* [the wolf] *became very frightened.*

TESSA/YOUNG GOAT: *Capture the wolf! Capture the wolf!*

TESSA/NARRATOR: She walks over to the chair. *Then they became terribly scared, frightened when he saw them. And then the three pigs came, but they were not*

(l. 145) *scared, you know. But the wolf was scared.*

TESSA/WOLF-SLAYER/PIG: She climbs up on the chair and hops onto the wolf, then returns to the chair and climbs up.

TESSA/NARRATOR: *'Help me!', said the wolf. 'Crocodiles, crocodiles!'*

In line 148, she associates to the crocodiles in *Peter Pan*, who are also predatory threats.

Dramatic monologue: Tessa's dramatic convention

As mentioned earlier, in the day-care institution where the field study was conducted, drama education is prioritized as a play-enhancing practice. Tessa's teacher has previously used the dramatic monologue-form to enact another fairytale. In dramatic monologue (Fo, 1991) the structure enables the storyteller/actor to shift among many role positions and perspectives in several situations and locations. First, in the position of a Narrator, the actor contextualizes the dramatic situation and comments upon it. Second, s/he shifts to the position/standpoint of the protagonist, the role-figure who drives the action forward. Thereafter, s/he continuously shifts between these standpoints and the mimed enactment of the protagonist and the characters involved in the dramatic situations that develop. Tessa adopts and adapts this convention, in order to perform her imagination about The Wolf. The convention gives her a flexible structure in which to explore and interpret the meanings of the fairytales, and to enact with ease the ideas that emerge in her imagination.

Tessa's consciousness moves back and forth among all the characters she enacts, but never seems to settle on one perspective for very long. Her moving consciousness ties in with her use of the monologue-form. The theatre form resembles not only a folk-cultural way of telling stories, it also resembles children's way of telling stories, which is: '[. . .] disconnected, full of impulsive insertions and multiple associations [which] appeals to an immediate receptiveness' (Fo, 1991: 8, my translation from Danish). Sensory receptiveness is a key-word in understanding the children's reflective process and sensory knowing.

There seems to be an ambiguous shift in perspective in all these movements, the in-between state of consciousness (between her memory of the fairytale narratives and her immediate meaning seeking) which creates tension and excitement. I view the full arc of lines 135–47 as an example of how the aesthetic form of her language and narrative storytelling seizes her senses and imagination and keeps her reflection and the dramatic situation in movement, bouncing ideas back and forth.

9.40 a.m.

(l. 198) **TESSA/NARRATOR:** After standing up from the mattress, Tessa is standing in the space between the mattress and the chair. *Ah! It was the wolf.*

TESSA/WOLF-SLAYER: *You don't give up!*

TESSA/WOLF/SOUND DESIGNER: She makes a knocking sound on the floor.

TESSA/A LITTLE PIG/SOUND DESIGNER: *What is it that is knocking?* She mimes that she is shoving a door open and at the same time, in her throat, she simulates the creaking sound of a door hinge that needs oil. *Is it the wolf? Just go away at once!* She shoves the imaginary door shut with much force. *Dong!*

TESSA/META-FICTIONAL COMMENTARY: *Wolves are so dumb, Hilde. I hate wolves.*

(l. 205) **TESSA/WOLF-SLAYER:** *Uff, what a wolf.* She pushes the chair forward, so that it is touching the edge of the mattress. She climbs up on the chair. *Now I'm going to hop on you, then you'll get ugly ugly.* She hops.

In the next episode, Tessa returns the action to the Mother/Wolf-slayers' hopping ritual where The Wolf is very much alive again. This pattern of moving from one dramatic time, place and situation to the other is repeated several times. Each time Tessa reverses the consequences of the climax (a finally dead wolf) by bringing him back to life. Her actions/her interpretation never resolve the problem of the ever-present Wolf-threat, even when she is too tired to continue the plot.

A critical and transformative process in dramatic form: mimesis

Both mentally and bodily, Tessa circles around a core dramatic action: tricking, torturing and killing The Wolf. She sets up several dramatic situations in which she explores how to accomplish the killing, on behalf of The Wolf's innocent victims. She explores how it has been done previously, in the fairytales; and she explores the possibilities for alternative solutions. She glues the episodes together with the Narrator's explanations and commentary on the action. Tessa also briefly enacts the roles and perspectives of the animal victims in *The Seven Little Goats* and *The Three Little Pigs*, perhaps a momentary identification with them and their situations.

The form-languages, including verbal language, afford Tessa a complex interpretive process that, in all probability, exceeds her ability to formulate her meanings in conceptual language alone. The form-making process is self-reflexive. It makes it possible for both girls to experiment with, and to experience, previously untried sides of themselves. Their role figures are imagined and enacted from the perspective of the Other thereby expanding their identities/subjectivities.

In Tessa's mimesis, in her invention of a new solution to the ever-returning Wolf in fairytale after fairytale, she transforms herself to a superior dramatist/plot-maker by clipping out and gluing together fragments, *across* the fairytales. Her intertextualization is an impressive critical reflection over the traditional tales, and how she might succeed in disposing of The Wolf once and for all. Tessa and Hilde both transform themselves into heroines who *play*. The Wolf to death. This is also an alternative spin on the fairytales. However, although Hilde seems content with the fact that The Wolf is finally, finally dead, Tessa maintains an ambiguous relationship to the finality of his death: She keeps The Wolf howling, even after they have buried him.

Toward the end of the hopping ritual, in a non-classical, folk-cultural aesthetic, and in an increasingly exaggerated physical exuberance, Tessa assigns *'spiky hair'* and a *'spiky tongue'* to The Wolf. He is, in her irreverent judgment, a *'fart-turd'*. In the second reality (Bakhtin, 1984) of their playing, with a symbolically enacted, omnipotent power that the girls do not command in the first reality, they actualize aesthetically a new life experience. This is a transformation and a transcendence of their daily experience as children/girls in an institutional setting – with strict rules for how to behave indoors.

With regard to Tessa's expressed relation to the wolf and what he might represent for her, I say with Bakhtin's words that her symbolic language contains 'a multiplicity of meanings, and its complex relation to the object' (ibid: 42; Guss, 2000). Her performance contains a sensory knowing about The Wolf, even though the knowing is full of contradictions and paradox that exist simultaneously. If we were playing with the children, would we have the urge to correct this ambiguity, or let it remain as a dynamic force, a sign of curiosity, a process of reflecting over who deserves to die or survive? (see Edmiston, 2008).

Tessa's actions embody what Bakhtin (1994) defines as the 'dialogic imagination': In the novel the dialogic imagination is present in an author's consciousness, when it moves back and forth among the various consciousnesses of the various characters – in continual dialogue with them, but without arriving at an authorial definition, for the reader, of which voice/perspective is the 'correct' one. From this state of consciousness, 'polyphony' (multi-voicedness) emerges. I understand Bakhtin to mean that dialog is not about reaching a synthesis of one truth, but rather is about listening and learning from the Other(s). On this dialogic threshold of Tessa's drama, she arrives at no definitive meanings and no final truth. She seems to *sense* the complexity of possibilities. In their playing, the children are both in dialog with each other and with all the voices in their imaginations. Their consciousnesses are in a state of continual becoming (ibid.). The play drama both *is* and *provokes* reflection on the world; it is a hermeneutic construction of meanings from the player's perspective. I interpret Tessa's movement among the various standpoints as a radical intervention in the original models and a destabilization of her perception (*ilinx*).

At the crossroad between postmodern pedagogy and children's aesthetic play-culture

There is a critical reflection in Tessa's 'improvising variations' (Diamond, 1997: vii) on her experience, that is 'a powerful instantiation of the role of subjectivity and cultural specificity of artist, viewer, speaker and reader' (ibid.: iv) – in contrast to the role of objectivity, cultural generalization and normative modeling. As a foundation for my aesthetic reconceptualization of play, and for understanding its reflective, self-reflexive and cultural significance for the players, I have illustrated *how* the children explore and reflect upon experience, as they perform in, and move back-and-forth among, the myriad aesthetic functions in the dramatic play medium; *how* they communicate and interact in a continuous, intersubjective interweaving of symbolic expressions and thematic perspectives; *how* they *think* in dramatic form. The children's minds/imaginations are intersubjectively at play in an aesthetic medium. Their dialogic relationship constitutes what can be described as 'mutual influence and regulation', in which 'both partners contribute to the quality of the relationship' (Teicholz, 2001: 12). Teicholz writes that '[. . .] subjectivity (identity) is constantly being shaped by its intersubjective context, while the context itself is being co-created . . .' (Teicholz, 2001: 16). In play-drama, the context itself is being co-created by what the play partners bring with them into their play-culture arena, where each child's subjectivity/identity is '. . . unfixed, unbounded, contextualized and open to mutual influence' (ibid).

My findings support postmodern pedagogical views of children as active subjects who can give voice, construct meaning(s), and transcend normative barriers. Therefore, they can participate, on their own reflective terms, together with adults, as significant members of society. With the distinction between unbound and rule-bound playing, and with findings about the richness of critical reflection in unbound play, I conclude that we should create a pedagogy in which we engage with the children in *paidia*, rather than using *ludus* for 'Project School Readiness'.

Bakhtin's concepts of the dialogic imagination and polyphony provide insight for realizing the goals of such a postmodern pedagogy of play. This would entail teachers and children in play dialogs that actualize differing perspectives on the same situation, critical reflection, and toleration of multiple perspectives (see Dahlberg *et al.*, 1999). In such play dialogs children and adults participate mutually, on their own reflective terms. In part, this could contribute to what Rogers and Evans' (2008) daringly envision with their concept of a co-constructed pedagogy of play. By placing the focus on enriching the children's expressive tools for self-steered meaning-seeking and construction, as well as the time, space and materials for doing so, we contribute to an ethical decolonization of the pedagogy of play (see Dahlberg, *et al.*, 1999; Edmiston,

2008). With evidence of the transformative potential of play-drama for forging both cultural identity and individual subjectivities, I conclude that we have a responsibility, now, to learn how to replace the game approach to play pedagogy with strategies that challenge ourselves to co-experience and co-learning with the children.

References

Bakhtin, M. (1984). *Rabelais and His World*. Indiana: Indiana University Press.

—— (1994). In Pam Morris (ed.) *The Bakhtin Reader*. London: Edward Arnold.

Baumgarten, A. G. ([1758] 1961). *Aestetica* [Aesthetics]. Georg Olms. Hildesham.

Callois, R. (1961). *Man, Play, and Games*. New York: Free Press.

Dahlberg, G., Moss, P., and Pence, A. (1999). *Beyond Quality in Early Childhood Education and Care: Postmodern Perspectives*. London: Falmer Press.

Diamond, E. (1997). *Unmaking Mimesis. Essays on Feminism and Theatre*. New York: Routledge.

Edmiston, B. (2008). *Forming Ethical Identities in Early Childhood Play*. London and New York: Routledge.

Fo, D. (1991). *The Tricks of the Trade*. New York: Routledge.

Gadamer, H. G. (1960/1996). *Truth and Method* (Second Revised Edition). New York: Continuum.

—— (1977/1991). *The Relevance of the Beautiful*. Cambridge: Cambridge University Press.

Gardner, H. (1983). *Frames of Mind: The Theory of Multiple Intelligences*. New York: Basic Books.

Guss, F.G. (2000). Drama performance in children's play-culture, in light of folk-cultural aesthetics. In F. Mouritsen and T. K. Marker (eds), *Tidsskrift for børne-og ungdomskultur* 41. Odense Universitetsforlaget. (Journal on child and youth culture)

——(2005)a. Dramatic playing beyond the theory of multiple intelligences. *Research in Drama Education*, 10(1), 43–54.

—— (2005)b. Reconceptualizing Play: aesthetic self-definitions. *Contemporary Issues in Early Childhood*, 6(3), 233–243.

—— (2008). *Performing and transforming. Children's social life in an aesthetic play mode. www.bin-norden. net* ('Online publikationer') Accessed March 2009.

Mouritsen, F. (1996). *Legekultur. Essays om børnekultur, leg og fortælling* (Play-culture. Essays on children's culture, play and storytelling. Odense: Syddansk Universitetsforlag.

Rogers, S. and Evans (2008). *Inside Role-play in Early Childhood Education. Researching Children's Perspectives*. London: Routledge.

Ryan, S. and Grieshaber, S. (2005). Shifting from developmental to postmodern practices in early childhood teacher education, *Journal of Teacher Education*, 56 (1), 34–45

Schechner, R. (1988). *Performance Theory*. New York: Routledge.

Sutton-Smith, B. (1979). *Play and Learning*. New York: Gardner.

Spariosu, M. (1989). *Dionysus Reborn. Play and the Aesthetic Dimension in Modern Philosophical and Scientific Discourse*. Ithaca: Cornell University Press.

Stern, D. (1985). *The Interpersonal World of the Infant*. New York: Basic Books.

Teicholz, J. G. (2001). The many meanings of intersubjectivity and their implications for analyst self-expression and self-disclosure. In A. Goldberg (ed.) *The Narcissistic Patient Revisited: Progress in Self Psychology*, Vol. 17. New Jersey: Analytic Press.

Wood, E. (2004). Developing a pedagogy of play for the 21st century. In A. Anning, J. Cullen, and M. Fleer (eds) *Early Childhood Education: Society and Culture*. London: Sage.

Chapter 10

Deconstructing the metaphysics of play theories

Towards a pedagogy of play aesthetics

Hae-Ryung Yeu

Introduction

In line with many other Westernized educational contexts, a play-based pedagogy is proposed as the principal approach to teaching young children in South Korea (Korean Ministry of Education, Science and Technology, 2008: 76). However, as in many other countries play-based teaching and learning is not without its problems, including the dichotomized thinking which exists between play and work, and instrumental approaches to teaching, where the value of play is interpreted only as an instrument for learning. Play, then, automatically comes to be viewed from a teleological perspective as a vehicle to get 'there', and therefore the genuine nature of play itself is not understood for its own sake. Within early childhood settings the play/work dichotomy is understood by children themselves (Rogers and Evans, 2008; Wing, 1995) as well as teachers, working in the pragmatic conditions of early childhood classrooms (Bennett *et al.*, 1997). Despite the fact that teachers may agree on the importance of free play they may still express a degree of perplexity, that they might miss something of educational value if the focus is only on the playful aspect. By concentrating our attention only on the surface 'educational' values of play, which lie outside play itself, we may neglect many important aspects which lie inside children's play (cf. Rogers and Evans, 2008). Goldman (1998: 18–47) says that behind our belief in the play/work dichotomy there lies the logic of representation developed throughout the historical traditions of play theories. From this perspective, children's play and an objective reality are seen as united together in a one-to-one corresponding relationship, and the value of children's play comes to be estimated by the degrees of representation. Children's role play is a good example of this. Because of the imitative nature of role play activity, its prime value has been simply assumed to represent adults' roles in an objective reality. Although the representational function is certainly one important element we should consider regarding children's role play, it cannot in any sense exhaust the pedagogical significance of this kind of play in educational settings. Similarly, Huizinga (1955: 2), reflecting on the traditional theories of play argued that 'Most of them only deal incidentally with the question of what play is in itself and what it means for the player . . . without first paying attention to its profoundly aesthetic quality'.

Within current dominant notions of play-based curriculum in early childhood education, play has seldom been understood for its aesthetic quality, which in itself may have pedagogical significance. With this in mind, in this chapter I attempt to deconstruct the logic of representation proposed in classic play theories by tracing back to their epistemological traditions and consider how and in what ways we can discuss the aesthetic quality of children's play in a contemporary context. I will try to highlight the complex, multi-faceted, and dynamic nature of children's role play, as it is manifest in children's living practice. This may lead us to identify ways in which we can re-think the pedagogy of children's play.

Drawing on postmodern aesthetics, freed from the modernist belief in an objective scientism of the subject/object split, I will bring to the fore some of the neglected aspects of children's role play. These include four major points. First, the signified nature of rigidly typified role enactments and the flexibility of meta-communication will be re-examined as they characterize the play to be both closed and open practice for children's meaning-making. Second, I will attempt to interpret children's fun-making trials, such as imitations of educational taboos, and some twists and encroachments on play rules in early childhood settings. These behaviours express how children transgress the limitations of a given reality controlled by educational rules, and how they construct the multiple layers of play by actively bringing the contingent elements of the everyday cultural environment into their privacy of play. Third, I will consider children's self-transformation into context-based storymakers, when some clues of specific identities and contexts are provided by the practitioner in advance through reading of a picture book. Play reality in this vein is a relational practice, a way of experiencing a new mode of becoming. Lastly, I explore some possible directions of a postmodern pedagogy, where our understanding of the aesthetic nature of play goes far beyond the corresponding logic of representation.

Deconstructing the logic of representation in classic play theories

Frost *et al.*, (2001) identify mimesis as one of the three routes (agon, mimesis, and chaos) to understand the human condition in ancient Greece, which enabled human beings to develop certain types of play. The Greeks created the art of 'mimes' to please the imagined behaviours of gods and goddesses. Mimesis in this context was simply the mimic in representational forms of play, but its notion can be extended to the discussion of the world views put forward by the ancient Greeks. Plato in his *Republic* (1941) understood the world as a triplex hierarchy, i.e., the worlds of ideas, original prototypes, of phenomena (and nature), and of arts (Bloom, 1968). Since arts were viewed as nothing but the imitations of the imitations (phenomena) of ideas, they were devalued by its far distance from the world of original prototypes of ideas. Imitative arts, including not only mimicry of the gods and heroes but also poetry and plays, were also devalued by its possible distortion in reflecting the original truths that exist beyond human expression. This Platonic view of mimesis has long been maintained throughout Western metaphysics of idealism.

Plato's concept of mimesis reveals the deeply rooted Western philosophical predisposition, which sets up the correspondence theory of truth as a firm backdrop for all discussion on the truthfulness of things. By means of human language, *logos*, it was made possible that the idealistic metaphysics of presence, as something true and always already there, has governed our gestalt of thinking throughout the Western history. However, the referential function of human language works in order to refer only to itself but not anything that supposedly exists above itself. With the recognition of this self-referential system any supposed foundation or ground like 'original prototypes' or 'ideas' can be deconstructed into a mere effect of differentiation process of signs in which meaning of ultimate referent is always deferred and differed from each other as Derrida's (1982) notion of 'differánce' implies. In this view Plato's concept of mimesis is entirely caught up by the logic of representation in logocentric tradition of metaphysics.

Sutton-Smith (1999) organizes the prominent characteristics of modern theories of play into three rhetorics (progress, imaginary, and self). We can trace in the theories of play another tradition of representational logic within modern metaphysics developed since the seventeenth century. What has been meant by Descartes' turn inward to self, *I*, is that in the cogito moment all knowing is anticipatorily contained, and thereby what is known in advance in this way as the precondition of encounters of the world can be secured as certain (Leder, 1985: 251). Such an elevation of the human subject as a conscious being to all importance in the act of knowing has provided the ultimate justification of the extreme subjectivism powerfully present in today's scientific objectification of the world. In this frame of thinking, arts as play are more than the representation of any transcendental truth as in the ancient Greeks' minds. They come to be rather the mirror reflecting the inner imaginary or consciousness. Freed from the ancient views of play as the mirror of nature or phenomena, play now began to be understood as a different type of mirror reflecting human inwardness (Goldman, 1998). We find here the tacit agreement on their conceptualization of play among modern thinkers and scientists like Piaget (1983), who identified children's play as the representation of inner intelligence. Strong dependence on faithful truth inside human beings is still clearly manifested in this rationalist perspective of play. Play is presupposed to represent its corresponding truth inside human beings.

While the strong influence of Darwin's evolution theory has dominated the areas of human sciences since the nineteenth century, human beings began to be understood in terms of their development following a series of linear and successive stages. Stage theories of human development have been formulated and are widely accepted as the most credible way of demonstrating how children live and find enjoyment, how they grow and perceive the world, problems in their development and growth, and how we could cure them. According to Cannella (2002), discussion on children's growth and education centered around the scientific theories of development as 'regimes of truth' in Foucault's term (Foucault, 1980). Play theories with specified stages of development are good examples of this. But empirical research on children's play shows that such stages are just as imprecice and unnatural, for those stages occur concomitantly (Reifel and Yeatman, 1993).

It can be said that most contemporary play theories share in common the traditions of the Western metaphysics of representational logic in their scientific belief in linear development. Moreover, these theories, presuppose the split between *who* plays and *what* is played as subject/object, and accept play as the representation of children's inner consciousness or intelligence. These perspectives reveal a lack of understanding of what play is in essence. This is evident in recent research on children's role play which shows the unbalanced inclination toward children's cognitive development. We simply believe that the more accurate and refined their imitative performance of reality is in their role play, the more advanced their cognitive development. Children do not, of course, play in order to develop. Rather they play for enjoyment and to be with friends (Rogers and Evans, 2008).

Gadamer (1996: 103) goes far beyond the horizons of either an ancient idealistic or a modern rationalistic conceptualization of play. He suggests that play is not an activity that can be performed and controlled by human subjects. In play there is no subject who plays, since the play is the 'occurrence of the movement' which has its own logic of evolvement, whose 'primordial sense is the medial one' constituting its own structure and making the 'transformation into mediation'. In the play phenomena there is no subject or object. Only play is playing. This process-oriented nature might be the very essence of what play is, that is, the self-evolving movement into somewhere we do not know in advance.

Exploring the aesthetics of children's role play

Role play as a sign system

The most distinctive aspect of role play is that the structure of play scheme centers on a series of already typified concrete actions, which children repeatedly continue whenever and wherever they come to be situated. In an earlier work, I observed that play actions varied in frequency, participants, and play materials used, especially in the case of four-year-old children (Yeu, 2004). Here is an excerpt of mommy/baby play enacted by four-year olds.

Sunah: (Lying down on a mattress with a baby doll in her arm) Baby, Let's take a nap. I am gonna sleep with my baby. Baby, you must be sick. I should make porridge for you . . . (Yejin is lying down next to her.)
Yejin: Mom, I'm hungry (moaning while laughing).
Sunah: Oh, honey. Don't cry. I'll get you delicious milk and take you to a doctor (She gets up, picks up a plastic bowl and brings it up to Yejin's mouth).

(Jul. 15, 2008. four-year-olds, E Daycare)

Mommy here is described as a person who gives comfort, helping baby to sleep, brings food, and takes baby to hospital. Baby is supposed to be 'hungry' or 'sick' waiting for mother's care. As such, children's role play largely consists of the variety of the types of typified behaviours as genre modality, whether they belong to doctor play, teacher play, or market play.

In a sense, these behaviours, on the surface, appear to represent the characteristic elements of adults' roles in an objective reality. Yet we can see that what young children imitate in their play is not simply what they experience or witness in reality. They pick up the most diverse and subtle stimulations from their environment and cultural texts such as storybooks and mass media representations. These are negotiated with peers and solidified into the fictional array of enjoyable actions. In order to be playful actions, their performance should obtain their peers' recognition. When these actions are overly serious by copying exactly the roles in real life, they come to lose their peers' attention as well as fun of play. For instances, a child who tried to imitate the details of his aunt's dentistry treatment on a patient was rejected by his play partners because it was too tedious (Yeu, 2004: 294).

A variety of typified behaviours associated with genres of role play indicate the existence of fixed repertoires. The imitations they express are mostly not what they can imitate from reality, but what they are supposed to imitate. As Goldman (1998) suggests, children do not naively 'pretend to' but rather, 'pretend to pretend'. This tells us that children's role play is a kind of sign system socioculturally constructed. Here we can read the children's participation as symbolic interaction within the sociocultural environment. Genre modality behaviours are indeed the signs drawn from the 'web of metonymy' (Ubersfeld. cited in Kim, 1999) constructed amongst intertextually circulating images in diverse cultural texts. In this complex web of influences, certain play topics, play materials, or role behaviours are linked together and form the signifying chains of each other, evoking interrelated images.

According to such typified actions children's imaginations are locked in the closed-circuits of signification. Because of this closed nature of signification systems, like the self-referentiality of human language systems (Derrida, 1982), actions of genre modality become stereotyped, and thereby call forth only certain simplified images. They do not signify the images of any specific persons with specific identities. They only signify the already circulating images of signs, playing with simulacra with no definite referents to represent. In other words, what a child imitates in her mommy play is not her real mom but 'unspecified' mom (see also Vygotsky, 1978). The meaning of representing my mother is continuously deferred and differed every time he/she plays. Figuratively speaking, such typified actions are the 'signs' of mommy/baby play, market play, or teacher play that children commonly share and utilize to establish the basis of their play reality. Yet the ultimate signifieds do not exist anywhere.

Playing the in-betweenness of meta-communication

Role play is by nature based on the imaginations of certain characters and the performance of their speech and behaviour in fiction. In this sense children's role play can easily be equated to adults' theatrical play. But the unique nature of children's role play lies in fact in a completely different domain from that of adult's theatrical play. Whereas the latter consists of a definite starting point, consistent development of plot and a definite ending point, the former flows in backward and forward movements between reality and fantasy with no definite starting and ending points. As Bateson's (1971) meta-communication theory indicates, children repeat the same scripts and actions over and over again, and construct, deconstruct, and re-construct the frames of imagination by situating themselves in and out of the frames. Accordingly, the dominance of meta-communication is the most distinctive component of children's role play that tells us 'this is the play of childhood not of adults'. This is why meta-communication is not something lying outside play but rather an important part of the play, namely 'metaplay', in which children enjoy the process of 'initiations, responses, and constructions' for play itself (Trawick-Smith, 1998). Here is a piece of meta-communication in the role play of wedding ceremony.

Jiyoung:	Who is gonna be a bride? Me!
Jeongwoo:	Me, bridegroom! (They change in a white dress or in a tuxedo.)
Sangsoo:	I wanna be a baby!
Eunjoo:	Uh, he wants to be a baby?
Hyunjoo:	Let's decide ages. I am an aunt, thirty-three. You [bride] are thirty-two, you [bridegroom] are thirty-five. Baby is one-year old.
Jiyoung:	Jeongwoo, honey! Oh, the baby's gone. Oh, god! . . . Oh, here he is! Don't make *a trouble, baby. Baby shouldn't move!* . . .
Jiyoung:	Who is officiator? (Pointing Minhyeok) You are? Mira can be a bride aid, lifting up the bride's dress. You are the officiator or photographer? Oh, honey! Baby disappeared again! Ah, I found him. You baby, stay just here! Don't move around!

(cited in Yeu, 2001).

Children here assign peers for roles for the wedding ceremony even including the role of baby without having good knowledge of what a wedding meant. They repeat a few times the same actions of searching for the frequently disappearing baby in order to make the play frames solid. They even set up ages and relations for the roles in a completely irrational manner. During the meta-communication, they usually forget to use official languages to partners by using regional dialects and non-honorific expressions, sometimes making conceptual confusions between the play of wedding ceremony with that of mommy/daddy play. Meta-communication in children's role play is the space of openness where they can freely make trial and errors in the process of building the frames of play fantasy. They come and go both in and out of the frames, blurring the boundaries between reality and fantasy, rules and freedom, and the rational and the irrational. Therefore, role play for children is not a linear process like adults' theatrical play that has definite starting and ending points. It is rather a dynamic circular process.

This also shows that children's imaginations in play are not confined to the one-to-one corresponding or representational relationship with reality. Although children's meta-communication may represent the degrees of cognitive development of their inner minds as developmentalists insist, it also indicates that they enjoy exploring an unlimited array of ideas and repetitions of them. It enables children to make and re-make the play, and intervene in any delimited preconceptual boundaries in order to have better make-believe than ever before. Children's role play in this light can be better called 'writerly text' in Barthes'(1987) term, as compared with the closed nature of 'readerly text' where meaning production is already complete. In a writerly text the author continuously writes and rewrites, so that the text is open to change, to go further for better meaning-making. Standing on the very edge of in-betweenness, children learn what it is like to live with the indeterminacy of life and to adventure into an uncertain world. This tells us of the pedagogical importance of role play as a living practice which is open to change and repetition with difference each time it is enacted.

Playing the taboos

Children do not always play only innocent imitations of lovely mommy, or good and kind teacher or doctor. They sometimes radically challenge through play actions the neatly controlled educational mood of classroom settings, especially when teachers' intervention is rare. Some research findings suggest that children challenge and even mock adult authority in play (Corsaro, 2005: 149). Sutton-Smith (1976) found in their play children critically challenged the order of adults' world. They sometimes deconstruct and reconstruct the order of play only for its own sake. Schwartzman (1978) also identified in children's play their trials to test many aspects of the adult world.

The kinds of challenges observed in classroom plays often include children teasing each other using ironical satires, mimicry of adults' pleasure habits like drinking behaviours, circulating the invented humorous play with the tabooed themes like excretion or slang expressions, using play materials in unexpected ways, intentionally speaking regional dialects, etc. (Yeu, 2001; 2004). These play behaviours in most cases appear and disappear in a short time, so that teachers are often unaware of them. But when they are allowed to be played under teachers' thoughtful consideration, they can develop into well-refined play activities of pedagogical significance. In a recent research on classroom play (Suh, 2008), it is reported that children's aggression towards peers were transformed in a period of three months into self-regulated and sophisticated war games. In this classroom, many boys were observed engaging in the mock yet physically wild aggression against each other. Teachers sought ways to positively acknowledge and transform those behaviours into a daily educational project. The project of war games, developed quickly in complexity and scope, satisfying the boys' and girls' natural desire to be 'wild'. This approach also enabled children and teachers to explore values such as mutual care, and cooperation as well as cognitive skills.

Such tabooed play behaviours may look trivial on the surface. But what they imply at a deeper level is that children are not immune from the mundane worldliness of our life environment. Children's life-world and that of adults overlap and intersect each other with inter-penetrating hybridity. Children do not live in a 'vacuum' with angel-like innocence, but they breathe and live the same world as their parents and neighbours. Therefore, some of the 'undesirable' behaviours children imitate might be an honest expression of their life experience. For example, while two five-year-old boys utilized the space of laundry play as a drinking bar and made mimicries of adults' drinking behaviours, they displayed happy smiles with the feeling of privately shared conspiracy and self-contentment (Yeu, 2001). Twisting the codes of hospital play into an unexpected way by putting a syringe into a peer's ear rather than onto an arm, a five-year-old boy violated the play regulations. When the teacher pointed this out, he tried to deny his deed and smiled at his partner with a sense of sharing a secret (Yeu, 1998). We read in these instances the strong feeling of connectedness and satisfaction among children by doing something which lies outside the rules of an educational setting. This is to say, rules exist for children not only to keep but also to violate. Children are always ready to transgress rules with their strong energy and curiosity. Role play offers children a place in which they can make active trials of these contradictory possibilities without guilt, although they also know that their actions will be sanctioned when their violations are noticed by teachers. It is also reported that preschool children reconstruct the teachers' teachings of linguistic socialization in play by humorously mocking them (Ahn, 2008). So, we can say, children play to violate rules as the existence of rules or taboos itself stimulates children to take risks and transgress boundaries.

Children sometimes choose to act in unexpected ways on the basis of their intuitive inclination toward what is good. The unofficial and old-fashioned Korean regional dialects of greetings by a three-year-old girl given to her play partner carried a deep sense of personal intimacy and natural warmth that could not be imitated by official standard languages of greetings (Yeu, 2001: 72–73). She chose the uniquely regional accents and more personalized expressions like those of an elderly lady such as 'Is today cold, isn't it? Is the room warm enough?' and 'Have you eaten a breakfast?' instead of saying 'Good morning' or 'Hello.' Despite her age, she demonstrated her intuitively well developed sense of judging what the language of personal greetings should be.

These instances leave us with the question of whether or not we can draw any clear line between what is educational and uneducational. Since the environment of children's role play in early childhood is surrounded by the existing adults' culture, mass media, and leisure industry, children often bring those mundane worldly elements into their play sites. What they express in play highlights the gap between the play children themselves enjoy and the educational play we adults assume that children would enjoy. They try to create flexible openings between these and make play more complex and multi-faceted. By lifting up and rupturing the rigid logic of play, children bring into the play their interest to deviate from the rules as well as the many voices of others around them.

Playing the concrete situation and transforming oneself

In a daycare in Korea, I recently observed a class of four-year-olds, engaging in role play that was enriched by the teacher's reading of a traditional Korean fairy tale titled

'Kongjwi and Padjwi'. In the story Padjwi and step-mom were characters with negative images of mistreating Kongjwi. After listening to the story, the children willingly participated in playing these characters and later transformed their character enactments into more positive characters (Note the italics in the excerpt later). This suggests that when children are offered alternative identities and specific contexts for stories, they can produce more elaborate play actions with empathic motivation. They also extended the play schemes into different sub-topics, for example, 'Kongjwi and Padjwi in a birthday party' and 'on a picnic'.

Sunyoung [Padjwi]:	(Making a bell ringing sound) Ting-a-ling, ting-a-ling, Hello? (Looking at Hamin) Kongjwi, your friend called. She is coming here soon.
Hamin [Kongjwi]:	Let me make a phone call, sister.
Sunyoung [Padjwi]:	This phone is not working well. You use your own!
Hamin [Kongjwi]:	(Taking a paper phone out of her bag) Tti-tti-tti, are you there, Shiyeon? Come over and wash my dishes with me. I need your help. . . .
Sunyoung [Padjwi]:	You, Kongjwi, Wash out all the dishes by 12 o'clock! *Oh, Hamin-ah, poor Kongjwi, I can help you. We can wash dishes together here (taking Kongjwi into a mock brook made of blue paintings). . . . don't forget your sack and shoes when you go out. The weather is cold.*
Bokung [step-mom]:	*Kongjwi, are you ready to go out? You'd better go out now with some cookies. You can be hungry.* I'll make a birthday cake for you, Padjwi, and then let's go on a picnic.
Sunyoung [Padjwi]:	Let's make a birthday cake, mommy. And then mommy and I will go on a picnic.

(October 22, 2008. four-year-old class, G Daycare)

The aforementioned play episode makes a good contrast with the example of simple repetition of mommy/baby play introduced in the earlier part of this chapter. With the specific names of 'Kongjwi,' 'Padjwi,' and 'step-mom,' children became better informed social actors, finding themselves placed in a concrete situation in which they could write and construct their own personal stories. They become more imaginative in making the play scenario by eagerly bringing many props and concepts into their play schemes, such as phones, friend, cookies, birthday cake, blanket, and picnic. More importantly, they widened and enriched the play schemes by extending their concerns over their play partners. As the class teacher commented:

> Children like to be different personae with concrete names in concrete relations with themselves. One day, I gave them the idea of playing 'my mommy and my daddy' after reading the picture book with the same title. They then began to express in role play lots of hidden stories of their own family life and personal hopes for daddy and mommy.

According to Barthes (1987: 5), interpreting a text as a 'writerly text' is essentially 'ourselves writing'. Through intertextually combining together the plot and the characters of traditional fairy tales with those of their usual mommy play, children were given the chance to be active meaning-makers of the surroundings. Even though Kongjwi and Padjwi was a typical fairy tale emphasizing the value system of rewarding the good and punishing the evil, children's enactments did not simply follow it. They began to 'write' their own narratives and develop personal relationships with peers and play materials. Only partially adopting the characters and rough plots of the tale, they invented a variety of altered versions of Kongjwi and Padjwi. As a result, their play enactments showed rather an eclectic mixture of common value systems different from that of the tale. Girls playing the roles of step-mom and Padjwi, step-mom's own daughter, did not express all the wickedness to Kongjwi but also offered frequent kindness and care at the same time in ambivalent ways. Caring much about others' feeling and attuning themselves toward others' situations, children participated in the active process of rewriting the tale and transforming themselves into more relational beings. The fairy tale provided only some specific clues for them to advance forward. But the children went much further by making concretely contextualized episodes with peers. What they in fact enjoyed in the play seemed to lie not only in the character enactments, simple representations of fixed roles, nor in the imaginations of them. More importantly, they seemed to getting fun out of 'personalising' the tale, stretching out the characters again and again in connection with their own specific situations.

Towards a pedagogy of play aesthetics

Structuralist perspectives developed in past centuries, whether idealistic or scientific, have placed much emphasis on schematic thinking in early childhood education, and evaluated pedagogical practice according to its instrumental rationality. The notion of a play-based curriculum might be one of the best expressions of such rationality. Play in this light is only an auxiliary element for learning, so that the desirable direction of children's play in a classroom is already presumed in advance to follow the pre-specified learning objectives. As a consequence, the complexity of children's play can easily be simplified into a few identifiable components of educational outcomes. Children's role play is indeed an exemplary site of this approach.

As I have discussed, the reality of children's role play reveals a hybridity of real and fantastic, rational and irrational, orderly and disorderly, and sacred and mundane elements. Freely incorporating what is different, uncertain, marginal, or irrational into play, children can practice how to make transgressions across the borders of any given rationality and transform themselves into different modes of thinking and acting. Although the typified genre modality actions confine children's imaginations to a closed realm, there are still flexible spaces created by all mixed and indeterminate nature of children's play. I discussed such flexibility while looking closely at the nature of children's meta-communication, worldly deviations, and situational meaning-making. Children's role play does not evolve in a linear direction like adults' theatrical play, but is rather a circular movement of repeatedly evolving and revolving dynamics that by nature allow many openings for flexible changes and new creations. Pedagogical consideration for children's play should start with our sensitive awareness of such hybrid and dynamic openness rather than solely with its representational logic.

In particular, children's attempts to deviate from play routines need to receive our attention. Unconsciously making fun of or mocking at educational canons behind the teacher's back, children twist, crack, and rupture the taken-for-granted views of a play-based curriculum. We find, in the types of deviations they make, children's play becomes a multi-dimensional reality where they can freely create and get in and out of different layers of meaning-making. Children's motives in play are drawn from multiple sources of their life environment. Everything can be transformed into more than itself and children experience the given reality in dramatically different ways. In this sense, we can re-think the children's humorous trials of educationally tabooed behaviours. For they would be the very signal of children's powerful vitality to make a leap of vision to see hidden possibilities of understanding the world beyond play regulations and educational principles. What children virtually mock at would be our rigid assumptions of what play should be in relation to learning.

Recently applications of poststructualist perspectives, and in particular the concept of the rhizome as an alternative to logic and linearity, are helpful here. Deleuze says:

> Unlike a structure which is defined by a set of points and positions, with binary relations between the points and biunivocal relationships between positions, the rhizome is made only of lines: lines of segmentarity and stratification as its dimensions, and the line of flight or deterritorialization as the maximum dimension after which the multiplicity undergoes metamorphosis, changes in nature.
>
> (Deleuze, 1987: 21)

Rhizomatic thinking here is a type of thinking whose principal characteristics can be expressed in terms of difference, rupture, heterogeneity, multiplicity, and connection. Children's strong vitality to twist and make heterogeneous the play routines could be a powerful momentum to transgress the 'bi-univocal' reasoning of representational logic in play education. Bi-univocal reasoning is nothing but the either/or type of thinking centred on fixed logic. Children's deviations during play could provide the possibility to make further segmentarity and stratification in their making sense of the world, so that they can be in the ever-renewed process of becoming.

In the play episodes cited earlier, we noticed that with the specific contexts and identities provided, children began to create the situational stories with empowered self-vitality, and produced personalized relationships with the roles they played. Rather than simply rerunning the predesignated series of typified behaviours of 'unspecified' mom and daughters, they personalized the roles in relation to those 'specific' names and contexts. They came to be actively engaged in the process of rewriting the stories of fairy tale and became more responsive to situational changes. Yet there were in fact no definite referents for Kongjwi and Padjwi characters since it was only a fairy tale. This means that they remained basically free from the logic of representation whose truth would be only possible under the condition of the original referents' existence. Producing many altered versions of simulacra with no originals to refer to, children enjoyed playing the roles differently every time according to a given situation. Properly responding to, in other words, being 'responsible [response-able] for' play partners and difference of situations (Yeu, 2006), they were in the process of self-transformation into more relational beings well-attuned to the Other. As Guss (see this volume) reports, children in dramatic playing can transform their own selves in the reflective process of *becoming*. This empowerment of children's vitality should be of a central importance in illuminating the future direction of pedagogy of play aesthetics.

Children live not in a self-contained vacuum but in a mundane world full of diverse stories and meanings. Role play by nature is children's narratives revealing the complexity of their life-world. Rather than delimiting the range of our pedagogical concern into narrowly defined educational principles, we as educators need to cultivate the sensitivity to hear what children truly narrate in this or that particular moment of play. Children's reckless trials to make their play reality even more complex and disorderly can sometimes hide in themselves deeply pedagogical strengths. It is because they might lead us into opening our imaginations in order to question which dimensions of the human world can be unfolded by them and what alternative perspectives of play education would be possible in appreciation of their attempts.

References

Ahn, H. J. (2008) '"Please pass me the mustache": reinterpretation and transformation in American middle-class socialization practice', *Korean Journal of Anthropology of Education,* 11(1): 235–53. [in Korean]

Barthes, R. (1987) 'S/Z: an essay' (tr. by R. Miller, preface by R. Howard), New York: Hill and Wang.

Bateson, G. (1971) 'The message "This is Play"', in R. Herron, and B. Sutton-Smith (eds), *Child's play* (pp. 261–66), New York: J. Wiley and Sons.

Bennett, N., Wood, E., and Rogers, S. (1997) *Teaching through play: teachers' thinking and classroom practice.* Buckingham: Open University Press.

Bloom, A. (1968) *The republic of Plato*, New York: Basic Books.

Cannella, G. S. (2002) *Deconstructing early childhood education* (tr. by H.-R. Yeu), Seoul: Changji-sa. [in Korean]

Corsaro, W. A. (2005) *The sociology of childhood* (2nd edition). Thousand Oaks, CA: Sage.

Deleuze, G. (1987) *A thousand plateaus: capitalism and schizophrenia* (tr. and fwd. by B. Massumi), Minneapolis: University of Minnesota Press.

Derrida, J. (1982) *Margins of philosophy* (tr. and notes by A. Bass). Chicago: University Of Chicago Press.

Frost, J. L., Wortham, S., and Reifel, S. (2001). *Play and child development*, Columbus, OH: Merrill Prentice Hall.

Foucault, M. (1980) *Power/knowledge: selected interviews and other writings 1972–1977.* New York: Pantheon.

Gadamer, H.-G. (1996) *Truth and method* (2nd revised edition), New York: Continuum.

Goldman, L. R. (1998) *Child's play: myth, mimesis and make-believe*, Oxford: Berg.

Huizinga, J. (1955) *Homo ludens: a study of the play element in culture*, Boston: Beacon Press.

Kim, D. H. (1999) 'Metaphors and Metonymies', *Korean Journal of Semiotics*, 5: 63–83. [in Korean]

Korean Ministry of Education, Science and Technology (2008) *An explanation of kindergarten curriculum: an general introduction*, Seoul: Ministry of Education, Science and Technology. [in Korean]

Leder, D. (1985) 'Modes of totalization: Heidegger on modern technology and science'. *Philosophy Today*, 29(3): 245–56.

Piaget, J. (1983) *Play, dream, and imitation in childhood*. New York: Norton.

Plato (1941) *The republic of Plato* (tr., intro, and notes by F. M. Cornford). London: Oxford University Press.

Reifel, S. and Yeatman, J. (1993) 'From category to context: reconsidering classroom play', *Early Childhood Research Quarterly*, 8(3): 347–67.

Rogers, S. and Evans, J. (2008) *Inside role-play in early childhood education:researching young children's perspectives*. London: Routledge.

Schwartzman, H. (1978) *Transformations: the anthropology of children's play*. New York: Plenum.

Sutton-Smith, B. (1999) 'The rhetorics of adult and child play theories', in S. Reifel (ed.), *Advances in early education and day care Vol. 10: Foundation, adult dynamics teacher education and play* (pp. 149–62). Stanford, CT: JAL.

Sutton-Smith, B. (1976) *The dialectics of play*, Schorndoff, Germany: Verlag Hoffman.

Suh, K. O. (2008) 'Beyond educational day toward children's day: fragments of relationship, argument, and play'. Paper presented at the Conference of Korean Association for the Reggio Emilia Approach, September 27. Seoul, Korea. [in Korean]

Trawick-Smith, J. (1998) 'A qualitative analysis of metaplay in the preschool years'. *Early Childhood Research Quarterly*, 13(3): 433–52.

Vygotsky, L. S. (1978). *Mind in society: development of higher psychological processes* (14th edition). Cambridge: Harvard University Press.

Wing, L. A. (1995) 'Play is not the work of the child: young children's perceptions of work and play', *Early Childhood Research Quarterly*, 10(25): 223–47.

Yeu, H.-R. (2006) 'Beyond monologue toward dialogue: understanding a pedagogy of responsibility in postmodern perspectives', *International Journal of Early Childhood Education*, 12(2): 29–53.

Yeu, H.-R. (2004) 'Aesthetics of mimesis and creation in children's role play', *Korean Journal of Early Childhood Education*, 24(3): 277–303. [in Korean]

Yeu, H.-R. (2001) 'Children's modes of experiencing role-play activities and their educational meaning: a phenomenological understanding', *Korean Journal of Early Childhood Education*, 21(3): 55–79. [in Korean]

Yeu, H.-R. (1998) A phenomenological study on children's modes of experiencing the educational media environment in free-choice activities', *Korean Journal of Early Childhood Education*, 18(1): 131–52. [in Korean].

Chapter 11

Digital play in the classroom
A twenty-first century pedagogy?

Tim Waller

Introduction

This chapter will critically appraise perspectives on the function and role of digital technology in early years pedagogy, with particular reference to children's play experiences both inside and outside the setting. A range of recent international studies will be drawn upon to analyse the growing appreciation of the impact of digital technology on childhood, children's lives and children's play and communicative practices. However, many children still do not have access to modern technology and the chapter also acknowledges the range of digital divides and the implications for children who are excluded from modern communicative practices.

The use of digital technology by children and young people has been a contentious issue in the media (in the UK and elsewhere), and a number of concerns have been raised over potentially inappropriate material (especially computer games) and the possibility of problematic contact and conduct of children in the digital world. This is compounded by a risk-averse 'culture of fear' (Furedi, 2002) in which some adults are concerned to have much greater control over children's lives and apprehension over rising childhood obesity and sedentary lifestyles (Tovey, 2007). One consequence for research in the field is that 'most of the research on computer and video games has focused on possible negative influences and the evaluation of policy designed to minimise risk to children and adolescents' (Salonius-Pasternak and Gelfond, 2005: 6).

Conversely, a number of recent reports in the UK have taken a more positive view. For example, *The Digital Beginnings Report* (Marsh, Brooks, Hughes, Ritchie and Roberts, 2005) found that most parents believed that digital technologies would play a significant role in their children's education and future careers, and the majority encouraged and supported their children's early experiences for this reason. Similar findings were reported in the *The Good Child Inquiry* (The Children's Society, 2007) and *The Byron Review – Children and New Technology* (Byron, 2008) which recognised the popularity and range of opportunities for enjoyment, learning and development that digital technologies provide children and young people.

However, the relationship between digital technologies and play is 'under-theorised' (Plowman and Stephen, 2005: 154) and there is a clear need to comprehend how the accelerating technological change in our daily educational and working lives impacts on both play and teaching and learning in the early years classroom. The chapter therefore considers recent research on the impact of digital technology on play in the early childhood classroom. Further, the chapter critically reflects on a number of possible tensions between these recent developments, 'traditional' pedagogy and practice in early childhood and children's digital play experiences outside school.

Finally, an example of how pedagogy can be transformed by children's perspectives of play revealed through the use of digital technology is discussed. Drawing on evidence from an ongoing research project conducted in the UK which focuses specifically on play in outdoor environments, the chapter explores possibilities for developing and documenting young children's narratives through digital technology. It asks what teachers can learn from children's play experiences with new digital technology.

The impact of digital technology on childhood, children's lives and children's play and communicative practices

Digital technology is now a significant part of many children's everyday lives and as McPake *et al.* (2007) point out, children grow up as part of an 'e-society' in which digital connectivity (use of the internet, mobile phones and other interactive technologies) is essential to daily life. Consequently, from birth many children across the world are immersed in a way of life where this digital technology is used for a range of complex cultural, social and literacy practices (Marsh, 2007). These practices, which are constantly changing, include using a range of hand held devices such as mobile phones, multimedia players (iPods) and games consoles, playing interactive games on digital and satellite television and accessing the internet to communicate images and text, hold telephone conversations and play games with participants across the world. Currently, social network websites (shared databases of photographs which facilitate group discussion) and blogging (contributing to online web diaries) are very popular, but as the technology develops new and different communicative possibilities and practices will evolve (Waller, 2008).

It is clear therefore, that many young children develop dispositions and competences with and through digital technology in the context of social interaction with their families and peers. For example, Marsh (2007) describes a number of cases which show that mobile phone use was firmly part of some families' communication practices with their young children, including the children's involvement in texting. Indeed, the BECTA (2006) survey of access and use of digital technology found that social interaction with peers, friends and family is emerging as the major driver for children's increasing use of Information and Communication Technologies (ICT). As Beastall (2008) surmises there can be little argument against the claim that (a significant number of) children and young people now have an advanced relationship with technology that has been developed right from birth.

Given that many children are immersed in a world where digital technology is increasingly used for a range of social and communicative practices it is inevitable that they will incorporate this technology in their play. As Wood (2009: 37) argues, 'play can be seen as a social practice that is distributed across a range of contexts and co-participants and is influenced by the tools and symbols of community cultures'.

Here key a question needs to be posed: is play with and through digital technology the same as play in other contexts or is play transformed by the context? Also, what are the features of digital play that make it different from non-digital play? Salonius-Pasternak and Gelfond (2005: 6) assert that, computer play is, perhaps, 'the first qualitatively different form of play that has been introduced in at least several hundred years . . . it merits an especially careful examination of its role in the lives of children'.

The main focus of research conducted on digital technology so far has concentrated on the use of computers by older children and young people and not with the range of digital technologies or with children under five. Despite these concerns four factors are evident from recent studies. First, it is clear that many young children develop significant competence with technology at home well before they attend an early years setting or school (Marsh *et al.*, 2005). Prensky (2005) developed the term 'digital natives' to describe the generation who have grown up with digital technology and 'digital immigrants' to refer those who have not. Similarly, Lankshear and Knobel (2004) use the phrase 'digitally at home' to describe a generation comfortable with and competent in the use of new technologies.

Prensky (2005) argues that these 'digital natives' think differently from other generations due to the types of technology they have been exposed to and the ways in which they exposed to these technologies. For digital natives, ways of acting and being in the social world are framed by their experiences with the technology. This involves not only the exploration of buttons on devices such as a remote control or mobile phone, but crucially, interacting in social worlds where devices are used for communication and young children re-construct this in their play. For example, I recently observed my grandson Hari aged 18 months playing with a mobile phone by exploring the buttons, pretending to have a conversation by holding the phone to his ear and talking and rushing to answer the phone when it rang. He also regularly incorporates an old disabled phone (that is part of his toy box) in his play. Yelland (2007: 11) makes an important point here when she observes that 'in much of the literature technologies are regarded merely as tools'. Yelland cites Castells (1996) who contends that technologies are also processes that affect how we can make sense of the world and communicate our views to others about it.

Second, children's play and participation in the use of digital technology helps to transform cultural, social and literacy practices (Marsh, 2005) and third, young children are deliberately targeted by global software and games manufacturers (Verenikina *et al.*, 2008). Finally, as Zevenbergen (2007) and McPake *et al.,* (2005) point out, exposure to such digital tools creates different experiences and orientations to learning and thinking and offers significantly different ways of playing from what had been possible in non-digital worlds.

Verenikina, *et al.* (2008) argue that for many children digital play and, in particular, computer games are a significant part of their daily experience. This experience has recently been given much greater recognition within an emerging literature, which they review. They draw attention to numerous studies that examine the value of computer play for learning and discuss arguments that this experience can impact positively on their academic achievements. Verenikina *et al.* (2008) conducted research (in Australia with children aged 5 to 7) to investigate the affordances and limitations of computer games and the features of children's traditional play that can be supported and further enhanced by different kinds of computer play. Usefully, they provide a classification of computer games according to game characteristics that support higher order thinking. Verenikina *et al.*(2008) showed that the games involved in the research afforded young children plenty of opportunity explore the environments in imaginative and make-believe ways, both within the games and beyond them to their everyday play. Interestingly, this research suggests that make believe play is at its best when children participate as a group.

Additionally, Plowman and Luckin (2003) who studied the use of interactive 'smart' toys by children aged between four and eight at home and in school, found that social interactions were significantly increased for the children participating in the research with the 'smart' toys. Consequently Plowman and Luckin argue that 'this increase in social interactions around technology is an appealing contradiction of the popular belief that technology leads to reduced socialisation' (2003: 2). As a result of their research, Verenikina *et al.* also argue that computer games do not necessarily constrain children's play to movements pre-determined by the game designer and that 'while it is possible that some games do inhibit imaginative play, the games chosen for the study appeared to enable developmental play in often unintended ways' (2008: 7).

Further, as Zevenbergen (2007) has pointed out, new and emerging play experiences are not restricted to digital media as there is an ever increasing amount of supporting matter. For example, many games are supported by television programmes, magazines, websites, trading cards and movies. As a result, children and young people have many worlds to explore that are separate but linked to these virtual games. Also Yelland (2007: 55) argues that, 'for young children the linking of three dimensional play things or television or movie characters with computer software provides a valuable context for learning that should not be underestimated'.

There is, however, much research to be done in order to distinguish the conditions under which computer games best facilitate play and higher order thinking in very young children (Verenikina *et al.* 2008) and to also to identify the features of digital play that make it different from non-digital play.

The range of digital divides and the implications for children who are excluded from modern communicative practices

Whilst it is clear that an increasing number of young children grow up immersed in technology and are 'digital natives' or 'digitally at home', it must be acknowledged that many children still do not have access to modern technology, both within the UK and across the world. This acknowledgement is informed, in the first instance, by a more straightforward position concerning economic digital divides. As Waller (2008) argues, there is not one, but multiple digital divides caused and reinforced by global capital's control of new technologies. There are clear divisions based on class, 'race', gender, age and geography. For example, in a current world population of six billion, less than one billion people have regular access to computers. In wealthy countries there are 563 computers per 1000 people but in less wealthy countries only 25 per 1000 people (Social Watch, 2008, *data available to 2005 only*). In the UK there is evidence of a class, race and gender based access and use of ICT, both at home and at school (Waller, 2008). Also, Zevenbergen (2007: 24), citing Judge *et al.* (2004), argues that in the American context there is a polarised use of technology, 'where schools serving Black, Hispanic and low socioeconomic status [SES] students have tended to have the lowest access to, and the most remedial uses of technology'.

However, McPake, *et al.* (2005) discovered a more complex pattern in their investigation of the impact of socio-economic disadvantage on pre-school children's development of ICT competences at home. They found it difficult to establish the impact of socio-economic disadvantage due to the complexity of the family contexts studied. Their research showed that parental attitudes and experiences and children's own interests and preferences have a greater influence on the development of early digital experiences than socio-economic disadvantage.

Recent literature has also identified a possible division between digital experiences and play at home and those in the early years setting and school. Zevenbergen (2007) explores the implications of young children's dispositions towards the use of digital technologies in contemporary early childhood settings. Drawing on Bourdieu's (1993) concept of habitus, she contends that young learners come to early childhood settings with a 'digital habitus', which is differently constructed in the home environment and needs to be considered in early childhood practice. Bourdieu (1993) uses the construct of habitus which is defined as being 'the embodiment of culture that provides a lens for seeing and acting on the world' (Zevenbergen, 2007: 20).

A further important divide, as Marsh (2007) and Facer *et al.* (2003) note, is that patterns of technology use are different from patterns of access. Some children have access to a range of digital technology at home but either chose not to use it, or it is used solely by the adults in the house.

Therefore, it is argued in this chapter that a more sophisticated understanding of the digital divides is necessary, as learning to participate in a 'networked society' involves using both economic and, cultural and social capital, to effectively engage with technology in a meaningful way. Castells (2001: 3) contends that 'exclusion from these networks is one of the most damaging forms of exclusion in our economy and in our society'. It is likely that many young children across the world will not necessarily have the opportunity to participate in social and cultural practices in which they will become 'digital natives' or 'digitally at home' and be able to draw on 'digital habitus' in their play and learning.

Recent research on the impact of digital technology in the early years classroom.

Whilst there is an international recognition of the potential of digital technology to create new learning experiences and environments for play, this has not been realised in the classroom and working digitally outside real time and space is an 'advantage that is as yet an untapped resource' (Beastall, 2008: 109). Findings from McPake *et al.* (2005), BECTA (2006) and Zevenbergen (2007) suggest that many pre-school and primary practitioners have limited knowledge of children's home experiences of digital technology and that, whilst they acknowledge the potential benefits, are therefore not in a position to build on these competences. As Beastall (2008) notes, although many children are ready for the digital era and e-learning, practitioners may need more strategic and pedagogical support in order to ensure the most appropriate use of technology in the classroom.

Yelland (2007: 51) summarises the beliefs of many early childhood educators that permeate curricula and pedagogy as involving 'the best conditions for learning are found where there is active learning, inquiry, and problem solving, whereby children are engaged and curious in their explorations'. Play is seen as a key aspect of learning and fostering positive dispositions, well being and confidence. However, there is also a belief that play and explorations are best kept within the real world and 3-D objects. For example, Zevenbergen (2007: 25) discussed a scenario where a group of children are playing cricket on an *XBOX*. The children's parents did not view this as 'play', but as Zevenbergen points out, the children's concept of play was different to their parents. The digital habitus of young boys allowed them to create a very different view of play than their non digital parents.

Three significant implications of this situation are apparent in recent literature. First, in order to enable young children to participate in 'authentic' forms of social practice and meaning (Lankshear and Knobel, 2004), early years settings and schools need to incorporate children's digital play experiences from home into the curriculum. Second, as children have differering levels of access and experience of new technologies at home (Plowman *et al.*, 2010) it becomes vital that schools equip children, at all levels, with the appropriate experiences and competences in the use digital technologies (Waller, 2006a). Third, there is a further significant *critical* role for the educational use of digital technology. The 'critical' dimension means that teachers and students need to be able to assess and critically evaluate software and other technology resources (Lankshear and Snyder with Green, 2000; McPake *et al.*, 2005).

There is therefore a strong argument that the role of the teacher changes as a result of the introduction of new technologies into the classroom. This new role includes providing opportunities and contexts to exploit the potential of children's experience of digital technology in the wider community. Teachers need to know their children's capabilities and interests, to understand how to organise their classroom and to structure the teaching of their children so that digital resources become an integral part of the learning (Waller, 2006a). Luke (1999) and Yelland (1999, 2007) maintain that the use of digital play opportunities can strengthen everyday teaching and learning in early childhood classrooms. Waller (2006a) contends that long-established play and literacy activities in early years classrooms can now be complemented with different experiences that have been made possible with the new digital technologies. These technologies, and the activities that children may engage with, have the potential to extend learning in new and exciting ways and strengthen everyday literacy teaching and learning in early childhood classrooms.

Two recent overviews of the international literature on digital technology in early childhood education are provided by Plowman and Stephen (2005) and Yelland (2005) and they suggest that we know little about the ways in which children react to and interact with the technology available in the early years setting. Most of the studies reviewed focused narrowly on how computers, rather than the range of digital technologies, support learning. The studies also acknowledge that this restricted view of technology was also evident in practitioners' planning, curricular and pedagogy. Further, almost all the studies concerned the application of the computer to curriculum areas (such as Maths) and did not relate to play. Plowman and Stephen (2005: 154) point out that although a relationship between play and learning is well established, this relationship is 'under-theorised with respect to uses of computers'. In one of the few reported investigations of classroom play involving computers Brooker (2002) studied children in a multicultural context in London. She observed that the technology acted as a catalyst for social interaction, mutually supportive collaboration in their problem solving and socio-dramatic play. Brooker concluded that 'the manipulation of symbols and images on the computer screen represents a new form of symbolic play, in which children treat the screen images as "concretely" as they do the manipulation of any alternative blocks and small-world toys' (2002: 269).

Plowman and Stephen (2005; 2007) studied early years settings in Scotland and reported little evidence that computer play acted as a support for learning. Typically, they found that children's use of computers usually took place during periods of 'free play' – where children could chose from a range of activities. Here children's interactions with the computer were frequently referred to, by adults and children, as 'playing with the computer' in the same way as they would talk about playing with construction or small world toys. There were few examples of adult involvement in computer based play, although practitioners intervened to ensure turn-taking and were observed occasionally making notes for records and the assessment of children's progress with technology. Noticeably, Plowman and Stephen found that, whilst there was explicit scaffolding of learning in other curriculum areas, it was absent in relation to children's play with computers. If early years teachers are expected to play alongside children to support their ideas and extend their thinking (Wood, 2009; DfES, 2007), then surely this role also includes play with digital technology? (See, for example, *Practice Guidance for the Early Years Foundation Stage* DfES, 2007b: 81–82).

Zevenbergen (2007: 20) therefore proposes that early childhood education be reconceptualised so as to incorporate notions of digital play in order to sustain and support the *habitus* of the children now entering the range of early childhood services, arguing that 'If the emergence of young children into the early childhood settings is to be seen differently as a consequence of their highly digitised home experiences, then the implications for practice are profound'.

An example of how children's use of digital technology can transform pedagogy

An example of transformative practice with digital technology is discussed briefly later in relation to an Outdoor Learning Project (see Waller, 2008). The project involves children aged 3 to 7 years in two different settings: a nursery school in England (Setting 1) and a primary school in Wales (Setting 2). The children are given regular access to extensive wild outdoor environments (such as woodland, riversides, mountains and beaches) and are afforded the opportunity to explore and play in the environment with minimal adult direction and intervention. The design of the project draws on the framework for listening to young children – the multi-method 'Mosaic approach' described by Clark and Moss (2001; 2005). The method uses both the traditional tools of observing children at play and a variety of 'participatory tools' with children. These include taking photographs, book making, tours of the outdoor area and map making (see Waller, 2006b and 2007).

Two examples from the project are now briefly discussed to illustrate the role and process of digital technology in transforming early years pedagogy. For the children (and adults) involved in the project, digital technology was used for two distinct purposes. First, children incorporated the technology into their play. For example, Ben aged three years was encouraged to film his favourite places in the country park. He had played with the digital camera and explored the camera functions on the bus journey to the park.

> Ben asked to use the video camera; he picked it up and turned it on. He then
>   walked up the path past a large open meadow.
> I am trying to find dinosaurs. Ssh Ssh. You have to be very quiet.
> That looks like where I play football with Mathew—he's my older brother.
> He then walked up the path towards the woods.
> You have to be very quiet to look for dinosaurs.
> After several minutes of filming, Ben put the camera down on the ground.
> This camera is too heavy now.
> He ran over to the wood and picked up a stick.
> The researcher then picked up the camera (for safe-keeping). After another two
>   minutes or so, Ben returned to the place he left the camera. He waved to his
>   friend Declan on the other side of the park and put his thumbs up. Then he
>   said,
> Let me look through the camera to see if I can see any dinosaurs.
> Ben looked through the viewfinder of the video camera,
> See here—it's fantastic, you can see them right over there. Look—it's pointing
>   that way.
> He put the camera down again and picked up his stick.
> This is to beat dinosaurs up with. Found some nearby dinosaurs.
> Ben ran off into the woods waving his stick in the air.
> Ssh. Only I can talk!
>   [From field notes reported in Waller, 2006b: 91–92]:

Second, the digital technology supported the distribution and extension of the narratives children developed in their play. For example, Gulpham aged 4 found an orange plastic pipe (used to build drains) in the woods [video and field notes]. He picked it up and started kicking it along the ground like a football. This incident was filmed both by another child and an adult on video and digital cameras. Gulpham took the pipe back to school and the images were viewed by a group of children on the electronic whiteboard. Consequently, a narrative about 'Bob the builder' developed which led to the construction of a builder's yard as an imaginative play area in the classroom. On the next visit to the woods, Beckham aged five found a knotted piece of wood which resembled a drill and he pretended to use it as, together with Gulpham and others, he played 'builders'. Once more Gulpham brought the pipe to the outdoor environment and along with the 'drill' and other artefacts this was used frequently as the narrative developed over a number of months. Shortly before the end of the school year Gulpham's family relocated to another part of the country and his mother informed me that he had taken the orange pipe to his new house and school.

Here, the model of interaction adopted was one where practitioners co-construct knowledge with a group of children (see also Waller, 2007). This pedagogy gives children the opportunity to play a central role in revealing their own priorities for interpretation with adults. Children can engage in (digital) play that is meaningful to them, whilst at certain times adults may also learn from children without a formalised agenda. In this space we can learn from the meanings that children ascribe to their different environmental experiences, e.g. the 'dinosaur land' and 'Bob the builder', as discussed earlier. In the process of 'making the space their own' the children developed enduring shared narratives around the specific locations in the outdoor spaces. These narratives were also supported and possibly enhanced by the adults as co-constructors. The role of digital technology was significant in that it was used as play (Yelland 2005, 2007) and also to reveal, distribute and reify narratives developed through children's play.

The potential of this model to be a *transformative* pedagogy (Larson and Marsh, 2005) is found in two key components; the willingness of the adults to build on children's digital experiences and involve the children as experts and engage in, support and reify their play activities. As Wood (2009) observes, play activities create transformational possibilities: children can reproduce and go beyond what is given. For Vygotsky, 'A child's play is not simply a reproduction of what he has experienced but a creative re-working of the impressions he has acquired' (Vygotsky, 2004: 11, in Siraj-Blatchford 2007: 16). When children use digital technology in their play it is possible that new and different forms of play may be created because the technologies offer extended opportunities for meaning making and representation that are different to other play contexts (Wood 2007). Whilst much attention at policy level is given to the technology, it is children, teachers and parents who hold the key to supporting and promoting the digital play emerging from contemporary communicative and social practices.

A transformative pedagogy is one where children's interests and intentions are revealed in their (digital) play and reified through the publication of pedagogical documentation aided by the technology. As Rogers and Evans (2007) argue, pedagogy tends to be defined principally from the adults' perspective with less attention to how children respond to and make sense of pedagogical practices within the contexts of their play. In the model outlined here, children are continually involved in the process through the co-construction of a pedagogy which is constantly evolving.

Conclusion

The chapter posed a key question concerning whether play with and through digital technology is the same as play in other contexts, or is play transformed by the context? Clearly, a research agenda needs to be developed around the impact of these social conditions on play and the potential for learning. Much further research needs to be undertaken with young children to establish the features of digital play that make it different from non-digital play.

The chapter has argued that recent literature and research in the field of digital technology and early childhood education has a firm message about pedagogy and practice in schools. If practitioners are to develop a *transformative* pedagogy (Larson and Marsh, 2005) then they will need to build on children's digital and online play experiences and involve the children as experts. However, there is also a clear need for much further critical reflection, discussion and articulation of possible models of classroom practice, particularly in relation to early childhood (Lee and O'Rourke, 2006). A significant aspect of pedagogy in early childhood involves teacher-child interaction and, as Plowman and Stephen (2005: 155) argue, 'if practitioners do not support computer play through guided interaction children will not fully benefit from using the technology in the early years setting'. The Outdoor Learning Project discussed briefly at the end of the chapter has shown that digital technology was significant in that it was used as play (Yelland 2007) and also to reveal, distribute and reify narratives developed through children's play. The role of the adults in guiding interaction, documenting, distributing and extending narratives with children through digital technology was seen to be crucial.

The challenge is for early years practitioners to do more with digital technology than use it to enrich or bolt onto traditional curriculum practices (Marsh, 2007; Knobel and Lankshear, 2007). As a result Thomas (2005) argues that professional development in digital and cyberliteracies for teachers is essential. Much further research is needed to inform pedagogy and practice in the use of digital technology in early childhood settings and particularly with children under three, as Aubrey and Dahl (2008) contend.

Much of the literature reviewed in this chapter considers school as a problematic site for play and learning with digital technology. Alternatively, Kent and Facer (2004) argue, there are already a number of ways in which children and young people's informal and formal learning experiences with digital technologies are coinciding and supporting each other both in the home and the school. Further exploration of this process might be most fruitful for further research to inform early years pedagogy, particularly in relation to digital play.

References

Aubrey, C. and Dahl, S. (2008). *A review of the evidence on the use of ICT in the Early Years Foundation Stage*. Coventry: BECTA. Available: http://partners.becta.org.uk/upload-dir/downloads/page_documents/research/review_early_years_foundation.odt. [Accessed 4 December 2008].

Beastall, L. (2008). 'Enchanting a Disenchanged Child: Revolutionising the Means of Education Using Information and Communication technology and e-Learning'. *British Journal of Sociology of Education*, 27 (1): 97–110.

British Education Technology Association (BECTA) (2006). *Evidence on the Progress of ICT in Education*. Coventry: Becta.

Bourdieu, P. (1993). *Sociology in Question*. London: Sage.

Brooker, E. (2002). *Starting School: Young Children Learning Cultures*. Buckingham: Open University Press.

Buckingham, D. (2005). *Schooling and the Digital Generation: Popular Culture, New Media and the Future of Education*. Professorial lecture at the Institute of Education, University of London, October.

Byron, T. (2008). *Safer Children in a Digital World* (Byron Review – Children and New Technology). London: DCSF Available: http://www.dcsf.gov.uk/byronreview/ [Accessed 10 October 2008].

Castells, M. (1996). *The Rise of the Network Society*. Oxford: Blackwell.

—— (2001). *The Internet Galaxy. Reflections on the Internet, Business, and Society*. Oxford: Oxford University Press.

Clark, A. and Moss, P. (2001). *Listening to Young Children: The Mosaic Approach*. London: National Children's Bureau.

—— (2005). *Spaces to Play: More Listening to Young Children Using the Mosaic Approach*. London: National Children's Bureau.

Department for Education and Skills (DfES) (2007a) *Curriculum Guidance for the Early Years Foundation Stage*. Available from www.standards.dfes.gov.uk/resources/downloads [Accessed 13 May 2008].

—— (2007b) *Practice Guidance for the Early Years Foundation Stage*. Nottingham: DfES.

Facer, K., Furlong, J., Furlong, R. and Sutherland, R. (2003). *ScreenPlay: Children and Computing in the Home*. London: RoutledgeFalmer.

Furedi, F. (2002). *Culture of Fear: Risk Taking and the Morality of Low Expectations*. London: Continuum.

Judge, S., Puckett, K., and Cabuk, B. (2004). Digital equity: New findings from the Early Childhood longitudinal study. *Journal of Research on Technology in Education*, 36(4): 383–96.

Kent, N. and Facer, K. (2004). 'Different worlds? A comparison of young people's home and school ICT use'. *Journal of Computer Assisted Learning*, 20(6): 440–55.

Knobel, M. and Lankshear, C. (eds) (2007). *New Literacies Sampler*. New York: Peter Lang.

Lankshear, C. and Snyder, I. with Green, B. (2000). *Teachers and Technoliteracy: Managing Literacy, Technology and Learning in Schools*. St Leonards, Sydney: Allen and Unwin.

Lankshear, C. and Knobel, M. (2004). Planning pedagogy for i-mode: from flogging to blogging via wi-fi, published jointly in *English in Australia*, 139 (February): 78–102 and *Literacy in the Middle Years*, 12(1): 78–102.

Lankshear, C. and Knobel, M. (eds) (2008). *Digital Literacies. Concepts, Policies, Practices*. New York: Peter Lang Publishing.

Larson, J. and Marsh, J. (2005). *Making Literacy Real*. London: Sage.

Lee, L. and O'Rourke, M. (2006). Information and communication technologies: transforming views of literacies in early childhood education. *Early Years*, 26(1): 49–62.

Luke, C. (1999). 'What next? Toddler netizens, playstation thumb, techno-literacies'. *Contemporary Issues in Early Childhood*, 1(1): 95–100.

Marsh, J. (2005). 'Ritual, performance and identity construction: Young children's engagement with popular and media texts'. In J. Marsh, (ed.) *Popular Culture, New Media and Digital Technology in Early Childhood*. London: RoutledgeFalmer. 28–50.

—— (2007). 'Digital Beginnings: Conceptualisations of Childhood'. Paper presented at the WUN Virtual Seminar, 13th February. Available: www.wun.ac.uk/download.php?file = 2488_Childrenpaper13Feb.pdf&mimetype = application/pdf. [Accessed 11 August 2007].

Marsh, J., Brooks, G., Hughes, J., Ritchie, L. and Roberts, S. (2005). *Digital Beginnings: Young Children's Use of Popular Culture, Media and New Teachnologies*. Sheffield: University of Sheffied. Available: http://www.digitalbeginings.shef.ac.uk/. [Accessed 15 March 2006].

McPake, J., Stephen, C., Plowman, L., Sime, D. and Downey, S. (2005). *Already at a Disadvantage? ICT in the Home and Children's Preparation for Primary School*. Coventry: BECTA.

McPake, J., Stephen, C., and Plowman, L. (2007). *Entering e-Society. Young Children's Development of e-Literacy*. Stirling: Institute of Education, University of Stirling. Available: www.ioe.stir. ac.uk/research/projects/esociety/ [Accessed 12 November 2008].

National Statistics (2008). Internet Access: Households and Individuals. Available: http:// www.statistics.gov.uk/StatBase/Product.asp?vlnk = 5672. [Accessed 4 December 2008].

Plowman, L. and Luckin, R. (2003) Summary of research: Exploring and mapping interactivity with digital toy technology. Futurelab conference paper Digital Childhoods: The Future of Learning for the Under 10s. Robinson College, Cambridge, March 2003.

Plowman, L. and Stephen, C. (2005). 'Children, play and computers in pre-school education'. *British Journal of Educational Technology*, 36(2): 145–58.

—— (2007). 'Guided interaction in pre-school settings'. *Journal of Computer Assisted Learning*, 23: 14–26.

Plowman, L., McPake, J. and Stephen, C. (2007). *Young Children's Learning with Technology at Home and in Pre-School*. American Educational Research Association conference,Chicago, April 2007.

Plowman, L., Stephen, C. and McPake, J. (2009) *Growing up with Technology: Young Children Learning in a Digital World*. London: Routledge.

Prensky, M. (2001). *Digital Game-based Learning*. New York: McGraw-Hill.

—— (2005). Digital Natives: How they think differently. Available: http://coe.sdsu.edu/eet/ articles/digitalnatives//start.htm [Accessed 11 February 2006].

Rogers, S. and Evans, J. (2007) 'Rethinking Role Play in the Reception Class'. *Educational Research*, 49(2): 153–67.

Salonius-Pasternak, D. E., and Gelfond, H. S. (2005). The next level of research on electronic play: Potential benefits and contextual influences for children and adolescents. *Human Technology*, 1(1): 5–22.

Siraj-Blatchford, I. (2007). 'Creativity, Communication and Collaboration: The identification of pedagogic progression in sustained shared thinking'. *Asia-Pacific Journal of Research in Early Childhood Education*, 1(2): 3–23.

Social Watch (2008). *Information, Science and Technology. Digital Gap, People Gap*. Available: http:// www.socialwatch.org/en/informeImpreso/pdfs/informationsciencetech2006_eng.pdf. [Accessed 4 December 2008].

The Children's Society (2007). *Good Childhood Inquiry*. London: GfK NOP (Job No: 451311).

Thomas, A. (2005). Children Online: learning in a virtual community of practice. *E–Learning*,

2 (1): 27–38.

Tovey, H. (2007). *Playing Outdoors*. Maidenhead: Open University Press.

Verenikina, I., Herrington, J., Peterson, R. and Mantei, J. (2008). 'The affordances and limitations of computers for play in early childhood'. *Proceedings of the World Conference on Educational Multimedia, Hypermedia and Telecommunications*, Vienna, Austria, 3–4 June, 2008.

Vygotsky, L. (2004). 'Imagination and creativity in childhood'. *Journal of Russian and East European Psychology*, 42(1): 4–84.

Waller, T. (2006a). 'Early Literacy and ICT'. In, M. Hayes and D. Whitebread (eds) *ICT in the Early Years of Education*. Milton Keynes: Open University Press. 36–53.

—— (2006b). 'Be careful – don't come too close to my Octopus Tree': Recording and evaluating young children's perspectives of outdoor learning. *Children Youth and Environments*, 16(2): 75–104.

—— (2007). 'The Trampoline Tree and the Swamp Monster with 18 Heads': Outdoor Play in the Foundation Stage and Foundation Phase. *Education 3–13 35 (4): 395–409.*

—— (2008). 'ICT and Literacy'. In J. Marsh and E. Hallett (eds) *Desirable Literacies: Approaches to Language and Literacy in the Early Years* (2nd Edition). London: Sage.

Wood, E. (2007). 'New directions in play: consensus or collision?' *Education 3–13*, 35 (4): 309–20.

—— (2009). 'Developing a pedagogy of play'. In, A. Anning, J. Cullen and M. Fleer (eds), *Early Childhood Education: Society and Culture* (2nd Edition). London: Sage.

Yelland, N.J. (1999). 'Technology as Play'. *Early Childhood Education Journal*, 26(4): 217–25.

Yelland, N. (2005). 'The future is now: A review of the literature on the use of computers in early childhood education (1994–2004)'. *AACE Journal,13*(3): 201–32.

—— (2007). *Shift to the Future: Rethinking Learning with New Technologies in Education*. New York: RoutledgeFalmer.

Zevenbergen, R. (2007). Digital natives come to preschool: Implications for early childhood practice. *Contemporary Issues in Early Childhood, 8*(1): 18–28.

Chapter 12

Taking play seriously

Liz Brooker

Introduction

From certain perspectives, the first decade of the twenty-first century seems to be a time when play, as an early childhood pedagogy, has finally come of age. Across the English-speaking world at least, the pedagogy of play is now enthroned in early childhood curricula; increasingly it has the stamp of approval of national governments and international agencies, policymakers as well as providers, parents as well as practitioners. A key battle of recent decades – establishing young children's 'right' and 'need' to play in a world which gave more value to traditional didactic instruction – appears to have been won. Children, a cynic might argue, are now *required* to play, in the cause of learning, whether they want to or not, though the suggestion that children may not always want to play is hardly voiced. In this climate then, a chapter proposing that we should *take play seriously* may seem itself to be seriously out of touch with its times. But I wish here to raise some persisting questions about the relationship of play to pedagogy, and about both the playfulness and the seriousness of young children's engagement in learning.

The chapter first outlines the current fragile consensus on play, before discussing some of the issues which arise from this: issues of culture and diversity, of power and pleasure, of home and school pedagogies, and of the work/play dichotomy. It concludes by discussing some examples of young children's self-initiated and serious play in early childhood settings, and the challenges which these play behaviours offer to conventional understandings of the play/pedagogy nexus.

The state of play

The persistence of play perspectives from the eighteenth century in the twenty-first century world of early childhood research and practice is a remarkable testament to the power of ideologies to outlast the circumstances that produced them – particularly since these beliefs now co-exist with other, often contradictory, perspectives on play. 'Romantic' views of play, originating with the philosophers of the Enlightenment but embedded in Western culture by means of the Romantic poets, are closely linked with the equally persistent Romantic constructions of childhood, which co-exist, similarly, with alternative and contradictory constructs. As Hendricks (1997) has shown, 'the child' in Western societies has passed through many phases and assumed many guises in the last two or three centuries, including a major shift in roles from a worker (who contributes to society through his or her labour) to a scholar (who receives the benefits of schooling provided by society). Yet the pre-school child continues to circulate in Western thought as a rosy-cheeked innocent who should be protected from the encroachments of adult anxieties and uncertainties; and the role of this child is still, on the whole, to play. Pellegrini and Boyd (1993: 105) described play as 'an almost hallowed concept for teachers of young children', and the adjective is apt. In Cannella and Viruru's formulation: 'Virtually all early childhood educators . . . espouse play as a sacred right of childhood' through which children achieve wellbeing (1997: 124). The type of play that is referred to here – hallowed, sacred – is the play described by psychologists (Smith 2006); it is characterised by spontaneity, pleasure and a lack of constraints or external goals; it is 'fun', the kind of experience William Blake ([1789] 1977) described in his images of children 'laughing on the green' until called in by their nurse. And it was institutionalized, as a principle if not as a practice, by the early educators: in Froebel's 'garden' where children could bloom and blossom under the kindly care of a 'mother made conscious' (Steedman 1988) and in Montessori's 'children's house' where children could follow their own interests and inclinations, and have charge of their own miniaturised world (Montessori 1967). Both the idea of play as the most important 'work' of young children, and the environments provided for children's play, have remained remarkably unchanged in many respects (Anning 1997), despite the dramatic changes which have re-shaped most Western societies.

Although the work of Bennett *et al.* (1997) exposed the gap between the rhetoric of 'learning through play' and the limited reality of 'teaching through play', the underlying premise, that early childhood educators can and should harness children's play towards adult learning objectives, is rarely challenged. In recent years the goal of perfecting a 'play pedagogy' – in other words, of discovering the most effective means to enable children to access the learning objectives of adults through their own pleasurable engagement in play activities – has come ever closer. Studies such as the Effective Provision of Preschool Education (EPPE: Sylva *et al.* 2004) and Researching Effective Pedagogy in the Early Years (REPEY: Siraj-Blatchford *et al.*, 2002), have provided evidence of 'what works' in this respect. Their findings have prompted, at a policy level, a recipe for early learning which is designed to enable those groups of children who have traditionally achieved less well to access the same chances as more privileged children. REPEY demonstrates that 'effective' settings achieve a balance between teacher-initiated tasks and 'the provision of freely chosen yet potentially instructive play activities' (Siraj-Blatchford *et al.*, 2002: 43). Yet it is not clear how children's 'free' choice of activities is guided, or how their participation can turn a 'potentially instructive' activity into one which achieves the curriculum objectives targeted by practitioners.

At the time of writing, therefore, practitioners are offered two apparently contradictory conceptions of young children's play: the play that is spontaneous and goalless ('free play') and the play that is planned and regulated to meet curricular objectives ('educational play'). This seems to be only the first of the problems of play.

Problematising play

The difficulties of defining play have been discussed for decades, despite the provisional consensus provided by Rubin *et al.* (1983). The challenge is a real one: how can a description be devised of a behavioural phenomenon that occurs in infants of seven months (Lillard 2006) and children of seven years (Van Oers 2010); in Australian kindergartens (MacNaughton 2009) and in Sudanese villages (Katz 2004); in homes, peer groups, preschools and schools in every society and culture? Common sense tells us that children's play behaviours change as they progress from infancy to middle childhood. Sociocultural theory (Rogoff 1990) tells us that these changes are linked to socioeconomic and cultural influences in their environments, as well as to biological and physiological factors. It follows that any description of what a play-pedagogy would look like must begin with 'it depends. . . .'

Cultural and structural variables

The variability of the environments for play, and the messages children hear about play from adults, is neatly demonstrated in a recent study (Göncü *et al.* 2006) of parental beliefs and behaviours in three poor communities – inner-city African Americans; rural European-Americans; and villagers from in the mountains of western Turkey. The study was prompted by concerns (e.g. Fleer 1999) that a great deal of empirical research has pointed to the apparent deficiencies and poor quality of the play of low-income children; and by a hypothesis that the roots of these 'deficiencies' lay in children's early communications from adults about the value of play in their communities. The cultural differences between parental messages, Göncü points out, are not arbitrary but derive from local socioeconomic factors: as earlier studies have shown (Göncü *et al.* 2000), families living in subsistence economies view children's activities, including play, in very different ways from those in communities even a little way above subsistence. In this study the parents in all three communities approved of their children's naturally-occurring play but none felt there was any need to 'encourage' their children to play, and all were to some extent concerned that play might distract their children from study, household chores or economically essential labour. The authors confirm that play is 'a supported activity of childhood in the low-income communities', but recommend that 'theories of children's play should be situated in children's context, taking into account unique dimensions of children's specific communities' (Göncü *et al.* 2006: 175).

In Göncü *et al.*'s (2006) study the children in both the American communities owned some toys, however poor the household, but families in the Turkish community, who were closer to subsistence levels, did not buy toys. Toys are not, of course, a pre-requisite for playing, as we know from cross-cultural studies. In *Growing Up Global*, Katz (2004) documents in great detail the ways that children in a Sudanese village community construct their play scenarios ('house', 'store' and 'fields') from scraps of straw, twigs, seeds and discarded food containers. Girls and boys, mostly in single-sex but cross-age groups, dedicate hours to developing their chosen scenarios

– dressing the twig dolls, ploughing the handkerchief-sized fields, bartering the carefully harvested crops of pebbles and seeds – and put away their treasured play props carefully at the end of each session ready to renew the game the next day once their work in the 'real' household or fields is over.

In this community play is not regarded by adults as a vehicle for learning, let alone the principal mode of learning. Yet the play described by Katz offers all the features we look for in observing children's educational play in the preschool settings of more affluent societies: intense involvement and engagement; high levels of motivation and persistence; collaboration and negotiation; problem-solving and planning (cf. Laevers and Heylen 2003; Siraj-Blatchford 1999). The tutoring of peers or 'more experienced others' in this study offers a textbook demonstration of a child's, or group's, Vygotskyan-style progress across their individual and collective zones of proximal development. The children's self-imposed or group-imposed 'rules' are aligned with the community's need for members who can participate in the activities which are essential for survival, and which if skilfully learned may improve their prosperity. The learning, however, is accomplished spontaneously and effortlessly, although the children's engagement is serious rather than playful. How can we draw comparisons between experiences like these – voluntarily entered into in the available time left when goat-herding and other chores have been attended to – and the tightly planned, resourced and evaluated play which is increasingly prescribed in early childhood curricula in the English-speaking world?

Pleasure and power

The association of play with pleasure is another problematic area. The notion that play is, or should be, pleasurable for children, is one of the key arguments proposed in its favour despite the fact that it has been repeatedly undermined. Vygotsky ([1933]1976) offered an early critique of the idea, most persuasively through a demonstration that the pleasure of play depends on the presence of constraints to action, rules which must be kept, the subjugation of individual wishes to the premises of the activity, and a host of other specific difficulties. In choosing to play, children simultaneously 'adopt the line of least resistance' and 'act on the line of greatest resistance' ([1933] 1976: 548):

> . . . by subordinating themselves to rules, children renounce what they want, since subjection to rule and renunciation of spontaneous impulsive action constitute the path to maximum pleasure in play . . . Play continually creates demands on the child to act against immediate impulse.
>
> (Vygotsky, 1933)

The constraining rules, Vygotsky emphasises, are properties of all play and not simply of the 'games with rules' described by Piaget as typical of school-age children's play: 'there is no such thing as play without rules', and imaginative or pretend play is rule-bound, just as surely as 'every game with rules contains an imaginary situation in a concealed form' ([1933] 1976: 541–43). Far from following their unconstrained impulses, children who play are constructing an edifice of constraints which, in making play more difficult, makes it more worthwhile.

An alternative critique of the simple association of play with pleasure is offered by more recent commentators, particularly through an analysis of the intimate association of play with power and domination. MacNaughton (2009), presenting a critical constructivist perspective on early childhood experience, describes four 'conditions of power' that constrain children's meaning-making in early childhood settings, and demonstrates that none of the free choices made by children or their educators is in any sense 'free' since the only choices available to us are those permitted by the discourses we have come to inhabit: 'Our meanings are constrained and constructed in and through the dynamics of power . . . Through processes of normalisation and regulation we come to learn that certain ways of thinking are normal, natural and preferred' (2009: 57). The force exerted by normalising discourses is illustrated here by an account of a small boy's effort to re-engineer the gender stereotypes available to him, but is also present in modes of being which are too deeply ingrained for us to perceive without a conscious effort. It is the task of critical constructivism, as MacNaughton argues, to 'explore the effects of cultural and structural positions on how and what children can and do know and learn' (2009: 60).

Re-phrasing only slightly, we might want to explore the constraints on *how and what (and why)* children are permitted to play in early childhood educational settings, in which apparently 'cognitive' tasks are frequently privileged over rough-and-tumble, and boys' self-initiated play is more likely to be frowned upon than that of girls. When children's spontaneous play ideas are compared with adult-provided educative play, it is clear whose agenda dominates. Adults' power over children in such settings, masked though it is by a discourse of kindness and affirmation, invitations to play rather than coercion to join in, shapes children's conceptions of their world, leading them towards a stance in which compliance is balanced by resistance (Rogers and Evans 2008). Equally importantly, it shapes the ways that educators relate to young children, and thus their whole professional and personal identity.

Discourses of power also underpin the important critiques of Cannella and Viruru (1997) and Ailwood (2003). The former link the pedagogy of freely-chosen child-initiated play with the universalising and normalising account of children's development which they see as permeating early childhood education. Citing Burman 'Child-centred pedagogy is just as coercive as traditional approaches but in more subtle ways' (1994: 70), Cannella and Viruru argue that play is a form of instruction which has been privileged as in some way respectful towards children, as well as promoting democracy and equality. Ailwood's critique goes further, arguing that play is a governing technology which subjugates children and parents, adults and institutions, with its plausible rhetoric of children's needs, rights and wishes. As she concludes (2003: 297), we can affirm the importance of play to children at the same time as being 'vigilant about the circumstances and discourses through which play's vital place has been produced' – and its place in pedagogy.

Problematising the pedagogy of play

Cultural beliefs: how do children learn?

The dominant discourses of Western early childhood environments may mask the fact that the close association between play and pedagogy which is taken for granted in English-speaking and European-heritage societies is an alien idea for many other societies – including the minority communities whose children attend our schools and preschools. Outside the Western-influenced world, the notion that children's freely-chosen play will promote their academic achievement can seem nonsensical (see Gupta this volume).

Tizard's (1977) report of parents' perspectives on the activities provided in nursery and infant schools was an early warning of the incomprehension that persists in many communities to this day. She describes the gulf in understanding, even after an intervention to involve parents, between teachers, who believed that water play taught children mathematical concepts, and parents who saw their children 'just filling bottles' (1997: 16). Decades later, the All Saints' study (Brooker 2002) described the rather similar experiences of sixteen children from both Bangladeshi and English families in one English Reception class. The study demonstrated that concerns about play still exist for many working-class families, and especially for parents whose own upbringing was outside the UK. As one mother implored:

> She has to work harder, you have to stop her playing . . . every day, play, 'what did you do?' – 'play', then after school – play; Monday, Tuesday, Wednesday – play . . . she has to stop playing!
>
> (Minara, Bangladeshi mother)

The range of views expressed by parents in this study formed a continuum; some English mothers accepted that play was a useful preliminary to school learning:

> yeah, the school's fine: even if they play now, you know they're going to learn in the end.
>
> (Gaynor, African-Caribbean mother)

> I think the school's OK, they have to learn to play before they learn to work.
>
> (Maisie, white UK mother)

Others covertly taught their children more didactically at home:

> We work with him constantly on letters and numbers . . . cover the pictures so he reads the words . . .
>
> (Charlotte, white UK mother)

Although many parents expressed some ambivalence over the school's methods, there was a clear polarisation between the views of 'Anglo' parents (those who were educated in the UK) and Bangladeshi parents, who received their own education in

Sylhet. Whereas the Anglo parents were vaguely sympathetic to the notion of learning through play, the Asian parents were not persuadable. Their own culturally acquired discourse (what Bruner, 2006, calls a folk pedagogy) would not admit such patently foolish ideas. The evidence of their own school experience, and of their pedagogic work with their children, confirmed that 'learning' requires both explicit teaching, by adults or older siblings, and hard work on the part of the learner. To suggest otherwise was nonsense.

But the learning-through-play which greets parents and children in a typical English reception class, and which may appear to prioritise *play* over learning, from other perspectives appears to place an undue emphasis on *learning* rather than play. In the Nordic countries for instance (Wagner and Einarsdottir 2006), practitioners are reluctant to view the kindergarten years as an induction period for the school curriculum, and most reject the term 'preschool' with its connotations of 'preparation for school'. The historical accident which provided universal elementary education for 5-year-olds in England from 1870 (Woodhead 1989) had no equivalent in most European countries (Bertram and Pascal 2002). In the Nordic nations, a typical daycare for six-year-olds may still offer a whole day's freely-chosen activity, indoors and out, with little requirements for formal learning or assessment (Wagner and Einarsdottir 2006). Within these comparative contexts, it could be argued that the English-speaking world's search for an effective pedagogy of play fails to take play seriously at all.

Taking play seriously: what about work?

Another problem arising from this focus on play as the appropriate activity for children is the concomitant repudiation of the idea of work. Physical labour, including economic labour, was the lot of almost all children until the mid-nineteenth century, and remains the lot of most of the world's children today (Woodhead 2007). There is a danger in romanticising such labour, however picturesque and carefree the goat-herding or basket-weaving may appear in photographs: there were good reasons why the industrial nations legislated to remove children from the hazardous world of work, and why, in the name of schooling, many developing societies are undertaking the same process (Woodhead 2004). But there is a danger too in viewing the concept of 'work', in all its forms, as anathema for small children, and this includes the 'work' of learning those things which have to be learned through an effort of practice, memorisation, and 'getting it wrong'. Teachers of 4-year-olds know that there are many children who ask for 'work', usually designated as sums or writing, when invited to play, and many others whose greatest pleasure apparently lies in sorting and tidying equipment, washing tables and sweeping sand in the classroom. Why should we be surprised that children, like adults, gain satisfaction from identifying a task and tackling it, solving a problem, creating order out of chaos – and that these pleasures are not confined to play activities?

It could be argued that early educators, keen to distinguish their own approach from the pedagogy of primary classrooms, have overlooked young children's love of work – or have disguised it with semantic formulae. The tradition, from Montessori and Isaacs, of describing play as a child's work is still upheld (see Paley 2004: *A Child's Work: the Importance of Fantasy Play*) but this sleight of hand both obscures the issues and fails to address the real questions: how should we identify, in any contexts, the activities that are important, developmental and meaningful for preschool children? Left to themselves, will young children follow such a pattern of activities? What do children's 'interests' really look like?

This last question is important because the early childhood rhetoric of 'following children's interests' may assume that children are only interested in childish things (toys, games and children's TV and media outputs) whereas, as Wood points out, their interests 'are often driven by their fascination with the world of adults, and their motivation to act more knowledgeably and more competently' (2009: 37). The segregation of children's worlds – whether the 'playrooms' of Scotland or the 'play-schools' of Iceland (Stephen *et al.* 2001, Wagner and Einarsdottir, 2006) – from the intergenerational world outside the nursery, makes such interests increasingly difficult to identify and to support. Without the research of cross-cultural theorists (Rogoff 1990; Göncü *et al.* 2000) it would be easy to forget that, for most of human history, small children have played and learned alongside older children and adults, through the process defined by Rogoff herself as 'participation in cultural activities': through 'guided' or 'intent' participation, in a gradual apprenticeship into the world of experts which builds on 'young children's eagerness to be involved' (1990: 18).

Whose culture, whose activities?

The cultural worlds introduced to Western readers by writers such as Rogoff, Göncü and Katz – Guatemala, Turkey, Sudan – appear integrated and organic, though complex. When we return our attention to the cultural worlds of western children we are faced at once with a multiplicity of co-existing or conflicting cultures: those of school and home, neighbourhood and nation, peers and other reference groups, as well as the media. Adopting Rogoff's definition of learning, as the transformation of participation in cultural activities, poses a particular problem when applied to early childhood settings, where the culture may be one of innocence, and the principal 'cultural activity' is play. Learning to participate in play is important, and recent research has clearly demonstrated the importance of acquiring these transferable life-skills (Broadhead 2001). But it is debatable whether a cultural environment which has been systematically disconnected from the world of adults – a Disneyworld of fun and fantasy – can contribute to children's development as participants in their community and the wider society, where the serious business of responsibilities requires continuous negotiation.

Children behaving seriously

I conclude by offering small snapshots of some two-year-old children's activity in their nursery setting – activity which defies categorisation as play-which-is-not-work, or even work-which-is-not-play, but which I would describe as both serious and purposeful.

Jack's sandpit activity

Jack, a child of mixed English and African heritage, had recently settled into the Toddlers (two-year-olds') area in his local children's centre, where he was a member of a small key-group (three children and a key worker) within a room accommodating twelve children in all. The toddlers had free access to their own garden once all the children had arrived, and the parents departed, in the morning, and Jack was in the habit of spending much of the day out of doors unless the weather was really wet or windy. Jack's mother reports that he has no garden at home, so the nursery is his first opportunity to spend time in this way. This brief observation could have been replicated on almost any day during the early weeks of his attendance.

Jack is alone in the middle of the sandpit. He spends some time carefully filling a large bucket using several spades, and then heaves it with considerable effort, and with two hands on the handle, to the edge of the sand pit and then over the low wooden fence onto the tarmac. He then climbs over himself with difficulty and heaves at the bucket again to carry it across the tarmac to the tree garden; he continues to drag the bucket round the garden, stopping for breaks, and at last shows it to an adult, apparently telling her what he has done. She tells him to take the bucket back to the sandpit and he does so, painstakingly.

He continues working in the sandpit for another ten minutes, using three plastic digger trucks to make a route or roadway across the sand, then carefully lifts each truck over the fence on to the tarmac, where he lines them up in a row.

An activity of this kind is so normal in our nurseries as to be all but invisible. But what is Jack doing and why? He appears to be purposefully engaged in a job that 'needs doing' (an 'imaginary situation' in Vygotsky's terms) and he works hard for 20 minutes, on his own, to achieve his objective. He does not appear concerned at being told to take the sand back, after all the effort of delivering it, because the pleasure or purpose of the activity is in doing it rather than in any outcome, and he moves immediately into another facet of the task (road-building?). If we describe Jack's activity as *play* (because it is spontaneous, pleasurable, without external goals or rules) we may ignore the seriousness implied by his solemn demeanour and concentration. If we try to identify his *learning*, we could tick a check-list about gross and fine motor skills but might ignore the important dispositions which underpin his planning and persistence. If we were to observe Jack undertaking similar activity alongside another adult (probably a male relative) we would be more likely to describe his activity as an apprenticeship to the appropriate activities in his local culture, or an effort to construct his identity within his local context. In the absence of such clues to interpretation, we watch and wait for Jack to demonstrate the meanings this activity has for him.

Yuk Yue in the kitchen

Yuk Yue, a little girl of Chinese heritage, joined the nursery in the same month as Jack, but belonged to a different key-group in the Toddlers area. For the first few weeks of her attendance she played at cooking, but her cooking, like Jack's outdoor work, appeared to be so serious and focused that 'playing' seemed an inadequate description. Here is one example.

Yuk Yue returns from the sand table to the home corner, searches in the cupboards and oven and comes back to the sand holding a wooden bowl; she holds the bowl out towards Davey who co-operatively fills it; then she takes it to give to a child at the table and after some 'giving' activity, removes it to the home corner and puts it in the oven. She finds a plastic spoon in the oven and retrieves and examines it; she announces, 'That sticky, that sticky' but no one responds because all are busy. She comes to me to give me more plastic food from the home corner (a steak, an onion, toast and an apple). By now there is a lot of sand in the home corner on the cooker and the floor, and she becomes very busy spreading it around on the cooker hob, and dumping more plastic food on top. She becomes so involved that at one point she pushes me out of the way quite forcefully to establish her place at the cooker-top.

Why is this activity so serious for Yuk-Yue? How does she understand the activity she initiates and pursues with such concentration? In Yuk Yue's case, her mother is able to offer further information on the little girl's remarkable planning and persistence – or possibly her coping strategies as she started nursery:

> She puts all her tea cups, her doll's set, because this is her favourite, in her bag, and she takes with her, that is her human being survival way: she thinks it makes her belong so she took that to nursery and she's happy! I say, Yuk Yue you can take it with you but you play with the nursery one, and she does that, but it is for belonging, for comfort. I didn't ask her but she just say Mummy, I like it . . . and then she takes back; because another thing, her sister and brother have their bag to go to school, maybe she thinks, that is my bag.
>
> (field notes; Parent interview)

Yuk Yue has formed a plan – taking her tea set to and from school in her back pack, but playing with the nursery equipment while she is there – which appears to have meaning for her. She works hard for many hours each day in the home corner, bringing plastic food or sand to the cooker, cooking it with careful inspections and constant stirring, and either delivering it to others in the room or simply dumping it before moving to the next task.

It is hard to establish Yuk Yue's own meanings with regard to play, work or learning, but her key worker does use her apparent interest to bond her with her key-group through shared cooking activities which require her to pass things to the other two children, and collaborate with them in stirring and spooning. Adult learning objectives for two-year-olds typically prioritise early skills in making relationships and communicating ideas and wishes, and Yuk Yue's integration into the nursery room is rapidly accomplished. But does she identify her own activity as play; as work; or is she simply building an identity for herself in this new and strange environment (hard work in itself)?

Taking children seriously

These somewhat enigmatic examples offer partial answers to the questions posed earlier: they illustrate what children do in an environment which supports them in their self-chosen learning journeys – as individuals, and as members of a range of cultural groups, including peer groups. In many respects these two children's 'play' resembles the cultural activity of the Sudanese children described by Katz: gathering the resources to carry out repeated, well-planned, careful rehearsals of activities common in the social world they inhabit outside the nursery. We might conclude on the basis of these observations that, rather than prescribing and structuring play activities directed towards the learning objectives of the curriculum, we need only to offer children spaces in which they can undertake activities which are important and meaningful to them, and resources which enable them to fulfil their intentions, in their own way and in their own time.

Both Jack and Yuk Yue have brought to the nursery the 'interests' which they have acquired in their early experiences of cultural activity in the family; because they are still very young, their key workers are content to watch, wait and take their cue from these interests. With increasing mediation from the adults and children around them, and from the cultural resources of the indoor and outdoor spaces, both children have opportunities to increase their participation repertoires, hone their skills, and move from being peripheral members of the group to full membership. Such apparently optimal conditions for development may not be offered, however, to children who are three, or four, and in the UK are rarely offered to five-year-olds attending school. Despite the recent moves towards play-based curricula (in Northern Ireland the Enriched Curriculum (Walsh *et al.* 2010); in Scotland the Curriculum for Excellence (Stephen 2010); in Wales the Foundation Phase (Maynard and Chicken 2010)), the curriculum content in all four countries is prescribed by statutory frameworks, and the pedagogy of play is directed to meeting adult-imposed targets.

Perhaps now is the time to acknowledge that we need a new term to describe the activities-based, adult-inspired and 'potentially instructive' tasks which practitioners so diligently and creatively organise for the children in their classrooms. We could then return 'play' to its original status as an activity which is voluntary, goal-less, spontaneous – but which for children is entirely serious.

References

Ailwood, J. (2003) Governing Early Childhood education through play, *Contemporary Issues in Early Childhood*, 4 (3), 286–99.

Anning, A (1997) *The First Years at School* [second edition] Buckingham: Open University Press.

Bennett, N., Wood, E. and Rogers, S. (1997) *Teaching Through Play*, Buckingham: Open University Press.

Bertram, T. and Pascal, C. (2002) *Early Years Education: An International Perspective*. London: QCA.

Blake, W. ([1789] 1977) *Songs of Innocence and Experience, in Collected Poems*. Harmondsworth: Penguin.

Broadhead, P. (2001) Investigating sociability and co-operation in four and five year olds in reception class settings, *International Journal of Early Years Education*, 9 (1), 23–35.

Brooker, L. (2002) *Starting School: Young Children Learning Cultures*, Buckingham: Open University Press.

Bruner, J. (2006) *In Search of Pedagogy, vol 2*. London: Routledge.

Burman, E. (1994) *Deconstructing Developmental Psychology*. [second edition] London: Routledge.

Cannella, G. and Viruru, R. (1997) Privileging Child-Centred, Play-based Instruction, in G. Cannella (ed.) *Deconstructing Early Childhood Education*, New York: Peter Long

Fleer, M. (1999) Universal fantasy: the domination of Western theories of play, in E. Dao (ed.) *Child's Play: Revisiting Play in Early Childhood Settings*, Sydney: Maclennan & Petty.

Göncü, A., Mistry, J. and Mosier, C. (2000) Cultural variations in the play of toddlers, *International Journal of Behavioural Development*, 24 (3), 321–29.

Göncü, A., Jain, J. and Tuermer, U. (2006) Children's play as cultural interpretation, in A. Göncü and S. Gaskins (eds) *Play & Development. Evolutionary, Sociocultural and Functional Perspectives*. NJ: Lawrence Erlbaum Associates.

Hendricks, H. (1997) The construction and reconstruction of British Childhood: an interpretative survey, 1800 to the present, in A. James and A. Prout (eds) *Constructing and Reconstructing Childhood: Contemporary Issues in the Sociological Study of Childhood* (2nd edition) London: Falmer.

Katz, C. (2004) *Growing Up Global: Economic Restructuring and Children's Everyday Lives*. Minneapolis: University of Minnesota Press.

Laevers, F. and Heylen, L. (eds) (2003) *Involvement of Children and Teacher Style*. Leuven: Leuven University Press.

Lillard, A. (2006) Guided participation: how mothers structure and children understand pretend play, in A. Göncü and S. Gaskins (eds) *Play & Development. Evolutionary, Sociocultural and Functional Perspectives*. NJ: Lawrence Erlbaum Associates.

MacNaughton, G. (2009) Exploring critical constructivist perspectives on children's learning, in A. Anning, J. Cullen and M. Fleer (eds) (2004 first edition) *Early Childhood Education, Society, Culture*. London: Sage

Maynard, T. and Chicken, S. (2010) Through a different lens: exploring Reggio Emilia in a Welsh context. *Early Years*. 30 (1), 29–39.

Montessori, M. (1967) *The Discovery of the Child*, [tr. J. Costelloe], New York: Ballantine Books.

Oers, van, B. (2010) Children's enculturation through adult guidance in the context of play activities, in L. Brooker and S. Edwards (eds) *Engaging Play*. Maidenhead: Open University Press.

Paley, V. G. (2004) A *Child's Work: The Importance of Fantasy Play*. Chicago: University of Chicago Press.

Pellegrini, A. and Boyd, B. (1993) The role of play in early childhood development and education: issues in definition and function, in B. Spodek (ed.) *Handbook of Research on the Education of Young Children*, New York: Macmillan

Rogers, S. and Evans, J. (2008) *Inside Role Play in Early Childhood Education*. London: Routledge.

Rogoff, B. (1990) *Apprenticeship in Thinking: Cognitive Development in Social Context*. Oxford: Oxford University Press.

Rubin, K., Fein, G. and Vandenberg, B. (1983) Play, in E. Hetherington (ed.) *Manual of Child Psychology: Socialization, Personality and Social Development* (vol 4), New York: Wiley.

Siraj-Blatchford, I. (1999) Early Childhood pedagogy: practices, principles and research in P. Mortimore (ed.) *Understanding Pedagogy*, London: Paul Chapman.

Siraj-Blatchford, I., Sylva, K., Muttock, S., Gilden, R. and Bell, D. (2002) *Researching Effective Pedagogy in the Early Years*, DfES, London: DfES research report 356.

Smith, P. (2006) Evolutionary foundations and functions of play: an overview, in A. Göncü and S. Gaskins (eds) *Play & Development.Evolutionary, Sociocultural and Functional Perspectives*. NJ: Lawrence Erlbaum Associates.

Steedman, C. (1988) 'The mother made conscious': the historical development of a primary school pedagogy, in M. Woodhead and A. McGrath (eds) *Family, School and Society,* Sevenoaks: Hodder & Stoughton.

Stephen, C., Brown, S. and Cope, P. (2001) Alternative perspectives on Playroom Practice, *International Journal of Early Years Education*, 9 (3), 193–205.

Stephen, C., (2010) Pedagogy: the silent partner in early years learning, *Early Years, An International Journal for Research and Development*, 30 (1), 1–14.

Sylva, K., Sammons, P., Siraj-Blatchford, I. and Taggart, B. (2004) *Final Report of the EPPE Project*. London: Institute of Education.

Tizard, B. (1977) 'No common ground?' *Times Educational Supplement*, 2 May, 15–16.

Vygotsky, L. [(1933) 1976] Play and its role in the mental development of the child, reprinted in J. Bruner, A. Jolly and K. Sylva (eds) *Play: Its Role in Development and Evolution*. Harmondsworth: Penguin.

Wagner, J. and Einarsdottir, J. (2006) Nordic Ideals as reflected in Nordic Childhoods and Early Education, in J. Einarsdottir and J. Wagner (eds) *Nordic Childhoods and Early Education*, Greenwich CT: Information Age Publishing.

Walsh, G., McGuinness, C., Sproule, L. and Trew, K. (2010) Implementing a play-based and developmentally appropriate curriculum in Northern Ireland primary schools: what lessons have we learned? *Early Years, An International Journal for Research and Development*. 30(1) (forthcoming).

Wood, E. (2009) Developing a pedagogy of play, in A. Anning, J. Cullen and M. Fleer (eds) (2004 first edition) *Early Childhood Education, Society, Culture*. London: Sage.

Woodhead, M. (1989) School starts at 5 . . . or 4 years old? The rationale for changing admission policy in England and Wales, *Journal of Education Policy*, 4: 1–22.

—— (2004) Psychosocial impacts of child work: a framework for research, monitoring and intervention, *International Journal of Children's Rights*, 12(4), 321–77.

—— (2007) Harmed by work or developing through work? Issues in the study of psychosocial impacts, in B. Hungerland, M. Liebel, B. Milne and A. Wihstutz (eds) *Working to be someone: Child Focused Research and Practice with Working Children*. UK: Jessica Kingsley, 31–42.

Index

abstract thinking 63
action vocabularies 114
actions with objects 64
activity 37
activity-based learning 82
'addressivity' 49
adult-determined goals for play 9
aesthetics of play 12, 112; 126–37; knowing and 115–16; v play-movement 113; role play 129–35
affective dimension of play 12
Africa 73–83; pedagogical implications 81–3; play and ECE in Africa 77–9; play and enculturation in 74–7; policy implications 80–1
agon (competition) 114
aisthanomai 115
alea (chance) 114
ambiguous power 24
analytical interpretations 117–21
Anglo-Saxon models 77
'answerability' 49
apartheid education 79
apprenticeship 75
Ashanti region of Ghana 77
'assign and rotate' 11
'auction' 11
Aurobindo, Sri 93
autonomy 32

Bakhtin, Mikhail 49, 50, 51, 52
'balanced compliance' 15
barriers to implementing play 43
barriers to play 40–2
barriers to play-based pedagogy 82
Basic Education approach 89
bi-univocal reasoning 136
blogging 140

boundaries of inclusion and exclusion 16
'Bridging Period Programme' 79
Byron Review, The – Children and New Technology 139

cameras as a data generation method 28
Carnival 116
child-centred teaching 94
child-centricity 94, 97
child-directed play 32
child labour 158
childhood obesity 139
children behaving seriously 159–61
choice 32, 37, 97
citizenship 97
classroom management as barrier to play 41
cognitive 'de-centering' 63
'cognitive learn as you play' regime 15
collaboration 155
colleagues as barrier to play 41
colonial curriculum 89
colonialism 87, 97
comprehensive assessment 95
computer games 139
'conditions of power' 19–22, 156
'conflict of interests' 5–16
Confucianism 105
consciousness, relational view of 51
constructivist approaches to play 39
continuum from free play to structured play 10
control 12
cooperative learning 82
correlations 66
correspondence theory of truth 128
creativity 9
cultural beliefs 157–8, 159
cultural understandings of children 26

cultural variables 154–5
Cultural-Historical Psychology 60
Cultural-Historical Theory 62
culturally embedded concept, play as 74
'culture of fear' 139
culture, play, early childhood education
  practice and 81
curriculum: assessment and 40; expectations
  as barrier to play 40; play-based 162; in
  South Africa 78; in South Australia 35;
  subject-based 33; tools of the mind
  68–70
Curriculum for Excellence (Scotland) 162
'curriculum kits' 107
cyberliteracy of teachers 148

'de-centering' 63
decision-making skills 95
decline of play 66
deliberate behaviours 63
Derrida, Jacques: notion of 'differánce' 128
Descartes: turn inward to self, *I* 128
design 77
developmental discourses of play 38
Developmentally Appropriate Practice
  (DAP) 34, 86, 100
Dewey, John 93
dialogic imagination 112, 123, 124
'dialogic' struggle 49
dialogizing discourses in position-play 55–7
Digital Beginnings Report, The 139
digital divide 142–3
'digital habitus' 143
digital literacy, teacher 148
'digital natives' 141, 142, 143
digital play in the classroom 139–48
digital technology: discourse of 'traditional'
  childhood 26; impact on childhood,
  children's lives and children's play and
  communicative practices 140–3; impact
  in the early years classroom 143–5; in
  transforming pedagogy 146–8
'digitally at home' 142, 143
discrimination in play 43
discursive struggle 49
'disposable camera' method 28
dramatic monologue 121–2
dramatic play 60, 69, 92; area 11;
  formation of ethical identities and 48–58;
  narratives 53

Early Childhood Education Focus Group
  Position Paper 90

early childhood educators 32–44
Early Years Foundation Stage framework 8,
  16, 100
Early Years Special Interest Group of
  the British Educational Research
  Association 34
Early Years: Curriculum Continuity for Learning
  (South Australia) 34, 35, 42
economic labour 158
educational games 77
'educational play' 126, 153
educators, early childhood 32–44
emotional disorders 67
empathy 9
empowerment of children 28
enculturation in African contexts: 74–7
engagement 155
Enriched Curriculum (Northen Ireland) 162
Erikson, E. 100
ethical action as answerability 49–51
ethical considerations in interviews with
  children 23
ethical dialogic 50
ethical identities 58; authoring 51–3;
  coauthoring in dramatic play 53–7;
  dramatic play and 48–58; formation of 9
ethical self 52
Euro-American models of ECE practice 74
European educational games 77
exclusion: boundaries of 16; classroom rules
  about 11
exclusionary discourses 20
extended play 54
external action 61
Extreme Adventures Travel Agency 49

'facilitating' play 39
facilitators, teachers as 42
fairy tales 135, 137
fantasy playing 114
feminist theatre theory 116
first year of school (FYOS) settings 34, 36
folk-cultural aesthetics 120
folk pedagogy 158
form-languages 112, 114–15, 123
Foucault, Michel: on power 19
Foundation Phase (Wales) 162
free play 9, 10, 12, 38, 113, 153
freedom within play 32
French models 77
Freud, Sigmund 100
Froebel, Friedrich 32, 93, 100, 153
'fully developed' play 64–6

'games with rules' 155
Gandhi, Mahatma 89, 93
gender stereotypes 156
genre modality behaviours 130
'give voice to' children 28
goals for play, adult-determined 9
Golden Rule 51, 53
Good Child Inquiry, The 139
Guide to the Pre-primary Curriculum 101
'guided' participation 159

habitus 143, 145
Head Start movement 78
hiding 27
High Scope approach 78
holistic development of children 90
Hong Kong 100–8; competence of
    teachers and their preparation 107–8;
    discrepancies between policy and
    practice 104; early childhood
    context 101–2; play and the assistance in
    classrooms 104–5; policy innovation and
    the beliefs of parents 105–6; quality of
    'play' implementation in 102–4; teachers'
    professional autonomy in theory and
    practice 106

'identities' 52, 97
ilinx (vertigo) 114
imagination 63, 128; development of 9;
    ethical action and 50
immediacy 116
inclusion, boundaries of 16
independence 32
India 86–98; early elementary
    classrooms 91–3; theory and policy
    influencing play and pedagogy 88–91
innovation 9
Integrated Child Development Services
    (ICDS) 91
intelligence, inner, children's play as 128
'intent' participation 81, 159
inter-cultural negotiation between colonizer
    and colonized 87
internal action 61
International Center of Education in
    Pondicherry, India 89
intrinsic motivation 37
Isaacs, Susan 32

Japanese Ministry of Education Preschool
    Guidelines 100

Kendra, Shishu Vihar 90
Kohlberg, Lawrence 49
Kpelle children of Liberia 75
Krishnamurty, Badheka 93

language delay 67
'leading activity' 62
learning by doing 89
Learning Stories 42
'learning through play' 10, 42, 103, 108, 153,
    158: in Hong Kong 101, 104, 109
literacy 33, 37, 38
Llewellyn Visiting Panel 100, 101, 103, 108
logos 128
ludus 112, 114, 124

Mahabharata 88
make-believe play 60–2, 64, 68
managers, teachers as 42
Mandir, Bal 90
'match-making strategies' 11
'mature' play 64–6
McMillan, Margaret 32
meaning-making 53
mental representations, development of 63
mental voluntary actions 63
meta-cognition 64
meta-communication 130–2, 135
metaphysics of play theories 126–37
mimesis 112, 116–17, 122–4, 127
mimicry (imitation) 114, 116
mirror of nature or phenomena, play as 128
mobile phone use 140
mock adult authority in play 75, 132, 136
Montessori, Maria 32, 90, 93
Montessori movement 78
moral development 9
moral development framework (Piaget) 49
'mosaic approach' 146
mother-child play 76
'mother-teacher' 90
motivation 63, 155
mythic play 53–4

Narrator, position of 121
National Council of Educational Research
    and Training (NCERT) 90
National Curriculum Framework 90
National Curriculum, Key Stage One
    (England) 8
Ndebele 76
negotiation 155

New South Wales 22
non-governmental organizations
    (NGOs) 77
numeracy 33, 37, 38
Nursery School Association of South
    Africa 78

'object-centred' role-play 65
observation 39, 75, 77
oppositional identity 58
'other-regulation' 64
Outdoor Learning Project 146, 148

paidia 112, 114, 124
parents: expectations as barrier to play 41;
    perspectives on nursery and infant schools
    activities 157
parodies 75
participation 75, 77
'participatory tools' 146
'pedagogy of listening' 13
pedogogisation of play 5
peers, socialization of play and 76
persistence 155
photography as a data generation method 28
physical labour 158
physical voluntary actions 63
Piaget, Jean 100;:moral developmental
    framework 49
Piagetian theory, influence on ECE
    curriculum 78
planning 69, 155
Platonic view of mimesis 127, 128
play and pedagogical practices 9–14
play and pedagogy in the early years 34–6
'play as learning' 37–8, 106, 108
play as 'pedagogical priority' 36
play as preparation for future tool use 62
play as work 5
play at home or in the neighbourhood 10
play-culture 114–15
play, definition of 7
play-drama 114–15, 117
'play experts' 67
'play novices' 67
play outside school 88
play reality 127
play scenarios, development of 68–9
'play school' 93
play scripts 43
play training 38, 43
play versus work 5, 7

play/work dichotomy 126
'play-based teaching' 93
players, teachers as 42
playing 113–14; with selves and
    identities 53–4
'playrooms' (Scotland) 159
'playschools' (Iceland) 159
'play-way method' 89, 93
pleasure and power 155–6
'polyphony' 123, 124
portfolio, child 95
positioning-play 54, 55–7
positive play 42
postcolonial theory 86
postcolonialism 86–98; perspectives
    on play 93–5; interplay between the
    dominant and the marginalized 95–8
postmodern pedagogy 112–25
post-structural research 21
post-structuralist frameworks 9
post-Vygotskian developments in the study
    of play 62–4
power 19–30: adult, over children 156;
    participation and pedagogy 28–9;
    pleasure and 155–6; relationships of 19–
    22, 29
'pre-cooked play fare' approach 15
presence 116
'pretend identities' 52
pretend play 9, 26–7
prior-to-school (PTS) setting 34, 36
privacy 21
problem-based learning 82
problem of relevance 74
problem-solving 9, 155
problematising play 154–6, 157–9
progress 128
'Project School Readiness' 124
props, used of play 64, 68
Provision of Preschool Education 153
Puranas 88

Quality Assurance Inspection (QAI) annual
    reports 102
quality of children's play 35

Ramayana 88
rational approach 12
'readerly text' 132
'reception class' (England) 7–9
recitation 75
reflective process of *becoming* 137

Reggio Emilia approach 6, 14, 19
'regimes of truth' 10, 128
regulation 20
'rehearsals for life' 54
relational pedagogy 6, 10, 12, 13
'relationship-centred' play of kindergarten-
aged children 65
relationship with a non-teacher adult 24
relationships of power 19–22, 29
relevance, problem of 74
representation, logic of, in classic play
theories 127–9
resistance 2
resources, classroom 94
respect for children as competent beings 29
rhizomatic thinking 136
role play 126; aesthetics of 129–35; in
an imaginary situation 61; as a sign
system 129–30
'role speech' 65
role-play 60
'role-related speech' 65
roles in play 64, 65; development and
maintenance of 68–9
'Romantic' views of play 152
rote memorization 75
Rousseau, Jean-Jacques 93
rules 155; development and maintenance
of 68–9
Russell, Trish 49

scaffolding 39, 60; of learning 145; play
68
school: administration as barrier to play 40;
consent for research in 23; games 25;
playing at: research project 22–4
school-based play 10
self 128
self-control 54–5
self-regulated learning 82
self-regulation 61, 64, 66
sensory 'knowledge' 116
sensory receptiveness 122
Shona games 76
siblings, socialization of play and 76
social constructivist educational theory
(Vygotsky) 53
social engineering 11
social identities 58
social network websites 140
social realism 5
social situation of development 67
social skills 38, 42

socialization of play 76
socially-guided learning 82
social-realistic play 116
socio-cultural theories 35, 39
socioeconomic factors 154
Sotho communities 76
South Australian Curriculum Standards and
Accountability framework (SACSA) 35,
40
South Australian Department of Education
and Children's Services (DECS) 33
South Korea, teaching young children
in 126
spontaneity 116
stage theories of human development 128
state of play 152–3
Steiner kindergarten 15
stereotypes 43
structural form 120
structural variables 154–5
structured play 15
subject-based curriculum 33
subjectivity 97
subversive play, 15
sustained shared thinking 43
symbolic action 115
symbolic place 115
symbolic play 145
symbolic play-modeling 113
symbolic role-figure 115
symbolic thinking and imagination 61
symbolic time 115
systems issues as barrier to play 40

taboos 132–3
Tagore, Rabindranath 93
taking children seriously 162
taking play seriously 161
'talking matter' 75, 76
Tallensi children of Northern Ghana 75
Tanzanian Chagga children 75
Te Whariki 6
teacher-child ratios 95
teacher definitions of play 36–7
teacher-directed play 32
teacher-led activity 10
teacher perspectives of play 35–8
teacher roles 38–40, 42
'teaching through play' 153
texting 140
theory of mind 9
thinking skills 42
Tools of the Mind 68–70

toys 154; interactive 'smart' 142; use of, in
 symbolic way 68
'traditional' childhood 26
transformative pedagogy 147, 148
transforming oneself 133–5

ubungani 76
universal efficacy of play 32
 utilitarian approach 12

Vedic period (2500–600 BC) 88
verbal language 123
violent discourses 20
voluntary actions 63

Vygotskian perspective: make-believe
 play 60–2
Vygotsky, Lev 50, 53, 54, 57

'watching' play 39
'web of metonymy' 130
'well-developed' play 65
work 158–9
work/play dichotomy 126
work-oriented pedagogy 12
'writerly text' 132, 135

Zone of Proximal Development [ZPD] 60,
 61, 66–7, 69